W9-BSI-207

TOUGHNESS

TOUGHNESS

DEVELOPING TRUE STRENGTH
ON AND OFF THE COURT

JAY BILAS

Foreword by
MIKE KRZYZEWSKI

NEW AMERICAN LIBRARY

NEW AMERICAN LIBRARY
Published by New American Library,
a division of Penguin Group (USA) Inc.,
375 Hudson Street, New York, New York 10014, USA
Penguin Group (Canada), 90 Eglinton Avenue East, Suite 700, Toronto,
Ontario M4P 2Y3, Canada (a division of Pearson Penguin Canada Inc.)
Penguin Books Ltd., 80 Strand, London WC2R 0RL, England
Penguin Ireland, 25 St. Stephen's Green, Dublin 2,
Ireland (a division of Penguin Books Ltd.)
Penguin Group (Australia), 707 Collins Street, Melbourne,
Victoria 3008, Australia (a division of Pearson Australia Group Pty. Ltd.)
Penguin Books India Pvt. Ltd., 11 Community Centre,
Panchsheel Park, New Delhi–110 017, India
Penguin Group (NZ), 67 Apollo Drive, Rosedale, Auckland 0632,
New Zealand (a division of Pearson New Zealand Ltd.)
Penguin Books, Rosebank Office Park, 181 Jan Smuts Avenue,
Parktown North 2193, South Africa
Penguin China, B7 Jaiming Center, 27 East Third Ring Road North,
Chaoyang District, Beijing 100020, China

Penguin Books Ltd., Registered Offices: 80 Strand, London WC2R 0RL, England

First published by New American Library, a division of Penguin Group (USA) Inc.

First Printing, March 2013
10

REGISTERED TRADEMARK—MARCA REGISTRADA

LIBRARY OF CONGRESS CATALOGING-IN-PUBLICATION DATA:
Bilas, Jay, 1963–
Toughness: developing true strength on and off the court/
Jay Bilas; foreword by Mike Krzyzewski.
p.   cm.
ISBN 978-0-451-41467-0
1. Bilas, Jay, 1963–.   2. Basketball players—United States—Biography.   3. Basketball
coaches—United States—Biography.   4. Lawyers—United States—Biography.   I. Title.
GV884.B54A3 2013
796.323092—dc23   2012037085
[B]

Set in Bembo   •   Designed by Elke Sigal

Printed in the United States of America

PUBLISHER'S NOTE
While the author has made every effort to provide accurate telephone numbers, Internet
addresses and other contact information at the time of publication, neither the publisher nor
the author assumes any responsibility for errors, or for changes that occur after publication.
Further, publisher does not have any control over and does not assume any responsibility for
author or third-party Web sites or their content.

Contents

To my wife, Wendy
You are everything to me

Acknowledgments

A great friend, the late Wake Forest coach Skip Prosser, used to say, "Never delay gratitude." I am grateful to so many for their guidance, inspiration and help throughout this process, and in my life. I have been positively influenced by so many people, and in writing this book I was able to better appreciate just how fortunate I have been to have these great people in my life. Each has made me better in so many ways, and helped to make me a tougher person.

In writing this book, I was able to delve deeper into the motivation and inspiration behind the toughness I admired around me. Specifically, Mark Alarie and Tommy Amaker were especially instrumental in helping me understand and define the qualities displayed by our teammates through the most challenging times of our journey together. I played with some extraordinary men, none more extraordinary than Alarie, Amaker, Johnny Dawkins and David Henderson. They have been, and always will be, brothers.

As a player and young assistant coach, I was incredibly lucky to serve under Mike Krzyzewski. Over the past thirty years, Coach K has acted as my coach, mentor, confidant and, most important, my friend. His insights and time were invaluable in this process, and throughout my life. I count my decision to play for Coach K as the second most important and meaningful decision in my life, the first being my decision to marry my wife, Wendy. The lessons Coach K taught me, sometimes against my will, shaped the way I live my daily life.

Over my years in basketball, I have been fortunate to get to know Bob Knight, and to call him my friend. He has been a truly positive influence and he has taught me a great deal; there is seldom a time when he speaks that I don't learn something valuable. I especially value his dining suggestions (should I survive the ride when he is driving), as he has never steered me wrong on a good place to eat.

In my years in basketball, I have met so many wonderful people and competitors. In writing this book, I could have chosen many to lend their voices, but Steve Kerr, Tom Izzo, Roy Williams, Tom Crean and Bill Self stood out. I have learned so much from each of them.

My understanding of toughness gained greater depth from my friendship with Dr. Henry Friedman. Through Henry, I was able to learn the importance of hope, which was personified in the inspiring story of Sabrina Lewandowski. I am so grateful that they shared their stories with me.

In putting this book together, I strove to draw upon the values and principles I learned and observed from people I have played and worked with over the years. I cannot thank enough Doris Burke, Herm Edwards, Sage Steele, Curtis Strange, Julie Foudy and Jon Gruden, all of whom I work with at ESPN. They are not only colleagues, but respected and admired professionals who inspire me every time I talk to them. Another great inspiration in the writing of this book was Mia Hamm. Mia is the finest player in her sport, but she is an even better person. I could not imagine writing about toughness without her input.

Growing up in Southern California, I had some outstanding coaches and teachers, none more influential than Dick Spidell and Billy C. Creamer. Coach Spidell taught me how to win, and Mr. Creamer taught me how to follow my passion so my job would never be work; it would be what I wanted to do.

I have tremendous parents, Anthony and Margie Bilas. In ways they cannot imagine, they have inspired everything good in my life through their belief and unfailing support, and there is not a single day in which I do not think about the values, principles and lessons they taught me. My parents were not and are not lecturers. They taught by example, and the example they set for me I could never live up to. It is a debt that I can never repay. My brother, Dave, and my sisters, Colleen and Sharyl, have been similar inspirations for me, and all have been amazing role models.

Last, I would like to thank my wife, Wendy, and my two children, Tori and Anthony. The biggest honor I have had in my life is to have been called Tori and Anthony's dad. And since the day I first met Wendy, I have had my best friend by my side, and have been able to walk through life with the smartest, most caring, and toughest person I have ever met. Wendy was incredibly helpful in putting together this book and guiding me through the writing process. After questioning her grammar advice and having every piece of resource material shoot down my argument, I will never question her again. She edit good.

Foreword

I am so glad that Jay Bilas wrote this book.

Jay made a tough decision to attend Duke University and to join our basketball team when my staff and I recruited him out of his California high school in 1982. I was young, I had not yet established myself as a winning college basketball coach, most people had never heard my name and, with a 27–30 record in my first two seasons at Duke, I did not have statistics or championships to help me "sell" prospects. I had only my value system, coaching style and great intentions of future success to offer. When I presented those things to Jay and his family, they listened with kind respect. Somehow those things were enough. He agreed to believe in me, and I in him. It is an unwritten contract we uphold to this day.

He was a tough basketball player on the court. During his Duke career, he was charged with some of our most difficult defensive matchups, including legends of the game like Ralph Sampson and David Robinson. He never backed away from these assignments and relished the opportunity to face the best. He was committed to hard work in practice as the only means of improving, he was a selfless and loyal teammate, and he possessed the mental toughness to never show weakness on his face in competition.

Jay and his class of 1986 collectively changed the course of Duke basketball and my career. I can never thank them enough for the belief that they had in me before I had any tangible reasons why they should. And I have admired each of them in the lives they have led since graduating from Duke. They are responsible, driven family men who have met with success in their professional lives because they deserved to. Toughness is evident in all that they do—mostly in the fact that they are all good men leading principled lives in the various professions they have chosen.

I have the privilege of seeing Jay more often than the others from that class because of his role as an analyst and writer for ESPN. In my opinion, he is the best in the business. He knows the game and he knows people. This combination along with his intelligence and wit make him very, very good at what he does.

In *Toughness*, Jay examines the way in which the true definition of toughness is being lost in the game of basketball and in our society. Then he reminds us, through the stories he shares, what toughness really is. It is not found in bravado. It is found in the heart of an individual willing to devote him- or herself to what he or she knows is right. On the court, it is manifested in committing to a difficult defensive assignment, diving for a loose ball or taking a charge. In life, it manifests itself in making a tough decision because it is the right one, and holding oneself to high standards of honesty and integrity.

Toughness is a rare commodity and, as Jay argues, can be a learned skill. I have had the great fortune in my life of seeing true toughness in some amazing people and I have learned from each of them. I have seen it in guards, forwards and centers. I have seen it in doctors, soldiers and CEOs. I see it in Jay and the rest of the Duke basketball class of 1986. And now, having read Jay's book, I see it even more clearly.

—Mike Krzyzewski

TOUGHNESS

TOUGHNESS DEFINED

I value toughness, and I value toughness in every aspect of life. I admire the toughness I see in others, and I strive to be tough in my daily life.

I saw toughness every day growing up, but it wasn't really defined for me, and I don't believe I grasped it. In my early years of life, I didn't concentrate on toughness, or truly understand what it meant.

It wasn't until I started playing college basketball for Mike Krzyzewski that I finally wrapped my head around the concept of toughness, and internalized it. I also realized that I had seen true toughness every single day displayed by my parents and a select few of my teachers and coaches. I just didn't really get it at the time.

Fortunately, I get it now.

The term "toughness" is used often these days, especially in sports while breaking down games and in evaluating players. Reporters and commentators reference and opine on the toughness of a team or player, and often make judgments on toughness based upon the final score, or whether a player or team has won or lost a championship game. Coaches are often quoted emphasizing the need for their teams to "toughen up" or "get tougher" in order to be champions.

Coaches on all levels are seeking toughness in their teams and players. But just as often, coaches lament a lack of toughness or emphasize it in their practices and locker room meetings, but their players don't know the true meaning of the word. There is a disconnect.

In almost coordinated fashion, I see player after player thumping his chest after a routine play to call attention to himself, angrily taunting an opponent after scoring or blocking a shot, engaging in a shouting match with an opposing player, or squaring up nose-to-nose with an opponent as if a fight might ensue. I see players jawing at and scowling at each other, trying to "intimidate" one another.

Is that real toughness? Is that what the word has come to mean?

I don't think so. I see those actions as nothing more than "fake toughness" or false bravado, and such actions have no real value in sport or in any other aspect of life. To me, it's a waste of time and energy. It is simply a false pretense of toughness, and falls short of what true toughness is all about.

So I wonder: Do most people really understand what coaches and leaders mean when they plead for "toughness" from their players and teams? Or is it just a popular buzzword thrown around haphazardly without clear definition or understanding?

It bothered me when I perceived commentators and reporters were misusing the concept and promoting false toughness. So much so that a few years ago, I was motivated to put pen to paper and write about what I knew and understood about toughness. In 2009, in an article on ESPN.com, I wrote about what I believed true toughness really means in basketball.

The response to my article on toughness was overwhelming and humbling. Hundreds of coaches, players, parents, teachers and administrators from all over the world, from the NBA to the military to the elementary school level, called and wrote me to tell me they had posted the article in their locker room, handed it out to their teams, studied it in class or gone over it in detail with their players, teams, families or coworkers.

A young high school coach in California wrote to tell me his staff had just read the article and it was enlarged, put on a poster board and hung in their locker room. Every player had a small copy in his locker, and as far as the coach was concerned, the article will be the team's bible going forward.

Kentucky coach John Calipari, then coaching at Memphis, told me he required each of his players to post the article above their beds. Countless other college basketball coaches, from young, up-and-coming coaches to Hall of Famers, told me that they had used the article with their teams and had posted it in their locker rooms.

A special operations pilot in Iraq, who flies C-130s and F-15Cs and works with the nation's most elite soldiers, asked me to write more about the subject: "Your demographic is, I fear, in dire need of hearing more on the subject. . . . I've known in my gut when I was up against toughness. . . . That's why we strive to be tougher than every enemy we face down for our nation. . . . I can only hope that you and others like you continue to talk about this character issue."

Finally, one of the more memorable demonstrations of the article's influence came at the expense of my son Anthony's AAU basketball team. A coach of an AAU team in Raleigh, North Carolina, approached me and said that he had based his entire program on my article. His players had the article posted in their facility, and each player was required to carry a copy with him when they traveled to games. The next day, my son's team faced that Raleigh team in an AAU tournament in western North Carolina. The Raleigh team did almost everything right, and beat my son's team by more than twenty points. The Raleigh team set good screens, finished plays, consistently boxed out, talked on defense, showed great body language, related well to one another, and played hard together for the entire game. It was impressive.

After the game ended and the teams shook hands, one of the players on the Raleigh team approached me and held out some worn papers, stapled together. "Excuse me, Mr. Bilas," he said, "but could you autograph this? It's the article on toughness you wrote. Our coach printed it out for our team at the beginning of the season, and he wants us to keep a copy of it in our bags. We use it very day as a reminder of how we want to play."

After I signed my article for the young player, several of his teammates asked me to autograph their copies. Then the coach asked me to be in a photo with his team under the scoreboard. After the photo, a fellow parent from my son's team approached me and asked, "Have our kids read your article? Maybe they should!"

It was a great lesson about toughness. The players on the Raleigh team weren't bigger or more talented than the players on my son's team, but they played better together. They were *tougher*.

These were young teenagers, not grizzled veterans. They not only understood the concept of toughness that their coach was teaching, but they embraced it. It was a standard they wanted to meet. I quickly got the message that this subject resonated with people in and out of sports, and I should expound upon it.

In the time I've spent studying the concept of toughness, I've learned that toughness may not be exactly what many people may think.

Toughness Is a Skill

I received a wonderful education in toughness playing for and coaching under Mike Krzyzewski at Duke University, playing in the Atlantic Coast Conference, playing for Gene Keady on the United States National Select Team, competing in NBA training camps, playing pro basketball in Europe, studying in law school, practicing as a trial lawyer, and in my current job as a basketball analyst at ESPN.

Still, I wasn't born with any real toughness. I don't believe any person is born tough.

Duke basketball coach Mike Krzyzewski agrees. Coach K is the winningest coach in college basketball history, with four NCAA championships and eleven Final Four tournaments under his belt.

"We are not born tough," Krzyzewski said. "We may be born into a great family situation, or a difficult family situation that forces or conditions you to be tough, but we aren't born that way. Toughness comes from how you handle your experiences, what you learn from them, and how you are guided through them by others in your life."

Toughness is something I had to learn the hard way. Although I had a foundation of toughness laid by my parents, I had not put it all together or fully grasped its definition and practical applications until I played for Coach K. When I played for Coach K, all that I had learned from my mom and dad became clear.

Early in my college career, I thought toughness was about being physical, and based upon how much physical punishment I could dish out, and how much physical punishment I could take.

Up to that point, I thought I was pretty tough. I quickly found out that I wasn't as tough as I thought I was. And I wasn't nearly as tough as I needed to be.

Toughness isn't physical. It has nothing to do with size, physical strength or athleticism. It's an intangible, an attitude, a philosophy. Some people may be born with the aptitude to be tougher than others, but I believe that true toughness is a skill that can be developed and improved in everyone.

The Dictionary Definition of Toughness

No examination of toughness would be complete without considering the dictionary definition of the word. The most common definition of "tough" is being able to withstand great force without tearing or breaking. In other words, something that is tough is strong and resilient.

In metallurgy—the science of metallic elements—toughness is a measure of how much energy a material can absorb before rupturing. Scientists have devised ways to measure a metal's toughness through lab impact tests, such as swinging a hammer from a pendulum at a metal object to calculate how much energy is required to break the object.

In technical terms, toughness is a descriptor of how much energy a material can absorb before breaking. For example, if a material withstands a great deal of energy before breaking, then it is a tough material even if it bends and changes shape in the process.

Hardness—in metallurgy, at least—is related to toughness, but it's not the same thing. Hardness describes how much energy it takes to bend or change a material. If the material takes a lot of energy to change only a little, it is said to be hard. Conversely, if the material changes shape without much energy, then the material is not hard. Glass, for example, is hard because it takes energy to change its shape, but it breaks easily, so it's not very tough. Rubber, on the other hand, isn't usually hard. In some cases, we can call it soft. It bends and changes shape much more easily than glass, but it takes more energy to break it. So rubber is tougher.

These same terms are often used to describe people. We are hard or soft, tough or weak, but those qualities are harder to define and measure when applied to human beings. We all have images in our minds of characters that epitomize the classic and stereotypical "tough guy": Rocky Balboa, Chuck Norris, or John Wayne.

In sports, I think of an Ironman triathlete, a football player like Ray Lewis, a basketball player like Kobe Bryant, or baseball Hall of Famer Cal Ripken, who played in a record 2,632 consecutive Major League games. In sports, we presume that it's a positive to be hard, but I believe it's much more important to be tough, or—in scientific terms—unbreakable.

In fact, I would argue that being able to bend or flex under pressure without breaking is a more important attribute than hardness. An athlete who bends without breaking and bounces back up will prevail over the hard athlete—someone who is resistant to bending under pressure but will break with enough force.

My Foundation of Toughness

It has been said that you cannot choose your parents. Well, if you could, I would have chosen mine. My parents are genuinely great people. They are nice, polite, smart, hardworking people who mind their own business but are always willing to help, and always strive to do the right thing.

And they are tough.

Toughness has no relationship to how nice a person is. There is no reason you can't be exceedingly nice and incredibly tough at the same time. Those two traits are not mutually exclusive.

Whatever toughness I have been able to muster as an athlete, attorney, broadcaster and person, I learned first by the example set by my mother and father.

I recognize that I am incredibly lucky. I grew up in a privileged background with every advantage and every choice, but my parents did not. My parents came from very good, hardworking families, but they had fewer choices, and had to work harder and sacrifice more for their family.

My father, Anthony Bilas, was born in San Pedro, California, in 1933, the son of Yugoslavian immigrants. English was a second language for him when he first attended kindergarten, and he began working at an early age.

My dad began working as a commercial fisherman, as his father did before him, and he fished all over the world as a young man. After several years of commercial fishing, he decided to attend technical school and go into the electronics business. He opened up his own television sales and service business called Anthony's TV in San Pedro, California.

Every day, my father always got up and went to work. I learned about his work ethic not from my father talking about it, but from watching him. Actually, I never really heard my father talk about how hard he worked, unless he was answering a question of mine. He didn't talk about it; he just did it.

I never heard my dad complain about working, or about how difficult a particular job or task was. He would plan for a task and concentrate fully on that task until it was completed. And he would always do it right the first time. Then he would move on. He never sought congratulations or a pat on the back. He just went to work every day.

Whether the task was relatively simple or more difficult, my father always approached it with the same demeanor. He was disciplined and thoughtful about things, and never rushed or crazed about anything. He was never rattled by any issues that arose, met challenges head-on, and always looked for the best solutions. Truthfully, he was everything I was not. As a boy, I was hotheaded and impulsive. Later I learned to be more like my dad, but I've never been able to match him.

When I was a kid, I played Little League baseball. One day I asked my dad to take me to the batting cages so I could get in a few swings against the pitching machines. I chose a cage that was too fast for me, but I wanted to hit against faster pitching. My dad didn't say a word.

After watching me swing and miss, swing and hit weak grounders, and swing and foul off pitch after pitch, my dad said, "Just relax and meet the ball. You're trying to kill it. Let the bat swing freely."

I was so frustrated that I couldn't get good wood on the ball. I thought he was getting on me, so like an idiot, I shot back at him, "If you think it's so easy, you do it!"

Without saying a word, my dad walked into the cage, took the bat and calmly dropped another quarter in the machine. Then, *whack! whack! whack!* He proceeded to hit hard line drive after hard line drive. I stood there stunned. Then he got out of the cage and said, "Just relax and hit the ball. You don't have to swing so hard. Just see the ball and hit it, and let the bat do the work." I never forgot that. He was so calm and matter-of-fact about it. The job was to see the ball and hit it. So he did just that. There was no need to make a big deal of it.

In his business, while my father had worked to make money, he was also forward-thinking and worked to make that money work for him. Early on after starting his television sales and repair business, he began buying commercial real estate properties in San Pedro. He did things step by step, and never got ahead of himself. First he started his own business, but he also bought the dirt underneath it. And he began buying other properties in the same area.

There were a few times I would be with my father at his TV shop, and when he would drive me home, he would stop and look at a local property for sale. He would consider what he would have to pay for the property, what would need to be done to make it profitable, and whether he wanted to take on the risk. He knew the area because he grew up there and worked there every day, and he knew what it took for a property to be successful for him. He told me about his general rule of "ten times gross" that he used to decide whether the property was worth pursuing further. If the building's price was around ten times its annual gross rent, my father would really dig in and evaluate the risks involved. When I asked, he told me that there was nothing easy in real estate or any other investment, and he tried to fully think through every aspect of the investment before he made a decision.

When I was in high school, my dad looked into buying a building that had been an auto supply store. It was a big space that seemed suited for only a large retail operation. I remember my father looking into buying that building, even though many of his friends believed the building was a loser, and that he shouldn't buy it.

But my dad saw something more than just one big retail space. He saw a building that could be turned into multiple retail spaces, and one that he believed was a steal. He didn't particularly care what other people thought about the building. Rather, he focused on his own evaluation and the opportunities that he saw. He bought the building and immediately worked to partition it into seven small storefront business spaces. I was with him during a few days of construction when he worked on partitioning the building, most of which he did and supervised himself. My dad took that one big retail space that sat empty for so long and quickly turned it into seven smaller spaces that housed small businesses like a salon, a furniture repair shop, and even a diner on the corner. My dad turned that "loser" into a net winner.

For a time, in part because my dad never bragged about anything, I thought he was just really smart in his business decisions, and had a magic eye that could see a winner at first glance. He was really smart, but his success was due to far more than that. His business successes didn't just happen. I might have been with him only when he initially looked at a property and did some calculations on a napkin while we were having a bite to eat. What I didn't see was how much work and thought went into that investment decision. For a time, I mistakenly thought my dad just took a quick look, did some math, and got a loan. He didn't. He gathered every piece of information he needed to make the best possible decision. He was disciplined and thoughtful in his decisions.

With considerable skill, time and effort, my dad became a very successful businessman. But with all of the work he had to put in, he never once said he didn't have time for me or my brother and sisters. He made time. My father never missed one of my high school games.

My dad essentially retired when I was in college. He still worked managing his properties, but his work was much easier than it had been all those years prior.

Of the many things I have admired about my dad, one stands out above all others: He is unfailingly honest and straightforward. If my father said he was going to do something, he did it. He was trustworthy, and you could count on his word. He didn't give advice often, but when he did, you knew he had thought about it, and it was going to be right.

And he is the toughest person I have ever known. My dad is big and strong physically, but he is much stronger in character. From the time he was young, he worked hard to make his own way without help from anyone. He never once complained or expected credit. It was just what he did. When he was sick or hurt, my dad went to work. When he was faced with a difficult task, he performed that task to the best of his ability. He provided a home and a great life for his family.

My dad was the consistent daily example of toughness early in my life. Each day of my life, I have known my dad as trustworthy, fearless, persistent, disciplined, committed, focused and resilient. My dad has always been the personification of the toughness I value, and the clear and simple stories of toughness I learned from him are the basis and foundation of this book.

I have often said that if I could be half the man my father is, I would be twice the man I ever thought I could be.

My mother, Margery Bilas, was born in San Francisco, California, in 1936, the daughter of a United States Merchant Marine lieutenant commander and a Scottish immigrant. My mother is a loving, caring person who displays tremendous toughness by always putting her family first, and being committed to her values and principles.

There is no way that my mother would fit any of the stereotypes of toughness. Her appearance is delicate and ladylike. She is quick to smile and laugh, and is unfailingly polite and nice. Until I got to high school and college, my mom had no earthly idea what certain curse words meant. So much so that I tried to get away with saying some of the things she didn't understand. That was the only area in which I could fool her. She is a very kind person, but I learned early not to mistake her kindness for weakness.

My mom has toughness of character, is very persistent and is totally committed to what she believes in. And she has always been committed to and believed in me. Without her belief in me, I doubt I would have ever believed in myself.

Today, my mom would be referred to as a stay-at-home mom. But she was really in the "development" business, and invested everything she had into her husband and children. My mom made it her job to prepare and develop her kids into self-sufficient adults who would have the skills to open all doors as they pursued their chosen paths. My mom wanted me to be able to handle myself in any situation, and to be able to feel comfortable in a classroom, courtroom, boardroom or even a ballroom. She wanted me to be "well-rounded," and to have my choice.

From the time I was little, my mother ingrained in me that I was smart enough and talented enough to do whatever I wanted to do in life. In school, my mother never told me she expected me to get straight As. But she told me often that she expected me to do my best. If I did my best, there was nothing to stop me from getting the best grade.

Like most kids, I was tested in school. I took the same IQ tests and standardized tests as everyone else. But my mother never told me my scores on those tests, only that I did well. She didn't want me to feel limited by a lower score, or that success would just happen for me because I had a high score. My mother knew that to have choices, I had to work hard and prepare. It was her belief that I was capable of anything I worked for, and I would be limited only by the amount of work I was willing to put in.

I used to think that my father was the most influential in instilling toughness in me. However, after studying the concept of toughness, I realized I owe a lot of it to my mother. It was my mom who encouraged and enabled me to push myself, who got me out of my comfort zone, and who prepared me for any situation I would encounter.

My mom drove me thousands of miles to different activities and opportunities. Even when I resisted, she convinced me it was the right thing, and I would do just fine. She was resolute that I was going to be prepared to go to the college of my choice, and so prepared that nobody would say no to me. I was the one who would be in the position to say no, but she would expect me to say, "No, thank you."

My mother fueled me, both figuratively and literally. I was a skinny kid growing up, and needed to bulk up and get stronger for sports. Every day my mother got up and made me breakfast before I went to school. Instead of watching me choke down unpleasant protein shakes, she would experiment at the blender and find creative ways to make them actually taste good. She made me lunch to take to school, when most of my friends just bought their lunch. She put two deli-quality sandwiches in my lunch to make sure I ate well, and they were so coveted that my friends used to try to trade for them or outright buy them. But they were so good that I never traded or sold them.

My mom also encouraged me to dress well, even as a high school student. Growing up in Southern California, I wanted to wear jeans and a T-shirt to school every day. Instead, my mom made sure I wore nice collared shirts and pants to present myself in the best way possible in any situation.

When I was a junior in high school, I took the SAT on a Saturday night. It was the day after a junior prom at my high school, so I went into the test a little bleary eyed and tired. I performed well on the test, but my mom was concerned that I wouldn't be able to get into the college of my choice with that score. Because I was being recruited for basketball, I knew my score was good enough to go anywhere, but that wasn't good enough for my mom. She wanted me to be able to get in anywhere without basketball as a consideration.

I made a deal with her. I told her that we would invite an Ivy League school in for a home visit, and if the coach said my SAT score would put me at any risk for not being accepted, I would take it again. At the home visit with the Ivy school, I asked the coach about my score, and he said I had no worries at all about gaining admission. I was almost giddy after getting the response I wanted, and I remember my mom rolling her eyes, then laughing, as if I were sneaking in the back door. I never had to take the SAT again, and that score got me into every college that recruited me. I still laugh when I think about that.

My mother had great perspective on most everything, and in this book I share some of the profound lessons she taught me.

Before I ever dribbled a ball or heard a word from Coach K, I first learned from my parents that toughness is a skill, and it is something I could improve upon. From that solid foundation, others added to my understanding of toughness. Over the years, teachers, coaches, teammates and even opponents have taught me, sometimes against my will, what it takes to be tough, and showed me what I needed to do to be tougher. In my judgment, toughness is one of the most valuable and admirable attributes in any person.

I'm nowhere near as tough as my parents, and I am nowhere near as tough as I want to be. But I am tougher than I used to be and, going forward, I know that I will be tougher than I am today.

That isn't true of just me. It is true of all of us.

Coaching Mental Toughness

Coaching legend Bob Knight has always said that in basketball, the mental is to the physical as four is to one. Knight was talking about concentration, but it also applies to the concept of toughness. True toughness is mental toughness, and has little to do with physical toughness. As we learned from metallurgy, it is mental toughness that makes a person, player or team unbreakable, whereas physical hardness can be more easily broken.

Most coaches agree that mental toughness is far more important than reliance on physical toughness. "Mental toughness leads to physical toughness," Coach K told me. "When you get knocked down, it's mental toughness that always gets you up, not physical toughness."

Michigan State coach Tom Izzo also believes that mental toughness dwarfs physical toughness in importance. "Some of the strongest guys in the world, physically, aren't tough, and some of the toughest guys in the world aren't physically strong. It's mental," he said.

"Toughness is doing what it takes to make a difference," Izzo said. "It is not thinking or accepting that you have a ceiling, but you have another notch, another gear. That takes mental toughness. Toughness is not about being big or strong, or being a bully. That displays the least amount of toughness."

On the Michigan State basketball floor, toughness is emphasized daily. Izzo believes that environment is a big part of who a person ultimately becomes, and players take real inspiration from people around them embracing toughness together. He highlights and accentuates toughness, and conditions his team for it every day in practice.

Toughness bears no relation to the physical, according to the great U.S. soccer midfielder Julie Foudy. "It is your mental character. I don't believe toughness or a tough person has this 'big muscle' or male quality. I see it as a 'fighter mentality.' Toughness is your willingness to fight through whatever comes your way. It is how you deal with adversity and what you learn from others you are invested with."

Foudy doesn't believe that people are born tough, but that it is possible to move that needle and become tougher. "A player can do mental training to improve her toughness. I was always working on it, and I am still working on it. You may not move the needle all the way from 'empty' to 'full,' but you can absolutely move it. I'm evidence of that," she said.

Former NFL star and NFL head coach Herm Edwards agrees that true toughness is completely mental. "The brain is a powerful thing, a powerful thing," Edwards said. "When you can weaken a man's brain, you've got him. When you can take a man's will away, take him beyond the limit of his toughness, you've got him. It is not about talent. It is about will; it is about how you go about your business." That's why, Edwards said, teams with more talent often don't win as much as teams with less talent.

When things get difficult, in sports and in life, too many people often give up the fight and quit. Edwards believes quitting is the easy way out. He has always said, "You finish, or you retire," and that truly tough people don't quit and they don't give in. Edwards believes that kind of toughness can be taught, and that players welcome it.

Super Bowl–winning NFL coach Jon Gruden also believes toughness can be taught, and he told me he always taught toughness to his teams and players. "You have to coach toughness, the effort and discipline it takes to be excellent, every bit as much, if not more so, than Xs and Os or strategy." Gruden believes toughness can be acquired, and if a leader sets a tough precedent, people will rise to meet a higher standard of toughness. About that he has no doubt.

"I watched Tom Izzo's Michigan State team put on helmets and shoulder pads to learn to attack the rim harder, to be more physical, and to be tougher on the glass," Gruden said. "I know toughness can be improved upon, and can be a strength of an individual and a team."

As a kid, Gruden was a ball boy for Bob Knight at Indiana. For years, Gruden has used Knight as an example of what it takes to be tough, and how a coach can positively impact his team's toughness level. "Do you think every player that ever showed up in Bloomington, Indiana, was tough when they got there?" Gruden asked. "No. But they were all a hell of a lot tougher after learning from Bob Knight. Hell, I was his ball boy and I got tougher from that."

Like Julie Foudy, Gruden understands that a coach cannot take every player's toughness level to elite status, but acknowledges that the proper mind-set and mental conditioning can make anyone tougher than they started. Similarly, Gruden can't make every player a superstar, but because toughness is a skill, he can help make players better and tougher.

To Indiana coach Tom Crean, toughness is a talent, and coaches and players have a responsibility to develop it like any other skill. "You have to be pushed and prodded. It's not about talk. You have to absorb it. You absorb what it takes," Crean said.

Crean puts a lot of importance on surrounding yourself with people who have similar values and a tough mind-set. "[If you] aspire to be great, to work with others that have similar aspirations, not just bought in but locked in both mentally and physically, you will have the capacity to do the hard things when you need most to do them. That's toughness," he said.

Crean is adamant that being totally locked in is a necessity in achieving the highest level of toughness possible. It is not enough to want to win. You have to be willing to do what it takes to prepare yourself to win, and willing to put in the extra work necessary to be great.

"It doesn't take toughness to lift a weight or start a fight," Kansas basketball coach Bill Self said. "It takes toughness to bring what it takes to win, and bring it every day." Self believes that toughness is a learned skill, and that a "willing" player can learn to be tougher. "And I think you can make a tough player a monster. I absolutely think you can build toughness in a person and in a group."

To North Carolina coach Roy Williams, toughness is one's ability to focus on what is important and to stay focused on the ultimate objective. "You can get whacked, the calls go against you, you can be physically challenged in a game," Williams said. "But you have to focus on what's important. You cannot be deterred, intimidated or thrown off from your goal. That's mental toughness."

Williams says toughness is not about getting into a fistfight, and he says he has never seen a real fight in a basketball game. "Toughness is, 'I'm not going to lose sight of what I want to do by what you do, or by outside influences.' That is a real form of mental toughness," Williams said.

Like his coaching counterparts, he thinks a player can improve his toughness. "You always have guys that take a hit, and it takes them a half hour to recover. That can get so much better," he said.

Taking a hit isn't just about the physical hit, but the mental hurdle that comes with it. Williams believes that mental toughness is vital in order to accept the physical challenges of the game.

And, as a coach and a teammate, when you see toughness and courage in competition, you need to acknowledge it. Doing tough things needs to be expected, but it also needs to be valued. Acknowledging and celebrating that those around you are doing tough things, and doing them for the good of the team, is important to a culture of winning.

Toughness and the importance of doing tough things need to be emphasized every day, but when a coach or a teammate sees toughness and courage in competition, it should be acknowledged. Boston Celtics assistant coach Kevin Eastman calls it "catching your players doing something right" rather than just catching them doing something wrong and correcting them.

Toughness is a skill that can be learned and developed. We can all be tougher.

What is true toughness? Who really displays true toughness? Why is it so valued and important? How can each of us demonstrate toughness in competition and in our daily lives?

How can I get tougher, and develop and instill that same toughness in those around me?

This book is a broad look at what true toughness really means, and I offer my own definition of the concept based on my own life experiences inside and outside of basketball, and the influences and lessons from my parents, coaches, teachers, teammates, friends, mentors and colleagues. I explore toughness through the thoughts and stories of people I know, respect and admire. And I relate examples and lessons of hard-won toughness I have seen up close, and that have made a positive and lasting impact upon me.

These lessons are not just for basketball players or other athletes. They are valuable for people of all ages, all professions and all walks of life. My analysis of toughness is broken down into specific ingredients, such as trust, preparation, courage, communication, self-evaluation, persistence, and resilience. The following chapters take a closer look at the individual elements that make up true toughness, as I define it.

Being tough is important on the playing field and the basketball court, but it's an essential part of success in everyday life as well. And these principles are emphasized daily by the best of the best, in every walk of life.

Through tested concepts, personal stories, strategies and directives, I will provide you with my own "recipe" for toughness and toughness building that I have learned from so many people I respect and admire. Because of what I've learned from some of the best athletes and coaches in the world, as well as some of my colleagues at ESPN, and what I have learned from people I have met along the way, I know I'll leave my career a heck of a lot tougher than when I started it. My only regret is that I didn't "get it" about toughness much sooner. I would have been much better as a player, teammate and person, and my teams would have been better, if I had been tougher earlier.

I appreciate true toughness in any person. I'll take true toughness over talent any day. Toughness wins. Toughness prevails. But when you combine talent and true toughness, that combination can be unbeatable.

CHAPTER 1

TRUST

It requires a certain toughness to trust in others and to trust and believe in yourself. I believe that trust is a choice. Trustworthy people deal in truth. They speak the truth and accept the truth from those they trust and respect. If you expect a culture of trust, you have to build and foster a culture of truth.

Coach Mike Krzyzewski deals only in truth. When I played for him at Duke, he was sometimes so brutally honest it could shake you to your core, especially if you weren't tough enough to process it the right way, handle it and act upon it.

Coach K was born in Chicago, the son of Polish immigrants. From the very first year I played for him, Coach K emphasized that his philosophy of honesty and hard work came from his parents, and our team heard their stories often. He credits his mother, Emily, as one of his greatest inspirations. Emily grew up in western Pennsylvania, and she raised her family in a poor, racially diverse neighborhood on Chicago's North Side. His father, William, was an elevator operator, and Emily scrubbed floors at night in the Chicago Athletic Club to help provide for Coach K and his older brother, Bill. Like my parents did for me, his parents instilled the foundation of his toughness and no-nonsense work ethic.

Krzyzewski graduated from the United States Military Academy at West Point in 1969, and played basketball under Bob Knight while training to become an officer in the army. He was captain of the Army basketball team his senior season, and after retiring from active duty in 1974, he started his coaching career as an assistant on Knight's staff at Indiana. After one year there under Knight, Krzyzewski returned to West Point as head coach of the Army Cadets.

In 1980, Duke athletics director Tom Butters hired Krzyzewski to replace Bill Foster, who resigned to go to the University of South Carolina. At the time, Coach K was considered an up-and-comer in coaching circles, but was largely unknown and unproven. After doing his homework, Butters, however, recognized Krzyzewski's potential and hired him despite the persistent questions from the media and Duke's rabid fan base. That hiring marked the start of the most decorated coaching career in college basketball history.

I first met Coach K in 1981 when he began recruiting me out of Southern California. I was part of a recruiting class that was ranked number one in the nation, made up of Johnny Dawkins, Mark Alarie, David Henderson, Bill Jackman, and Weldon Williams. All of us were highly ranked and highly sought-after national recruits, and we each committed to a young coach who had never coached a single game in the NCAA Tournament.

For me and that 1982 Duke recruiting class, the learning curve was steep. Despite the number one ranking as a freshman class, we struggled mightily in our first season. After being nationally ranked in 1984 and 1985, reaching as high as the number two ranking in the country, we were a seasoned team of veterans. In our senior season of 1986, and with a starting lineup of Dawkins, Alarie, Henderson, Tommy Amaker and myself, Coach K led us to an ACC regular season championship, an ACC tournament championship, an NCAA East regional championship, and Coach K's first Final Four. We had winning streaks of sixteen and twenty-one games that season, went undefeated at home, and advanced to the NCAA championship game in Dallas, and we won more games in a single season than any other team in college basketball history, finishing 37–3.

In 2000, Krzyzewski's numerous accomplishments at Duke were recognized: the Cameron Indoor Stadium court was named Coach K Court in his honor, and on November 15, 2011, Krzyzewski got his 903rd victory, passing his mentor Bob Knight's record for most Division I wins.

Coach K's numbers at Duke are staggering: four National Championships; twelve national Coach of the Year honors; eleven Final Four appearances; 405 weeks ranked among the nation's top-ten teams; 104 weeks ranked number one in the country. *Time* magazine and CNN named Krzyzewski "America's Best Coach" in 2001 as part of a joint venture between the two media outlets. The criteria for the selection were not limited to any sport or any level of play.

I learned a lot about what it takes to win from Coach K, and I learned a great deal about the toughness it takes to win at the highest level. And I was not alone. Coach K cultivated toughness in every player he coached. You showed toughness, or you did not survive.

"I learned a lot about toughness from Coach K," said former Duke All-American and NBA star Grant Hill. "To play for him, I think you have to be tough, or mentally strong, or you can get weeded out."

Coach K was the first coach I truly trusted. I had a few good coaches growing up, but once I became a sophomore in high school, I felt that I couldn't trust the coaches I played for. They were not bad people, but they did not foster a culture of trust. When it came time for me to go to college, it was the first time in my life that I got to choose the coach I played for. And playing for a coach I could trust was my most important consideration.

In the recruiting process, I learned quickly that I could trust Coach K. When I played for him, I learned that when he told me something, I could believe it, even if it was difficult to hear. I believed it because he never lied to me, and always told me the truth.

When Coach K was recruiting me, other coaches negatively recruited against him by telling me that he would make me play out of position in college. I was a forward who was projected to play inside and out in college, but some coaches told me that if I went to Duke, Coach K would bury me inside at center, and that's where I would stay during all four years in Durham. It was such a frequent topic that I finally asked Coach K about it.

"People are telling me that you will make me play center if I come to Duke," I said. "Is that true?" Coach K replied, "For your freshman year, yes. We don't have anyone better to play it, so I will ask you to play that spot. But I will recruit another big guy next year and allow you to move back to your natural position."

Coach K could have easily told me what I wanted to hear—that he would not play me at center—and then instructed me to play there anyway because the team needed it. I knew plenty of players who had false promises made to them in recruiting, and then had to live with it or leave.

But he didn't do that. He told me straight out that he expected that I would have to play center for at least a year because it was what the team needed, and that he expected that I would be the best person to play that role in my first year. I always respected that, and never doubted him—in large measure because of that.

In the Duke locker room, my locker was right in front of where Coach K stood to address the team. When he stood before us to deliver a pregame speech, to talk about winning or to share his expectation for the team, he would get goose bumps on his arms and legs.

I have heard my fair share of rah-rah speeches from coaches, and I am certain that some coaches have faked anger or enthusiasm to make a point.

But I have never seen anyone fake goose bumps. I knew instinctively that I could trust those goose bumps and believe in them. To me, trust and belief go hand in hand; and trust and belief are essential ingredients in toughness.

When you trust and believe, you can be challenged and held accountable. Once a coach earns his players' trust, he can push them to new levels mentally and physically, where less trustworthy coaches might not dare tread. When I played for Mike Krzyzewski at Duke, the players' trust of our coach was a crucial component of our success. It allowed Coach K to speak openly and sometimes harshly to our team, and to point out truths that softer, weaker players don't want to hear or might shrink from.

Most players believe that accountability means blame. It doesn't. Accountability is being held to the standard you have accepted as what you want, individually and collectively. Trustworthy coaches and teammates can help you be at your best by challenging you to do your best, even when you think you can't. For tough players and teams, accountability is an obligation coaches and teammates have to each other.

Belief in a Common Goal

The greatest compliment to any player is that he or she is a great teammate. We can't all be great players, but we can all be great teammates. And the key characteristic of a great teammate is belief. Belief, like trust, is a choice.

The toughest players and teammates believe in what their coaches and their teammates are striving to accomplish, and what they are capable of doing together as a team. Great teammates choose to commit fully to the team's goals and understand in the big picture what is required of each individual, even in the face of setbacks or tough competition. It is not some blind or naive acceptance of a coach's instructions or individual exercises, drills or games. A great teammate acknowledges the loftier goals and is willing to sacrifice for the benefit of the group. There is no true sacrifice without belief.

Belief can be an incredibly powerful force. And it goes both ways. There is nothing more powerful than having a team behind you that believes in you.

In my playing career, the player who best personified true belief was David Henderson. David was a teammate of mine for four years at Duke, and he will always be my teammate.

David grew up in rural Warren County, North Carolina, where, as a wiry, country-strong six-foot-five wing guard, he led Warren County High School to the North Carolina 3A state championship in 1982. Despite his talent, Henderson was overlooked among higher-profile, big-city players with more publicity and loftier reputations. Our 1982 Duke recruiting class was ranked number one in the nation in 1982, and David was, in fact, the lowest-rated player of the class, and the last player in that class to sign a letter of intent.

David's ranking as a high school prospect is all the evidence one needs to demonstrate that rating systems are imperfect.

In 1981 and 1982, Coach K was recruiting another North Carolina player ahead of Henderson, an outstanding prospect named Curtis Hunter. Hunter was a heralded recruit, a McDonald's All-American, and ultimately chose to attend North Carolina to play for Dean Smith. Coach K was waiting for Hunter to decide before offering David a scholarship. It was Hunter or Henderson, and it was Hunter's choice. Fortunately for Coach K, and for us, Hunter chose North Carolina, and David then decided to accept Duke's scholarship offer, even though Hunter was Coach K's first choice.

I say this without reservation: There has never been a tougher player at Duke than David Henderson. He was a ferocious competitor who refused to back down to anyone on the basketball court. No player believed in himself and his teammates more than David did. It did not matter with whom David was matched up; he expected to win and to be the better player that day. And he expected the same from his team.

"David's voice was meaningful and respected," teammate Tommy Amaker said. "From his background, he had to grind to get to the highest level, and we always had a clear recognition of the road David traveled."

My first season at Duke, Coach K started four freshmen: Johnny Dawkins, Mark Alarie, David Henderson and me. We were thrust into a veteran league with several of the best teams in the country, including Ralph Sampson's Virginia Cavaliers, Jim Valvano's eventual national champion NC State Wolfpack, and Dean Smith's defending national champion North Carolina Tar Heels. It was, at times, a brutal education in what it took to win at the championship level.

On a somber bus ride back from a loss at number one–ranked University of North Carolina, a young member of our team was in the back of the bus talking quietly, but in glowing terms, about how good North Carolina was, and just how good Michael Jordan, Sam Perkins and Brad Daugherty were. Of course, he was correct. North Carolina was ranked number one during that season, and its long list of All-Americans and future NBA stars was truly impressive. North Carolina was better than we were, and the Tar Heels had just demonstrated that to our painfully young team.

But David Henderson did not want to hear about it on that bus ride.

After listening to the platitudes about the rival opponent that had just beaten us, David walked to the back of the bus and went off. "We didn't go there to suck up to those guys! I don't want to hear how good you think they are. We were going there to win, and we should have won. If you didn't go there to win, then you shouldn't have made the trip. There is no reason we should not have won. No reason at all."

Henderson may have understood that he was not the best player in the country or the best player on that floor, but he never accepted it in competition. He believed that he would be the best player on the floor in that game, on that day, and that ours would be the best team. He believed that there was no player he could not outplay, outwork or "out-tough" on any given day. If we were playing, David Henderson believed we would win, and he would do what it took to win.

His confidence and belief were incredible and inspiring. His toughness and will made the rest of us believe.

"David amazed me," teammate Mark Alarie said. "He was the toughest guy on our team. He not only had a willingness to accept the assignment of guarding Michael Jordan, he *wanted* it. He *asked* for it. I didn't want to do it. But he relished it. And he believed to his core that he was better able to handle that than any of us."

Henderson's expectations of himself and his teammates were high. For David, when expectations are high, there are two choices: You can meet them or exceed them. More often than not, David Henderson exceeded them.

And when David got on you about your effort or performance, you automatically accepted his criticism because you knew how incredibly hard he worked. He had competitive credibility because of how hard he competed, and the fact that he never once backed down to anyone, no matter how talented or accomplished his opponent.

"He was fearless, which was far different than I was," Alarie said. "Off the court, I feared failing, and that drove me. David didn't fear anything. His toughness made me tougher. It made all of us tougher."

Henderson's attitude, words, actions and body language projected strength. I know that David had the same fears and insecurities as the rest of us, but he faced them, and didn't let them get in the way of his performance. He wanted to win, and he prepared himself to win.

Henderson certainly wasn't afraid of making a mistake. One thing that Coach K stressed was that he would never get on us for taking and missing a good shot, but he would get on us relentlessly for taking a bad shot, or for missing an assignment. If you didn't do what you were supposed to do, when you were supposed to do it, Henderson would fight you.

After our freshman year, David accepted and embraced a role change. He went from a starter and hearing his name called out at the beginning of every game to coming off of the bench as our "sixth man." Back then, the role of sixth man wasn't as celebrated as it is now, but David accepted that role and embraced it, even though he was one of our top three scorers. But at that time, coming off of the bench wasn't celebrated, and David's abilities and contributions were easier for the media to miss.

In our senior season of 1986, David returned to the starting lineup, and had a great season. David started out the season as MVP of the preseason NIT, and we all thought he would gain All-ACC recognition at the end of the year. Our star players, Johnny Dawkins and Mark Alarie, had All-American seasons, with Dawkins named National Player of the Year, but when the All-ACC teams were announced, Dawkins and Alarie were named to the first team, but David's name was nowhere to be found.

I saw David walking through the gym before practice, and I told him I thought it was ridiculous that he wasn't named All-ACC. I told him he should have been, because he was one of the best players in the league, and he had proven it. Without hesitation, David said, "Who gives a shit? Let's just win."

Henderson cared; I know he did. But he didn't let it show and he didn't let his disappointment get in the way of what the team set out to accomplish that season. That taught me a lot. All-star teams, rankings and honors are important. But the only people who truly know and understand the value of a teammate are his or her other teammates and their coaches. Outside honors are not enough. Great teammates need to let each other know how valued and important they are, and great teammates need to be celebrated internally. The ACC voters missed it on David Henderson. His teammates didn't.

David Henderson was the toughest player I ever played with. He was tough because he believed that he could win whenever he stepped onto the court to compete. His belief led all of us to believe, and we all took confidence from David's toughness.

Without David Henderson, Coach K would not have won as early as he did, or as big as he did. After playing with David, I have no doubt that Coach K was fortunate that his recruiting target chose a rival, and David Henderson was willing to come to Duke. Because wherever David Henderson went, that team was going to win. And that team was going to be tough, because David Henderson was tough.

David Henderson was never afraid to challenge a teammate and hold himself and others accountable; nor was Coach K. One of the things I have always admired about Coach K is his willingness to confront any issue at any time and get it out in the open before it becomes a bigger problem. I gained a greater appreciation for that as an assistant coach under Coach K.

I was on Coach K's staff when he won his first National Championship in 1991. This was Coach K's fifth Final Four, and he had yet to guide his team to a victory in the championship game.

The 1991 Final Four was played at the Indianapolis Hoosier Dome. Number one and undefeated UNLV, Kansas, Duke and North Carolina won their respective regions to earn the right to play for the National Championship in Indianapolis.

"I thought a lot about rationalization with regard to those previous Final Four losses," Krzyzewski said. "Toughness is the ability not to rationalize. Rationalization is to make an excuse for not achieving more than you have to that point."

To Krzyzewski, the 1991 Final Four had, in his words, "two big mountains of rationalization": one, Duke had to face the unbeaten juggernaut UNLV with archrival North Carolina playing in the opposite bracket, and two, Duke had to break through and win the championship game.

In the first national semifinal on Saturday evening, Duke's archrival North Carolina would take on Kansas, and Duke would play UNLV, the number one–ranked, undefeated and "defending" national champion.

The game against UNLV came with plenty of emotional baggage. The Runnin' Rebels had drubbed Duke the prior season in the National Championship game by a record thirty points. During Duke's week of preparation, some of Krzyzewski's assistant coaches—myself included—felt we shouldn't show the team the tape of the beating UNLV put on Duke.

Krzyzewski disagreed. He wanted to show the tape of the record-setting thirty-point loss and demonstrate to the players that if Duke cleaned up the errors it made in that game, Duke would be in the game at the end with a chance to win. And because Duke operated in close games all season long in '91 and UNLV didn't, Duke would have the advantage and would win.

While the Duke players and coaches were in the locker room preparing for the game against UNLV, the buzzer in the North Carolina–Kansas game went off. Kansas had upset the Tar Heels.

There was an audible and easily discernible sigh of relief in the Duke locker room. I felt it. Everyone felt it. It was a natural reaction. And Coach K felt it too.

When North Carolina lost, Coach K could feel the sense of euphoria and relief from the Duke players. "And it pissed me off. Their loss, in a way, could lead to us losing, and that was a big moment," Krzyzewski said. "A really big moment."

Krzyzewski came out of a small coaches' locker room into the main locker room where the players were making their final preparation to go out onto the floor for pregame warm-ups. And he lit into them.

"It is not okay to lose because Carolina lost," Krzyzewski told the team. "It is not okay to lose."

That simple acknowledgment of what we were all feeling snapped everyone out of that initial feeling and placed everyone back on track for the task at hand. I really believe that most people would have simply tried to ignore that feeling we all had, or simply "hoped" that the team would overcome it without confrontation, so as not to rock the boat just before such an important game. Krzyzewski couldn't ignore it. It was real, and he believed it needed to be addressed. It took toughness to address it.

"We're human. We, myself included, sighed and thought, 'They won't get farther than we will, and they won't win the championship over us,'" Krzyzewski said. "That's why I said something. It was not okay for us to rationalize and to think it was okay to lose just because we weren't losing to North Carolina."

With that mind-set, Duke went onto the floor of the Hoosier Dome in Indianapolis and pulled off one of the bigger and more improbable upsets in NCAA Final Four history. And it provided a tremendous opportunity to win a National Championship and at the same time overcome several obstacles.

"We ended up beating UNLV, and then we had another mountain of rationalization," Krzyzewski said. "Everyone around us was not only happy, but deliriously happy. Even right after the game, when I was shaking hands with Jerry Tarkanian, I had to tell the players to settle down, to take it easy."

Krzyzewski knew that Duke still had to beat Kansas to win the ultimate prize—the National Championship that had eluded Duke in four prior attempts. "We had to move on to the next play," Krzyzewski said.

Krzyzewski's coach and mentor, Bob Knight, gave him some significant words of wisdom that night on how to handle this situation. He called Coach K before the UNLV game to say good luck; then he added, "If you win, take immediate action to set the stage for your next win." That was an important piece of advice for Krzyzewski, and it prepared him for what he was to face next.

"Coach Knight knew how to do it," he said. "He helped me to be armed with knowledge for when the moment comes. It's a really great lesson. You're not tough alone."

That one phrase bears repeating: *You are not tough alone.* The best teams have a collective toughness, and that toughness is contagious.

On that Sunday, the day before the NCAA championship game, Duke had just gotten on the bus for practice and a final scouting report for the NCAA championship game on Monday night. Immediately upon the players' getting on the bus, Krzyzewski knew something was very wrong.

"Some of the players were wearing those Indiana Jones hats, whatever they call them, fedoras," Krzyzewski said. "They weren't carrying themselves right. Something was wrong. There was no way we were going to win like that. When we got into the locker room, I blew them out," Krzyzewski recalled.

Coach K walked into the locker room and lit into the players. "I don't like the way you're walking. I don't like the way you're talking. I don't like your body language. I don't like your attitude. You guys think you have won something, and you haven't won anything. And you won't win tomorrow night."

Unlike the tough message Coach K delivered to the team before the UNLV game, some coaches may have let slide the nonverbal signals Coach K saw from the team, thinking that challenging and holding everyone accountable might negatively affect the their confidence or knock the players off track mentally before the championship game. Coach K refuses to ignore such "small things." He believed the team was already off track, and he believed he had the trust of his team such that they could be challenged and held accountable.

Kansas coach Bill Self believes much the same as Krzyzewski with regard to the powerful messages sent by body language. "In the last two minutes of the 2008 title game against Memphis," Self said, "our body language never changed. Our guys didn't believe that they could lose. Their body language was the culmination of years of working on it, valuing it, believing in it."

Body language is so important to Self, in fact, that he talks about it every single day in practice. "I don't want a bunch of guys with their shoulders down and sighing when something goes wrong," he said. "I don't ever let body language go. Ever."

Body language is also important to Krzyzewski. Since I first played for him, he has consistently pointed out how we subtly communicated to each other and our opponents nonverbally through our body language. Coach K always wanted our body language, collectively and individually, to project strength and power, not weakness.

On that day in Indianapolis before the 1991 championship game, Krzyzewski pointed out, in a strong way, the poor body language and attitude of his team. He was honest with them and didn't tiptoe around the subject because of the lofty stage his team was about to take. He let them know how disappointed he was in them. Then he told them to go out on the floor and practice, but he wasn't going out there with them, not that way.

Some may have thought that approach to be a risky strategy, but Krzyzewski believed his players were tough enough to trust in his judgment and leadership, and he trusted that they would respond positively to being challenged in that way.

"I told them to go out onto the court by themselves, that I wasn't coming," Krzyzewski said. "I told them to look around, have fun, but I wasn't going out there because there was no way they'd win, not like that. After about ten minutes, a few players came back in and said they had a meeting, and they were ready. When I saw them on the court, I knew we would win. I knew it."

Coach K knew his team and, more important, knew what he wanted to see from his team. When he didn't see exactly what he wanted, he refused to ignore what others might consider "little things" the day before the title game. He wasn't simply going to hope things would improve and everyone would get into the right mind-set. He wanted to address them right then, right there, and he had to trust that the players understood his motives and would quickly adjust their approach and focus on the task at hand. And the players had to trust that Coach K was getting on them to make them better and give them the best opportunity to perform.

Would they retreat or shrink from the criticism? Or would they "lock in" and trust in and believe what they were being told?

"That's where Krzyzewski is the absolute best," Self said. "All of his players believe in him and what he is doing. That's not an accident."

What might have been a risky strategy for other coaches was exactly what Coach K needed to do for his team that night. He kindled the spark they needed to focus on the game and improve their chances to win.

Trust was a crucial component of the player-coach relationship. Coach K had earned his players' trust over years and years of telling them the absolute truth, both positive truth and negative truth, and they knew he was being honest with them. If he said it, that was what they needed to do. They listened, and they acted upon what they heard.

That Monday evening in Indianapolis, the Duke Blue Devils won their first NCAA men's basketball National Championship. They won, in no small measure, because they were tough enough to trust each other.

Belief in Yourself

There is nothing more powerful, motivating and inspiring than having people in your life, especially your teammates and coaches, truly believe in you. When I was in eighth grade, I played on an all-star travel team in basketball. The team was made up of all of my friends I grew up with, and was coached by Dick Spidell, a man who had coached just about every good player in our area for the prior twenty years. As it turned out, Coach Spidell provided me with a sense of belief that marked a turning point in my life.

I knew I was a pretty good player, but I didn't really understand how good I was, or where I fit into the big picture. The truth is, I never really thought about it. I just played, often without a real purpose.

After the final practice of our eighth-grade season, I was walking out of the gym with Coach Spidell into the parking lot, where my mom was waiting to pick me up. He had mentioned the adjustment to playing in high school the very next year, and I asked him whether he really thought I could play successfully at the high school level. I was headed to a public high school of more than two thousand students, and a big athletic program.

Spidell stopped, paused and looked at me with a scowl. He said, "Play at that level? Jay, you are going to be the best basketball player that Rolling Hills High School has ever had. Ever."

I really couldn't believe it. But after that day, I started to look at myself as worthy of being the best player, and I expected to play at a much higher level, and held myself to a higher standard. I looked at it that way in large measure because my coach believed in me, and allowed me to view myself that way. That was the first time anyone outside my family had told me I was really good.

Golf professional Curtis Strange, too, understands the power of belief. Strange joined the PGA Tour in 1976 and quickly became one of its most consistent, grittiest players. In the 1980s, Strange was among the world's best golfers, and topped the PGA Tour money list in 1985, 1987 and 1988. In 1988, he became the first man to win a million dollars in official money in a single tour season. Strange won back-to-back U.S. Opens in 1988 and 1989, becoming the first player since Ben Hogan to win consecutive opens.

Strange was born in Norfolk, Virginia, where his father, a local country club owner, introduced him to golf at age seven. He later attended Wake Forest University and was a member of an NCAA championship golf team.

Strange looks back to his high school basketball career as a turning point in his confidence level due to the belief his coach had in him.

"It's amazing how important it is when others have confidence in you," Strange said. "When I was a sophomore in high school, I played varsity basketball. We were in the district finals with around eight seconds in the game, and the coach said, 'Strange, get in there.' He wanted me to take the last shot."

Strange was incredulous, surprised his coach would put him in the game with the responsibility of taking the last shot.

"The fact that my coach had confidence in me to do that made a big impact on me," Strange said. "I will never forget that for as long as I live."

For me, Dick Spidell was that first coach who believed in me, and that belief provided a new sense of confidence that I could achieve whatever I put my mind to. It started with the base of self-confidence and assurance that my mother instilled in me. Parents can lay the foundation, but coaches can serve as a tremendous springboard for that confidence.

"I want every one of my players to know that I believe in them," Kansas coach Bill Self said. "I believe in what they are capable of doing, and I believe in them enough to hold them accountable for doing what they can do. I want them thinking nobody can guard them, and that they will win. If I don't believe in them, they'll know it. They'll feel it."

The confidence instilled by a coach knows no age limit. Bob Knight still inspires confidence in his former player Mike Krzyzewski. Given Coach K's incredible success and status among the elite coaches of any sport, it wouldn't seem as if he would ever need a confidence boost. But he says that he does, and that everyone does.

In 2006, Coach K was named the head coach of the United States Men's National Team, the team that would represent the United States in the Olympic Games two years later. Coach K was not only taking on the challenge of building a new program for USA Basketball with Olympic chairman Jerry Colangelo, but he was going to be coaching and working with NBA superstars. Many questioned the selection of a college coach to credibly lead NBA pros in the Olympics, and it would have been understandable for Coach K to internalize that criticism.

Just prior to the 2008 Olympics in Beijing, Bob Knight placed a phone call to Krzyzewski to wish him the best of luck. On that call, Knight asked his former player whether he thought the United States team was ready to play in Beijing. Coach K told him yes, he thought they were ready.

Then Knight said, "I want you to think of one thing. Remember that you are better than they are." Krzyzewski, thinking Knight was referring to the international competition his team would face, agreed that yes, he believed his team was better than Spain, Argentina and the rest.

"No," Knight corrected him, "you are better than the players you're coaching."

Krzyzewski took great confidence from Knight's advice. "Whether it was true or not didn't matter," Krzyzewski said. "He didn't want me to let any insecurity limit me. It helped me to be natural, to be myself, and to perform with that extra confidence."

That was an important moment and a great lesson for Krzyzewski. Notwithstanding his status as a coaching legend, even Coach K is not "tough alone" and needs the support of others. "You are not tough alone, and you are not at your most confident alone," he said.

Because of the belief that Coach Spidell had in me, I believed I could succeed at my high school, but I wasn't really sure beyond that. After all, I lived in Los Angeles, a big city full of great athletes. I had no idea how I fit in with the city's best players. After my sophomore year of high school, I got the chance to find out when I saw an article in the *L.A. Times* sports section about a tryout for the South Bay entry in the prestigious USA Olympic development summer league in Los Angeles.

The article gave the details of a two-day tryout at Loyola Marymount University, and listed the names of prominent alumni of the summer league who were now playing in college and the NBA. The two or three players from the South Bay area who had been named first team All-CIF or All-American were automatically on the team, and the tryouts were to fill the remainder of the South Bay team's roster spots.

My dad thought I should go and try out, even though I could participate in only the first day of the tryouts because I was scheduled to have my wisdom teeth extracted on the second day. We both agreed that it would be a good experience, and neither one of us thought I would make the team anyway.

When I entered the gym, I was one of more than a hundred players from the area at the tryout. I was given a number, and felt somewhat anonymous through the process. I felt like I played as hard as I could in every drill and scrimmage, and held my own against the older, more experienced players in the gym. I certainly hadn't embarrassed myself, which was my only real goal. As I packed up my gym bag at the end of the day, I felt good that I had proven I could at least hang with the best players in the area, and I was a little bit more confident because of it.

As I walked out of the gym with my dad, we bumped into Frank Burlison, a respected writer for the *Long Beach Press-Telegram*, and a legend in the Southern California high school basketball community.

"See you tomorrow," Burlison said.

"Well, no, sir," I said. "I can't be here tomorrow. I'm having my wisdom teeth taken out tomorrow, so I can't come. I'm not making the team anyway. I just wanted to do this for the experience of it."

Then Burlison turned to my dad.

"Mr. Bilas," he said. "You might want to reschedule that appointment. Your son was the best player in the gym today. He's making this team."

Of all the moments that helped me believe in myself, this was one of the most powerful. Along with Mr. Spidell telling me that I was going to be the best player ever at my high school, Frank Burlison telling my dad that I was the best player in the gym that day was a benchmark in my development as a confident, tough player and person. Those thoughts never occurred to me before they were verbalized to me.

I did reschedule my dental appointment and went back to tryouts the next day, and made the team. Right after believing I wasn't good enough to make it, I was a starter, and named to the All-League team later that summer. Because of the belief I gained from Spidell and Burlison, I started to really believe in myself, and started to expect more of myself.

Belief is a powerful thing, especially when those around you believe in you. Belief is one of the characteristics that leads to toughness. How can you be truly tough unless you believe in yourself? How can you believe in yourself if those around you do not?

As teammates, it is imperative that we let our fellow teammates know how important their abilities and contributions are, and then we can hold each other accountable for them. As coaches, it is important to let your players know their importance to the success of the team and why, instead of only correcting them and emphasizing their weaknesses. If players know you believe in them, it is easier to then hold them accountable and expect them to meet high standards. Your belief allows you to push them harder, and have them respond positively. Your belief makes them tougher.

When a player is tough enough to accept challenges from teammates and coaches, the rewards go far beyond the field of play. "Whether it is Bill Parcells or Bob Knight, even I have experienced it," former NFL coach Jon Gruden said. "Players will come to you ten years later and thank you. They say they appreciated you being on their ass, making them better and making them want to get better.

"My mom was an elementary school teacher," Gruden said. "If little Johnny got a B on one of her tests, if he got eighty-five percent, she would tell him that she thought he was capable of getting a ninety. Then she'd tell him he could get them all right. She would push him to get them all right, and the kid would respond."

To Gruden, with anything worthwhile, whether a game or a business venture, you're really chasing after perfection. He learned it first from his mother, and he has pursued it every day since then. As a Super Bowl–winning coach, Gruden starts with a positive belief in what his team and players can do, then challenges them to meet the highest standard and get better while doing it.

"The challenge you provide to a player or a coworker can be tough and even harsh, but it has to be fair," Gruden said. "I'm not out to embarrass or browbeat you. I'm focused on standards being high and expectations being high, to the point of soaring. If you want to soar, you have to put in the work."

Belief Through Adversity

It is easy to believe in yourself and your team when everything is going well, and wins are piling up. But what about when you and your team face adversity? Adversity is where your belief is tested, and where true toughness is tested.

Coach Jon Gruden has always taught his players to expect adversity, and to be prepared to use their resources to overcome it and do something better. Every year, Gruden tells his team, "Men, despite our goal to win every game, there's a good chance we're not going unbeaten. You have to have contingency plan for adversity, because you are going to face it. Period. Your only choice is how you respond to it."

Gruden points to the 2011 Super Bowl champion New York Giants as a great example of a team that used adversity to show the true level of their toughness. "They're seven and seven, lose to the Redskins, get booed out of their own stadium, and look like they'll miss the play-offs," Gruden said. "What do they do? Instead of sitting around feeling sorry for themselves or quitting, they showed the mental toughness, individually and as a team, to win the last two games and go into the tournament and win the Super Bowl.

"And I promise you one thing," Gruden said. "They did it one snap at a time." Gruden's mantra of "one snap at a time" is a crucial theme among successful players and teams, and an essential characteristic of toughness.

To Kansas coach Bill Self, true toughness is best measured when you face adversity. "It takes no courage or mental toughness to be tough when everything is going your way, and when the wind is at your back," Self said. Self isn't as concerned with how his players react when they are playing well. He wants to know what they will do when they are in the midst of a struggle, when facing difficulties in the classroom, after a breakup with a girlfriend, or when the coach is all over them in practice. Will his players deal with good times and tough times with the same resolve?

"If you meet those circumstances differently," Self said, "you're not tough. If you react to those things differently, you're soft." To Self, the difference between "tough" and "soft" is simple. "Soft is when you choose the easier path when the right path is the harder one," Self said. "That's soft.

"Soft is thinking you should have help on defense, and that thought causing a letdown," Self said. "Toughness is the anticipation that you won't get help, so you do everything in your power to stop your man. But at the same time, you know and trust your help is there. That's toughness, to me."

Self believes that toughness is a learned skill, and that it is infectious. "If the people around you are tough, and they are willing to do tough things, I think you are more likely to be tough too," Self said. "That's good peer pressure. Peer pressure can make us do things we shouldn't do, but it can make us want to do the tough things, the right things, too."

Self will never allow his players to compromise, to take the easy path in favor of the tough path. He conditions his team to expect the tougher path, and to want it. "I won't let our players switch a screen or go under a ball screen until January every year," Self said. "That is the softer way, the easier way. I never want to give them the easier way, or allow them to think there is a way they can allow themselves to be soft."

My former teammate Tommy Amaker didn't look tough as a college player. He was small and looked like he couldn't move the needle when he stepped onto the scale. But Amaker was an incredibly tough and focused competitor who studied the game and the tendencies of his teammates and opponents. Amaker was not just a student of the game; he was a student of the nuances of the game. His preparation and thorough knowledge of the game, including the tendencies of those playing, led to his confidence as a player and a leader on the court.

When Amaker and I were teammates on the 1985 U.S. National Select Team, we roomed together for part of the trip. One afternoon, one of our assistant coaches came into our room to give Tommy an extra bit of scouting information in preparation for our next game. Every time the coach started a sentence to inform Tommy of the tendencies and abilities of the point guard of our upcoming opponent, Amaker finished the coach's sentence, and he was right every single time.

I was impressed, and I told Tommy so. But I also asked him why he didn't just sit there and let the coach tell him the information. It wouldn't have occurred to me to finish my coach's sentences.

"He needs to trust me with the ball, and with the team," Amaker said. "I wanted him to know that I already knew those things because I had watched that team and point guard play myself, and I was already on top of it." Amaker opened the coach's eyes as to just how engaged he was. I already knew Tommy was "on it" in so many ways, but I had never thought about the trust factor between a coach and a point guard. Tommy's tremendous preparation helped to build the trust between coach and player that is vital to success and an important ingredient in toughness.

Amaker has always been tough through adversity too. One of the toughest times for Amaker and his own belief system was when he was a player and was cut by the NBA's Seattle Supersonics in

1987. He remembers it as the first time he was ever told that he wasn't quite good enough.

"Not that I wasn't good enough to play or start," Amaker said. "But that I wasn't good enough to even make the team, to be on the roster. That was a tough blow."

Amaker was born and raised in Falls Church, Virginia, and was the first freshman to make his varsity basketball team at W. T. Woodson High School, where his mother was a respected English teacher. Amaker joined our team at Duke in 1983–84 and immediately became our floor leader and a four-year starter at point guard who led Duke to the NCAA Tournament four times. Amaker was an instrumental part of our 1986 ascent to the NCAA championship game and a 37–3 overall record. In 1987, Amaker was named an All-American and the winner of the Henry Iba Corinthian Award as the nation's top defensive player. Amaker's playing career also includes a gold medal as part of the U.S. National Team at the 1986 World Championships, and a silver medal, with me, on the U.S. National Select Team in 1985.

Amaker went on to become the head basketball coach at Seton Hall and Michigan, and then in 2007 he was named head men's basketball coach at Harvard University, making him the only African-American among Harvard's thirty-two head coaches. His tenure at Harvard quickly sparked a long list of firsts for the school: first appearance in a top-twenty-five ranking; first win against a BCS school; first win over a ranked team; first Ivy League championship; and first bid to the NCAA Tournament since 1946.

Competition in life is also accompanied by the occasional tough blows. Hall of Fame basketball coach Pat Riley calls such events "thunderbolts." For Amaker, getting cut by the Seattle Supersonics after he was drafted in 1987 was something to come back from, not to shrink from.

"It takes toughness to endure, to get up and to come back with some fight in you," Amaker said. "And to do that with a positive attitude. That takes real toughness."

Amaker has faced adversity in coaching, as well. After a successful tenure at Seton Hall, he took over a Michigan program that was
hit by NCAA probation and sanctions for violations that occurred
many years prior to his arrival. After six seasons in Ann Arbor, including an NIT championship, he was fired.

"It isn't easy to be told you're no longer wanted, and it's meaningful to fight your way back and accomplish what we have accomplished together at Harvard," Amaker said. "It was a hard, tough
journey, with a lot of grit and grind to it. To take a program in the
Ivy League that had never won the league title, ever, and win back-
to-back Ivy League titles? That took toughness on the part of this
group."

But Amaker did not look at his success at Harvard as "bouncing
back" from being fired, but as a "comeback." To Amaker, bouncing back connotes something you do every day from simply getting
knocked back. Getting fired didn't knock him back; it knocked him
down. But because of his belief, it did not knock him out. Amaker
was tough enough to come back. His mother used to tell him,
"A setback is a setup for a comeback." Comebacks are hard, whether
you're coming back in a game, facing adversity on the road, or picking yourself off the deck after getting knocked down. To Amaker,
it all comes down to being mentally tough, and enduring.

Curtis Strange believes his toughest moment was recovering
from and coming back from falling short of winning the Masters in
1985. Strange had a lead on the back nine at Augusta, but couldn't
finish it. "I threw up all over my shoes down the stretch," Strange
said. "I should have won, but I didn't. That was the first time I felt I
should have won and I blew it.

"I had a choice to make. I could stay on the ground, grovel in
my tears and go away forever," Strange said. "Or I could pick myself
up, put my boots on again and just go do it. I needed to just get back
in it. That's the best thing, to get back in the fight, to suck it up and
fight it. I didn't win. But I can win and I will win again. That takes
toughness."

Setbacks are short-term and changeable. And failure isn't a lasting condition either. Setbacks and failure linger only if you allow them to.

Failing doesn't make you a failure. Failing makes you a competitor. Every competitor fails. If you lay it on the line, you will come up short at times. Failure is a part of competing, and embracing that fact is an important component of toughness. Tough people fail, but tough people are not failures. The only failures are those who give up, or give in.

One person whom I have never seen give up or give in is NBA and former Duke great Grant Hill. Hill believes it takes extraordinary mental toughness to fight through adversity. "It is easy to be tough when things are going your way. But what about when your shot isn't falling? What do you do when Kobe Bryant is lighting you up? Do you concede, give in? Or do you continue to fight, to compete? Those are the tough players and the tough people, the ones that fight through adversity," Hill said.

Grant Hill may very well be the best basketball player who has ever played at Duke. He is also one of the toughest players who ever played at Duke. But that wasn't always the case. Hill learned to be tougher, and his coach and teammates helped make him tougher.

Of all the players he's coached at Duke, Mike Krzyzewski calls Grant Hill the most talented. Hill played in three NCAA Final Fours, won two National Championships, and came within a single basket of winning three. In his college career, Hill was the first player in ACC history to amass more than nineteen hundred points, seven hundred rebounds, four hundred assists, two hundred steals and one hundred blocks. He was named All-American and National Defensive Player of the Year.

Then, in his first six seasons in the NBA, Hill performed at a level worthy of the Naismith Basketball Hall of Fame. Over those first six years, Hill totaled 9,393 points, 3,417 rebounds and 2,720 assists. In the history of the NBA, only Oscar Robertson, Larry Bird and LeBron James have reached those numbers in their first six seasons.

Hill was not only an amazing talent, but he has shown admirable toughness throughout his great career in overcoming injuries that could very well have ended his career, and ended his life. Grant Hill is incredibly tough, but he didn't start out that tough.

Early on in his basketball career, Grant Hill felt that he was labeled a "reluctant superstar." "I always resented that," Hill said. "I mean, I had really good players around me at Duke, but we won two straight titles. I wasn't reluctant to do what it took to win."

Another label that Hill faced was that he was a child of privilege, and that made him soft, or lack toughness. "Grant has always been privileged," Tommy Amaker said. "He grew up in a world of privilege. But that did not mean that he did not have high expectations on him, and that he did not need to be tough to accomplish what he accomplished. Nobody reaches the heights Grant has reached without being tough."

A major hurdle for Hill was accepting and overcoming the fact that he was a special talent, and stood out from his age group and his peers. "Grant was uncomfortable with that, uncomfortable with being seen as special," Amaker said. "At that time, it meant being different. To him, it was more important to belong."

Part of Hill's mind-set stemmed from not wanting to be different or to separate from his friends. "But part of it was that I doubted I was good enough for that. Even in high school, I was unsure." As a high school freshman, Hill was chosen to play varsity basketball at South Lakes High School. He didn't want to play varsity as a freshman. He wanted to play on the freshman team with his classmates.

"To me, that was the beauty of Grant Hill, and a real form of mental toughness," Amaker said. "He had the talent and ability to stand out, but the willingness to fit in. To me, that's beautiful."

Even as a prep player, Amaker was floored by Hill's humility, especially given his extraordinary talent level and national acclaim. "Grant called me one day after he had committed to Duke. He said, 'Do you really think I can play in the ACC?'" Amaker said. "I said, 'Are you kidding? Grant, you're the best player in the country!'"

Hill admits he was a bit unsure of himself, but he found a way to get over his insecurities and toughen up his game.

"Let's not fool ourselves," Amaker said. "Duke didn't win a National Championship until Grant Hill got there. The things he did as a freshman at Duke proved he had tremendous toughness, both mentally and physically."

Krzyzewski echoes Amaker's opinions. "The reason we won a National Championship was Grant. His defense on Stacey Augmon and then Alonzo Jamison was amazing. He was amazing," Coach K said.

Amaker believes a part of Hill's toughness emanates from Hill's unselfishness. "Grant is exceedingly unselfish," Amaker said. "He was that talented and that good, but he was not disruptive to the team dynamic in any way. It was never about him."

Amaker said that Hill bristled at being thought of as selfish. "He never wanted to be seen that way," Amaker said. "So, to get him to be more assertive, we flipped it." Coach K told Hill that he was actually being selfish by trying to be so unselfish. Coach K and his teammates wanted more. They wanted Hill to be more assertive, to look to shoot more, to take over more responsibility, and to impose his will in every game and practice.

"A real strength of Grant's, and a sign of his toughness, is that he would not take over the team, but he would take over a game or a possession," Amaker said. "He was respectful of older players, recognized leadership and the chain of command, but he could follow that lead and still break out."

Krzyzewski also attributes Hill's toughness to his strong foundation. "Grant has an incredible set of values, as strong as anyone's," Krzyzewski said. "Those values have really helped him, but they have also been a weakness at times. He has rationalized and deferred at times, especially early on in his career."

Coach K had to be forceful with Hill to help him become the best player he could be. He knew it wasn't easy for Hill to stand out because of his skill level, because he just wanted to fit in and be a member of the team. Krzyzewski believed in Hill, and needed only to communicate that belief. He did it using various methods and modes of communication, especially communicating through Hill's teammates. And Krzyzewski credits a single play where nonverbal communication delivered the message.

"In the 1991 championship game, Grant made one of the best plays ever in the Final Four, that lob pass he caught from Bobby Hurley," Krzyzewski said. "That was when he recognized his place." On that play, Hurley and Hill made momentary eye contact that communicated that Hurley was going to throw a lob pass to the rim, and trust that Hill would go get it.

The pass was high, and seemingly out of reach. Hill soared to reach the pass with his right hand, and dunked the ball while his momentum carried him away from the basket. It was a play only a few in the game's history were capable of making, and Grant Hill made it. To Hurley and Krzyzewski, it wasn't surprising. But it was transforming.

Earlier that season, Krzyzewski had a meeting with teammate Christian Laettner and Hurley. He asked them to name the best player on the team. Neither hesitated. They both said it was Grant Hill.

"I told them he was the most talented, but he would only give you so much, because he is not tough enough yet to show all that he can do," Krzyzewski said. "I told them they had to let him know that."

Coach K also credits another teammate, Brian Davis, who, along with Christian and Bobby, let Hill know how much the team believed in him. "Davis was like a corner man in boxing. He'd say, 'Grant, you're the best player; they can't stop you; you're unbeatable,'" Krzyzewski said.

Krzyzewski communicated to Hill, directly and through Hill's teammates, his belief in what Hill could do. He wasn't afraid that

Hurley, Laettner or Davis would be jealous. He was honest and straightforward in his opinions on what was best for the team. From that, Hill blossomed, and they all became champions.

"That lob play was a great communication and belief play, but not just the eye contact and communication between Bobby Hurley and Grant Hill on the play itself, or the belief they would do it," Krzyzewski said. "Further, the connection was symbolic of what those guys had done the whole year to help Hill reach that point. They expressed their belief in who Hill was, and as a result, he was also able to believe in his own abilities and feel free to be who he was."

The play was symbolic of their collective and individual toughness. Hill, Hurley, Laettner and Davis were tough enough to believe in each other and in their coach, and they were tough enough to communicate that belief without personal agenda. To me, the story of Grant Hill's development has always been a story of great teammates who were willing to bring out the best in each other without concern for their own individual benefit. But when the team won, every individual benefited far more than they would have otherwise.

That takes trust, belief and communication. That takes toughness.

CHAPTER 2

PREPARATION

One of the things I take pride in is being prepared. In my job as a trial lawyer and as a broadcaster, I take meticulous care in preparing my cases and for games and studio appearances. My preparation leads to my confidence, and allows me to react quickly under pressure.

I once heard Bob Knight say that everybody has a will to win, but not everybody has a will to prepare to win. My will to prepare has been a guiding principle in my career, but that wasn't the case when I was young. Whatever I learned about preparation, I learned from my father, though it took some time for those lessons to take effect. My dad set down the foundation for my preparation and my will to prepare.

Before I was born, my dad worked as a commercial fisherman out of the Port of Los Angeles in San Pedro, California. My grandfather was a fishing boat captain, and commercial fishing was hard, backbreaking work that kept my dad at sea, often for months at a time. But I never knew my dad as a fisherman. I knew him as the owner of his own television sales and service business, and as an investor in real estate. I remember my dad as a hard worker who was always prepared.

When I was a kid, I always looked forward to my dad getting home at night. There were many days when he left for work before I woke up, but he usually made it a priority to get home at night before we went to bed. One night, after my dad had gotten home, I expected him to hang out in the den with me and watch a baseball game on television.

Instead, I found him sitting at the kitchen table with a bunch of papers around him, working on a yellow pad.

"What are you doing, Dad?"

"I'm preparing for the day tomorrow," he said. "I'm setting out all the things I need to get done." I didn't get it. My dad was home from work. I thought he did his work at work, not at home. I thought he was finished.

"But you just got home from work," I said. "Can't you do that stuff tomorrow? I thought you were your own boss?"

He chuckled. My dad never lectured me. I asked him a question, and he answered it.

"I'm preparing now, so I can get a clean start first thing in the morning. I can't just wake up and then decide what to do. I'm taking a little extra time to prepare now, so I don't waste time tomorrow," he said. "And I am my own boss. But that also means I don't have anyone to remind me what to do. I have to plan it, and then do it myself. You'll see someday."

I look back on the things my father told me about preparation and concentration, and everything he told me was right. My father never went to work unprepared. When he was working on a project, he had it planned out, and had a contingency plan for things he expected might go wrong. He never left things to chance.

In his coaching career, Bob Knight was much the same way. Knight prepared meticulously for games and practices, and his greatest concern was whether he had anticipated and planned every conceivable detail heading into a game, and he was willing to do whatever it took to do so. "The biggest fear I had going into any game was, did I do everything I could to fully prepare our team to play this game?" Knight said.

To Knight, toughness didn't have anything to do with the physical. It was mental, and about the will and concentration necessary to prepare, mentally and physically, to play.

For former NFL star and NFL head coach Herm Edwards, toughness flowed from the preparation he put into his physical fitness. The better shape Edwards was in, the tougher he could be. "By far, the most important thing to me is the mental toughness necessary to put in the physical preparation, the conditioning, the fitness, especially in the off-season," Edwards said. "No one was in better shape than I was, and I made sure of that. I worked so that I would never have to check out physically."

As a player, Edwards found confidence in his preparation and his ability to play at the same speed on the first play and the last play. That is a consistent theme among the tough people that I know. They each take confidence from their work, and their confidence is the payoff from the investment they have made through their work. "For me, because of the level of my preparation, survival was never an issue. I never had to concern myself with just making it through," Edwards said.

Edwards is right. How many players start practice with the intention or goal of simply "getting through" practice? Instead of "getting through" a workout, players need to "get from" a workout—to get the most from it, and the most from themselves. No player ever got better by just getting through something. True toughness is competing through the end of a practice or workout after having prepared yourself mentally to compete. That is a key mind-set of the toughest players.

In the classroom and behind the coaching scenes, Edwards concentrated on staying mentally focused. He knew and emphasized his personal goals and knew exactly what his team was trying to accomplish. "I knew the objective," Edwards said. "Your eyes don't lie. I've seen it. I know what to do, why we are doing it, and how to do it. Now, let's go play. Let's go compete."

Edwards played nine seasons as a defensive back with the Philadelphia Eagles, never missing a game. After a very good high school and college football career, Edwards was overlooked by the NFL. "I went undrafted," Edwards said. "Undrafted! The NFL basically said they didn't want me."

To make it in the NFL, Edwards had to go to Eagles' training camp as a free agent. He had an opportunity, but he wasn't sure what kind. He only knew it was up to him to be prepared for his opportunity, whenever it came. If it was only one series of plays, Edwards had to be prepared for his opportunity. That opportunity was all he felt he was owed.

"When it's your turn, when you have a shot, an opportunity, you have to be prepared for it and take advantage of it," Edwards said. "You may not get the same number of snaps or the same opportunity as some other guy, but you will get an opportunity. It is up to you to take advantage of it."

There were 125 players in the Eagles' training camp, twenty-two of whom were at Edwards's position of defensive back. "Twenty-two people at my position," Edwards said. "And only six make it! I was a free agent. I wasn't getting a second look or the benefit of the doubt. Nobody was invested in me or invested with me."

Edwards had the mind-set that, even though nobody believed in him, nobody could keep him down, either. He knew that there were naysayers, people within the organization who felt he couldn't do it. Edwards's issue was how he responded to that. "How do you deal with it when you are better than the guys around you, but you are not *the* guy, not the first guy?" Edwards asked. "How do you deal with it when you play well, but are not rewarded?"

The answer was mental toughness. "I had to have toughness," Edwards said. "I had to have real mental toughness. And when the smoke cleared, when we got to the first preseason game," Edwards said, "I was the starter."

Edwards credited his preparation, the work he had put in, for the toughness required to make the team. He was fully prepared and willing to do the necessary things, the tough things, that others were simply not willing to do. Edwards did extra conditioning and film study so he was fully prepared to compete at training camp. He didn't just make up his mind in training camp to do those tough things; he had prepared himself mentally and physically before training camp even began, and that preparation continued throughout his career. His preparation led to who he was as a player.

"Others were not willing to endure what I was willing to endure. Others were not willing to do the hard things I was willing to do," Edwards said. "Others could not perform at my level every day. I believe I made that team and was a starter on that team because of toughness. I was mentally tough, and I was mentally tough *consistently*."

Edwards learned early on that his opponent, his competition, didn't matter. Someone is going to be lining up opposite him every play, and whoever that player is, he will be good. "I don't care who it is," Edwards said. "I was going to be prepared when I stepped between those lines, and I was going to cover whoever lined up against me." To Edwards, what mattered was his will to keep preparing, to keep competing. He couldn't control the identity or preparation of his opponent, but he could control his own preparation. For Edwards, it was not about competing against an opponent, but competing against himself so he was best prepared to take on any opponent. "I have to compete against me," Edwards said. "I have to compete against my will. I have to push through and compete against me, every day."

When you are fully prepared, you can go out and perform. You can react without having to think your way around the field or the court. The prepared player is more athletic, because the prepared player is reacting instead of thinking. Preparation allows you to be tougher. It is an investment in your toughness, and it pays off.

Preparation isn't about talent. In fact, often the players with the most talent feel they can rely upon that talent, and may not feel they need to prepare as diligently. The less talented player can often feel that preparation and work is the thin margin by which he can remain competitive, and set himself apart that way. "Most of the players with more talent, I was in better condition," Edwards said. "They felt like they didn't have to be in better condition because they had more talent."

North Carolina coach Roy Williams likes to say "persistence prevails when all else fails" and agrees that preparation is an investment. "It is like the stock market. The more you invest, the more it means to you. That's ownership. Everything important starts with your investment in it. People say 'all in,'" Williams said.

Williams perfected his preparation habits under his former boss, Hall of Fame coach Dean Smith, whom Williams calls "the master of preparation." Dean Smith had his teams and his players completely ready in every conceivable way, and from that total preparation, Smith gave his teams great confidence, and freed them to go out and just play. And play to win.

"His teams were totally prepared down to the last detail. And every day they gave maximum effort," Williams said. "From that, preparation and effort, they had the confidence and focus they needed, and that would not allow them to give in."

Williams wants his players to be so invested in their mission that they can function through errors and finish in style. "When my players say, 'My bad,' after a mistake, it drives me crazy. I saw it; I know it was your mistake," Williams said. "Saying, 'My bad,' is just a way to relieve yourself of responsibility for the mistake.

"At some point in every game," Williams said, "and I mean every game, somebody gives in." Preparation is the best tool for working through those moments of distress and weakness.

A player who is prepared can face negative situations with confidence and belief that he can turn a negative into a positive. Tough players keep plugging, keep believing, and keep playing. Tough players don't quit. When a player is fully and completely prepared, it is harder to quit because of the investment made. Nobody can be tough when they are unprepared.

Concentrate on What You're Doing While You're Doing It

After one of my high school basketball games, my father asked me whether anything was bothering me, because I looked distracted on the court.

"Yeah, I guess so. I have a couple of tests tomorrow, and a paper due," I said. "I have a lot to do, and I probably left too much until the night before."

My dad paused for a while; then he spoke.

"You know, it's okay for you to concentrate only on the game while you're playing," he said. "You're committed to being out there, so you might as well devote all of your attention to it. It didn't do you any good to think about school while you were playing. It didn't get you any closer to getting it done, and it didn't get you any closer to playing your best.

"But when the game is over, you move on to the next thing, and concentrate fully on that."

That's what my dad always did: He concentrated on one thing at a time. He made it look easy, but I learned that it wasn't easy for him or anyone else. It took concentration and mental preparation, and those were skills that you had to work on.

My dad went on to tell me that there was no use thinking about things you couldn't do anything about. I had set aside time to play in a game, and no amount of thinking about school was going to make me a better student or player during that game. That was time set aside only for basketball. I knew what time the game was, and I should be prepared for it by getting my schoolwork done and off my mind.

But my dad also said that it was a waste of time to think about basketball when I was studying. Whether I set aside the time to play ball, study or spend time with friends, I should devote my full attention to that until it was over. Then move on.

I guess my dad wouldn't be considered a multitasker, and neither would I. In large measure because of the great example set by my father, I strive to concentrate on one thing, I strive to get it done right, and then I strive to move on to the next thing and concentrate fully on that.

One Step at a Time

When I was in high school, my mom and dad thought it would be a good idea for me to work with my father over the summer. My dad owned some retail store properties that required construction renovation to bring them "to code" for California's new earthquake standards. I may have been cheap labor, but I think my mom and dad wanted me to have a better idea of what a real day's work was all about. I really had no concept of work. My father had once emphasized to me that I should work hard to one day make my living sitting down rather than standing up. I had no clue how hard a "standing up" job really was.

My dad had planned out the construction project down to the last detail. He had hired a small crew to work with him, and he was the hardest and most focused worker on the crew. When the crew took a break, my dad kept working. It was incredibly impressive. Here I was, this hotshot, highly recruited athlete, and I couldn't keep up with my dad. He wore me out.

One day my dad gave me a task. He asked me to take the tools and materials from the ground to the roof. I had to haul the gear up a ladder, about fifteen to twenty feet from the ground. Like a fish story, the height probably increases as the years go by!

That task seemed small and somewhat unimportant to me, and I didn't take it as seriously as I should have. Thinking I was really smart, I figured if I carried a bigger load up the ladder, I would have to make fewer trips up and down. By carrying more, I figured I could save myself some time and effort.

On my first overloaded trip up the ladder, I carelessly missed a rung, slipped and fell to the ground. I wasn't very far up, and I was embarrassed rather than injured. But I was probably lucky I wasn't farther up, and that I didn't get hurt. My dad saw me fall and that I was all right. He laughed a little bit, and shook his head.

"You need to concentrate on what you're doing, while you're doing it," he said.

Then he said something really profound, which I have never forgotten.

"You can't get to the top of that ladder in one step. But you can get to the bottom in one step."

I'm not sure my dad knew at the time that he was providing me with a piece of advice that I would use throughout my adult life. Every rung on that ladder was important, and there was nothing more important in my world at that precise time than getting up and down that ladder safely, and doing that job correctly. Why would I think about anything else? What else could I do but what was in front of me? I needed to concentrate.

That seemingly small, unimportant task demanded my full attention, and it demanded from me the discipline and toughness to get it done, and to get it done right. Even though I was the last man on that small crew, and probably of little real help on the job, other people were relying upon me to do my small job well so that they could do their jobs well. If I failed to do my job correctly, especially if I had been injured, someone else would have to do my job for me, or have to leave their job to take care of me.

The truth was, I wasn't disciplined enough or tough enough to concentrate on my small job, and to do it right. There should not have been any task that was "too small" for me to do, and to do right. That job was important because my boss, my dad, asked me to do it. It was a test of my toughness, and I failed it.

Coach K used to say, "Discipline is not punishment. Discipline is doing the right thing, at the right time, to the best of your ability." Whether my job was to carry materials on a job site, set a screen in a play diagrammed by my coach, or to provide support to a colleague that some may consider "below my pay grade," there is no task too small for me to execute to the best of my ability.

I have had the great pleasure of working with Boston Celtics assistant coach Kevin Eastman at the Nike Skills Academies. Eastman played college basketball at Richmond, and is the former head coach at Belmont Abbey, UNC Wilmington and Washington State. He is as fine a teacher of the game as I have ever been around, and is one of the most thoughtful people in basketball. Eastman often says that "discipline" is doing what you should do over what you want to do. Maturity, Eastman says, is when what you should do is what you want to do.

Several years ago, Wake Forest coach Skip Prosser was telling me about some of the issues he was having with his team's discipline, focus and concentration. While we were talking, I shared what my dad had told me, and the story of the ladder. Skip loved the metaphor.

The next day, when the Wake Forest team came out for practice, there was a ladder under the basket. On each rung of the ladder, Skip had the next game, and wanted his team to picture each rung on the ladder as an important step toward the top, their ultimate destination.

Skip credited me. He should have credited my dad. I do, every day.

Everything We Do Is Important

As an eighteen-year-old college freshman, I thought I understood what a "big game" was, and what it took to perform in one.

Early on during my freshman year, Coach K came into the

locker room to deliver a scouting report for a game against one of the "lesser" opponents on our schedule. We were playing a team we should beat, even if we played less than our best. It was not a game that would attract much media attention or excite the casual fan. And it was not the kind of opponent that would excite a normal player.

Well, it excited Coach K.

"This is the most important game on our schedule," he said.

What? We had number one Virginia, defending national champion North Carolina, and Final Four participant Louisville coming up on our schedule, and *this* game was the most important?

"It's the most important game on our schedule because *we* are playing it," Coach K said. "And everything we do is important."

Coach K stressed to us that if we truly wanted to play for championships, we needed to approach every single game as a championship game and give championship effort in every single practice. Our opponent did not determine our standard of performance or our level of preparation. We were striving to meet a standard of excellence, not just trying to beat this team. If we met our standard of excellence, winning would take care of itself.

It's funny to me now, but I had never really put together the similarities between my dad's work ethic and preparation and Coach K's. When I heard Coach K's approach about there being nothing that was more important than what we were doing, I thought of my dad and his advice to concentrate on what you were doing while you were doing it, and the importance of each rung of the ladder in getting to the top.

It was the same thing, just communicated in a different manner. Coach K was helping me build on the foundation set by my father, and those lessons made a profound impact upon me, and shaped the way I have approached my work since.

My very first game announcing for ESPN was Charleston Southern versus UNC Greensboro. It was not a game that would grab big ratings or attract much attention. But it was a "big game" for me, because it was my game and, based upon what my dad and Coach K taught me, everything I do is important. That game was the first rung on the ladder, and an important one. The reputation of the teams or how many people will be watching should not, and does not, change the standard of excellence I am striving to reach. The job is the same whether it is Charleston Southern in a Big South game or Kentucky in the Final Four.

But there were more reasons to treat my game as the most important game being played that day.

While the vast majority of people watching college basketball that day would not consider the game important, it was of great importance to the people who were watching it, including the players' families and my bosses at ESPN. For both Charleston Southern and UNC Greensboro, that game might very well have been the only time each team would be on television that season. And, just starting out, it might very well have been the only time I was on television if I didn't perform to a high standard.

I prepared for that first ESPN game as if it were the NCAA championship game, and for me, it was. I watched tapes of the two teams. I talked to coaches on the other teams in their league. I scouted the two teams in person. I went to the practices of both teams and watched film with one of the teams that invited me into their scouting report. I was as prepared as I could be when the game started.

My preparation allowed me to watch the game intently and react to what I saw. I was inexperienced, so I was hardly relaxed, but I was more relaxed than if I had been less prepared. The game was a close one, and came down to the last shot. After a time-out, Charleston Southern had the ball, trailing 67–66, with a chance to run a play for the last shot and to win the game. As the teams stepped out onto the court, I was asked what I expected in the game's final play.

I expected to see Charleston Southern run a play for their best players, Eric Burks or Brett Larrick, who had twenty-two and nineteen points, respectively, in the game to that point. But, I said, what

I would be most concerned with would be an offensive rebound. The initial shot was important, but the offensive rebound and tip-in was often a higher-percentage shot. I emphasized to watch the offensive rebound.

Larrick took the last shot and missed. Burks grabbed the rebound and put in a shot at the buzzer to win, 68–67.

Of course, when Burks scored on the offensive rebound, I looked smart. The truth is, I got lucky. But had I not been fully prepared for that game, I would have been scrambling at the end, and likely could have missed the opportunity to react to the situation. My preparation allowed me to take advantage of my luck on that last play.

Today I take the same approach to preparation as I did for my very first ESPN game in 1995, although I am far more efficient now. I am constantly looking for better and more efficient ways to prepare, and to find better techniques.

In my job with ESPN, I really have no control over how people respond or react to my performance. This is a subjective business in which people have opinions. If people like or dislike me or my work, whether they are players, coaches, fans or my bosses, there is not much I can do about it. There are simply significant elements of broadcasting that are matters of individual taste and individual judgment.

The only thing I control is how I prepare, and how I react to every situation.

I take my preparation seriously, and I put my time in. I love what I do. I love basketball, and I love being in the gym. I cannot think of a time when I would rather be somewhere else.

For me, preparation is like shaving: I do it every day. I study the game, I study the players, and I do it every single day. I strive to be excellent in my preparation. If my preparation is up to a standard of excellence, I am more likely to reach my highest level of execution. How can I possibly expect to be excellent if my preparation is not up to the level of excellence?

During the season, when I sit courtside to broadcast games as a color analyst, I study the two teams that are playing, and I prepare as if I were a coach in that game. I begin with one team, and I watch the most recent tapes of that team's games. I take notes and prepare a thorough scouting report of the tendencies of each player, his strengths and weaknesses, and important statistics from that player's last four games.

I also break down the offensive and defensive tendencies for that team, whether it plays man-to-man defense, whether it is denial defense or allows passes, whether it switches screens or fights through them, how it defends pick and rolls, how it defends the post, and how it defends out-of-bounds plays. I even have play diagrams for its most often used set plays that I may choose to point out during the course of a broadcast.

I spend time talking to people in and around the game, including the coaches who have recently played against those teams. Often an opposing coach will tell you much more about a team he has just played than about his own team. I take advantage of that.

Then I do the exact same thing for the other team.

I usually arrive at a game site the day before the game. I attend the practices of both teams, and the "shoot-arounds" on the day of the game. If coaches are open to it, I will sit in on any team meetings, coaches' meetings, scouting reports or film sessions of any team that will have me. Fortunately, most coaches are kind enough to invite me into those private sessions.

Once I have gathered every possible piece of information in preparation for the game, I next prepare a "game chart." I produce a handwritten chart, which is essentially a scouting report for each team, for every single game that I do. It is that exercise, of preparing those charts by hand, that gets the relevant information in my head. The process of producing those charts prepares me for the game, and my preparation allows me the freedom to follow my instincts.

I keep the chart with me during the game, but I rarely look at it, unless I am retrieving a key stat or a key piece of information at an appropriate time. In the average broadcast, I may use only 10 percent of the information I have on my chart during the game. But I never know which 10 percent will be called for by the circumstances.

My preparation allows me to simply watch the game and react to what I see on the floor. Essentially, my preparation allows me to say what I think, without some script prodding me to work something in when it may not fit. I have a chart there to consult if I need it, but I usually look at it only during time-outs or at halftime.

Through the best and most accomplished coaches allowing me in, I have learned a great deal about the game, and have seen it from so many different perspectives. From my seat as an ESPN college basketball analyst, I have had the privilege of learning the game from many of the very best coaches in the game's history. And that has allowed me a better understanding of the game from every conceivable angle, as both a person and a professional.

And I'm always continuing to observe and learn. I watch games, college and pro, all season long and into the off-season. I watch DVDs of games; I watch player and team breakdowns with Synergy Sports Technology; I attend coaching clinics, and read books on the game. I strive to constantly learn more about basketball, from X and O strategy, to the newest teaching methods and drills, to the rules and how the game is officiated, to the history and tradition of the game. I want to know everything I can about basketball, and I am always willing to learn. During the summer, I have been a skills instructor for the Nike Skills Academies, and I teach at camps and lecture at clinics. Put simply, I try to immerse myself in the game.

I take notes. I take a lot of notes. I take notes when watching games, attending games, attending practices, sitting in meetings, or having lunch with someone from whom I can learn. I keep those notes in a book, and I carry that book with me wherever I go.

And I steal ideas from the people I work with. I watch how others prepare, the materials they use to do their jobs, and I ask questions so that I might incorporate something more efficient or effective into my routine. Over the last seventeen years, I have adjusted the charts I use based upon seeing how others do it, and I have learned different approaches to studying the game.

I used to say, "I have to prepare." I usually said it when I had to turn something down, and would respond to an invitation by saying, "I can't. I have to prepare for a game."

I suppose preparation can be seen as obligation, but I don't view it that way—at least, not anymore. I *want to* prepare, and I have come to really enjoy the preparation and enjoy the process. I love diving deeper into the game and learning from those who play and coach it. I learn something new almost every game, every day that I am around the game. To me, it isn't work. I have really come to enjoy it.

I like to be complimented like anyone else, but I am also open to criticism. I have a simple rule for myself: My opinion is of no greater value than the opinion of any other person. Just because I am on ESPN, or just because I have played and coached, doesn't make me right. And just because a critic of mine or someone who disagrees with my positions didn't play or coach, or isn't in the business of basketball, doesn't make that person wrong.

Whenever I speak to people in and around the game, whether to coaches, administrators or referees, I provide them with my cell phone number. I also tell them that if there is ever a time that I say or write something with which they disagree, I want to know about it. I encourage them to call me and let me know, and I promise them that it will be well received.

I want to get it right, not just once in a while, but every time. There is a difference between being confident in your opinion and thinking you're always right. I am the former, but I am not the latter.

When I state an opinion, of course I believe I am right in that opinion. Otherwise I wouldn't state it. But I am also willing to accept and acknowledge that I can be wrong. When I am wrong, or when others believe I am wrong, I need to know about it.

If I am alerted to a differing opinion or interpretation, I can address it, explain my position or consider and assess the validity of the opposing view. If I believe something, I have researched and carefully considered it, and I have a basis for my judgment. I will stand behind it and stand up for it, unless convinced I am wrong. That is how I learn, and that is how I grow. There is nothing wrong with people challenging your opinion. That is what debate is all about, and what people in my job should welcome.

I have the pleasure of working with the great Bill Raftery, analyst and former college basketball coach, and one of the finest people I have ever known. I have never heard a single person say an ill word about Bill. He is the best among us, both personally and professionally.

Of the many great Bill Raftery lines, I always remember what he said in response to someone who approached him to take issue with something he had said on the air.

"Geez, I must've missed all your thank-you notes for the good stuff!" Raftery quipped, with a big smile and laugh. The two of them started laughing together, and Bill patiently explained the basis of his opinion.

I remember thinking, *If Bill Raftery gets criticized or disagreed with, what makes me think I shouldn't be criticized or disagreed with?*

I view my job simply. My job is to say the right thing, at the right time, and in the right tone. Most often I get the latter part wrong. To get your point across, tone is very important. I never want to come across as angry, but when I am emphatically making a point, that can sometimes happen. And with limited time to make a point on the air, it is not uncommon to state your position in the wrong tone, or at the wrong time. When that happens, I address it honestly and straightforwardly. And I strive not to make the same mistake again.

Look, I would really be pleased if everyone out there liked me and everything I said. But I know that is impossible, and I try not to get worked up over opinions or judgments that are matters of taste. If there are people who do not like me personally, do not like my style, do not like my delivery, or do not care for my perspective or where I went to school, I have no problem with that. People are allowed to dislike me as a person, a broadcaster or both. That is a matter of personal taste, and that is absolutely fine with me.

When I meet criticism that is more factual in nature rather than a matter of taste, I ask myself two important questions: Is the criticism correct? And is the criticism reasonable? If the criticism is correct, I use it to get better, and I will thank anyone who brings it to my attention. If it is incorrect, I address it in a professional manner, state my argument justifying my position, and work toward a better understanding with the other person.

If it is unreasonable, I dismiss it. Sports are emotional, and sometimes emotional ties to a team or player can make people say and do some unreasonable things. I accept that as part of the business.

Every year, without fail, I get mail from fans of both teams from a game I have called where both sides strongly suggest that I was clearly biased toward the other team in the game broadcast. And, remember, those two dueling charges of bias are coming from the two different sides in the exact same game!

The truth is, I don't care who wins the game. I have too much respect for the competitors in any game. In my job as a basketball broadcaster, the only thing I root for is a compelling game. I couldn't care less who wins. That is up to the teams.

I believe that, in a public job, one has to be open to criticism, and willing to accept it. When praised, I never seem to question the credentials or credibility of the person praising me. Why would I question the same of someone who criticizes me? If I can dish it out publicly, I had better be able to take it. And I can take it.

When I opine on competition and make judgments on the actions of those involved, I owe it to each and every competitor and coach, and to the game, to be prepared and to be right. And when criticism comes my way, from any direction, I assess it and focus on the solution, the right answer, and not the complaint itself.

When I am wrong, I want to know about it. I believe I am

tough enough to handle it, and handle it the right way. And because I am prepared and thoughtful before I speak, I can defend my position.

It requires a certain toughness to put your opinions out there, especially when those opinions may not be flattering to people you know, like, respect and admire. The subjects we cover—the players, coaches and officials—all work hard to compete successfully, and all lay it on the line in a very public manner. They all strive to reach a standard of excellence in competition, and I respect that very much.

It is too easy for us to say, "It's just basketball," or, "It's entertainment." This may be just a game or just entertainment for those watching, but this is competition, and there are careers and livelihoods on the line. These games are important, and I treat them as such. That doesn't mean that we cannot have fun while doing it, but it is important.

The approach I learned from my dad and Coach K has also been important in my ability to handle pressure. If I treated every game as being important, and strove to reach my own standard of excellence instead of being driven by outside factors or expectations, I would be in a better position to handle pressure. Nothing is different in my preparation and execution when the stakes are bigger to outsiders. No rung on that ladder is more or less important than any other. Thanks to the lessons my parents and Coach K taught me, the stakes are always high for me. This is what I do, and the way I do it, all the time, not just for "big games."

Preparation isn't just for big events; it is a daily thing. If I could go back and be a player again, one area in which I would strive to be better would be my daily preparation. I would take more time to mentally prepare myself for practice.

I was usually early to arrive to practice and workouts, and I think I was a hard worker as a player. I was always physically prepared for practice, but I was not as mentally prepared as I could have been, or should have been. Looking back, even though I was there early, I spent too much time "waiting" for practice, rather than "preparing" for practice.

Like my father simply taking time to prepare for the next day's work, it would have made me a far better player if I had consistently taken the extra time to mentally prepare myself and focus on what I expected to get out of that day's practice, and to mentally prepare myself to truly compete that day, from the first drill to the last.

I have heard this from others, and I believe it to be true. At certain times when I played sick or hurt, at less than 100 percent physically, I often performed better than if I had felt my very best. I believe the reason was that, when I played at less than 100 percent physically, I mentally prepared myself differently. I placed a singular focus on what was important to be competitive, and I kept it simple, and didn't try to do too much.

If I could do it all over again as a player, I would strive to take that approach to each practice, preparing myself mentally for what I needed to accomplish, and the areas in which I needed to improve as an individual, and areas of improvement for our team.

Each game is different and singularly important; so is each practice. I needed to acknowledge that I might be a different player each day as I went to practice. Perhaps I was tired or ill one day, or coming off a poor effort in a game. I needed to prepare thoughtfully for that difference. Or perhaps I was coming off of a great game, and just thought that my confidence and good feeling would carry me through practice, when I really needed to concentrate on competing that day at the highest level.

Over the years, I have worked on concentrating on doing one thing at a time, then moving on to the next thing and concentrating fully on each task I set out to do. I cannot concentrate on two things at the same time. I can be responsible and accountable for completing multiple tasks, but I can concentrate fully on only one thing at a time. Looking back on my playing days, I regret that I did not always approach practices in that manner. It would have made me much better, and I would have been able to give more to my team.

Really, I am talking about toughness: the "maturity" to take a professional approach to my work. It is easier, and more common, to go to practice and simply try to get through it, or survive it, and to let your coaches set the agenda and the tone.

But I did not want to be common; I wanted to be uncommon. I did not want to do what was easy; I wanted to do what was hard, and do it consistently. To get the most from myself and to get the most out of practice, and to give the most to my team, I should have put more effort, energy and thought into preparing myself for each practice. Each practice is an opportunity. It is an opportunity to get better, and an opportunity to make a breakthrough and reach a new level. I should have done a better job of preparing myself for that opportunity, instead of treating some practices as "just another day."

It seems like such a small thing, but it is a big thing. It is a mental thing. It is a toughness thing.

"Making" Shots

One former teammate of mine who never shied away from the intense, hard work it took to prepare was Mark Alarie. It was a trait I always admired in him. Alarie was a thoughtful and focused worker.

Alarie was my roommate at Duke. He was born in Scottsdale, Arizona, and graduated from Brophy Prep, where he was the Arizona Player of the Year for 1982. At Duke, he was a two-time All-ACC first team selection and an All-American as a senior in 1986, when we played in the NCAA championship game.

Alarie scored 2,136 points at Duke, making him and Johnny Dawkins the first classmates in NCAA history to each score more than two thousand points. When his NBA career ended because of injury after five seasons, Alarie went back to the books, earning an MBA at the Wharton School of Business in 1995, and he went on to work as an investment banker and the president of a software company.

Every basketball practice includes shooting drills, and coaches and players often talk about "getting up a lot of shots" or "taking a lot of shots." In fact, many players say that they took a certain number of shots per day, from five hundred to a thousand, in the off-season to improve their shooting.

Alarie didn't think that way. He wasn't just taking shots; he was practicing making shots. For every shooting drill, he had a goal in mind of how many shots he expected to make. And he wanted to make each shot he took. When taking ten shots in a drill, even if he had made nine in a row, he burned to make the last one.

"If the game matters, the last one is usually pretty important," Alarie said. "I just didn't let the story dictate the next action. I really concentrated and focused on the present, washing my mind of the last play, or the last action."

Boston Celtics assistant coach Kevin Eastman has a great way of framing perfect preparation, and it captures Alarie perfectly. "We focus on excellence in every single action," Eastman said. "We are not taking five hundred shots. We are taking one perfect shot five hundred times."

Alarie didn't think about missing. He thought only about making it, and taking the necessary steps and work to prepare to make it. "Once the game starts it's a waste to think about missing," Alarie said. "It's better to think positively about making it."

And when he didn't hit his benchmark in practice, Alarie would get angry, like he had just lost the NCAA championship game with his miss. At first, I would shake my head when he did that, but I just didn't get it. Alarie was competing, in everything, all the time.

Anger is not a bad thing, as long as you don't lose your composure and fail to make the next play. Often, as a competitor and as long as it is controlled, anger can be a really good motivator. When Alarie didn't hit his number, there were a few times when, after the drill was over, he would get really angry. He constantly put game pressure on himself in practice situations, and made those everyday, sometimes mundane drills important. Alarie tried to simulate game pressure every day, so during an actual high-pressure game moment, that pressure was normal.

I asked Mark why he got so worked up over not hitting the very last attempt of a shooting drill, even though he had hit his benchmark.

"Because I had washed my mind of the prior shots. The last shot was the only shot. Right then, I missed the only shot, and that's what pissed me off," Alarie said. "And I didn't have any defense on me. If there is nothing technically wrong with my shot, then it's just concentration and stamina. I knew I could concentrate, but I worked on improving my concentration too. Especially when I was tired. Most of the truly important plays in a game have to be made at the end, when you are going to be tired."

Bob Knight believed in putting additional pressure and stress on his team in practice to build up a level of individual and collective toughness.

"Practice, for better or worse, is going to be re-created in a game," Knight said. His goal was to correct mistakes in both practice and games, and he posted a sign over the locker of every player that read, "Victory favors the team making fewest mistakes."

Knight never worried about a player's confidence when he corrected his teams' mistakes. If the correcting of a mistake caused a player to fear making a mistake and retreat from playing, Knight said, he didn't really want that player on his team. His style was to acknowledge when something was done correctly, and to correct it when it was done incorrectly, or not the way he wanted it done. He wanted players who could handle positive and negative feedback.

When he was a player, Kansas coach Bill Self struggled with that issue. "As a player, I was so soft for a time," Self said. "When I missed a shot and my coach told me that we could've gotten a better shot, I took it that he was telling me not to shoot. That was soft, and I needed to get over it. I needed to take the criticism, learn from it, and let the rest roll off my back and go play my ass off."

That resonated with me, because as a player, I was the same way early in my career. When I made a mistake and got yelled at or challenged, I didn't want to make that mistake again. But I could feel that I was simply retreating, and not putting myself in the position to make another mistake.

That was a mistake in and of itself. I had to toughen up, take the criticism or correction, and just play. I could be mad or think, *I'll show you*, but I had to channel those emotions into positive action. That isn't always easy, but it is something that tough people and tough players do. And it is a challenge of concentration, the ability to focus on the task at hand instead of being distracted from it by what just happened.

Knight believes that concentration is one of the most overlooked and undertaught issues in sports, and he had specific tactics to improve his teams' ability to concentrate.

"I used to call time-outs in practice, bring the players over, and in the time normally taken for a time-out, I would give them three things. Then I would send them back out on the floor," Knight said. "Before play started again, I would call them back one more time and ask them to write down the three things. We'd be lucky if each one of them would get two. That is just simple concentration. It is the most underrated thing: the ability to concentrate on what is going on. There is nothing more important than your ability to concentrate, and you can improve it."

When he was at Indiana, Knight had a drill he called "Change." It was a five-on-five drill. When he would yell, "Change," the offensive player would put the ball down on the floor and offense would go immediately to defense, and vice versa. The only rule was, no player who had just converted to defense could guard the player who was just guarding him. Each player had to find another player to guard. While the defense was looking for a man to guard, the newly converted offensive team was allowed to try to score.

"In 'Change,' you have to communicate, be alert and make quick adjustments," Knight said. "Nobody can tell you or diagram for you exactly what is going to happen. You have to figure it out under stress. I was trying to develop a toughness in players."

Knight did the same thing by incorporating "no dribble" into every practice and putting the offense at a disadvantage. The offense was forced to overcome the inability to dribble with better passing, player movement and cutting.

In defensive play—five on five—Knight would often make the defensive players practice with their hands behind their backs. His philosophy of putting them at a physical disadvantage trained them to adapt to the disadvantage and overcome it.

"Plus, defense is not a game of hands; it is a game of feet," Knight said. "Your feet have to dominate on defense. Your hands put the other team on the free-throw line. That's why the feet, the development of the feet was so important to me. I wanted to take the hands out of it. It is tougher to play with your feet."

Knight designed many four-versus-five situations in practice to have four players on defense against five players on offense, or vice versa. He called it "Advantage-Disadvantage."

"When the defense becomes offense and vice versa, it was designed to be more difficult than a game," Knight said. "As time passed, we came to rely on the toughness and resiliency we developed using those simple drills."

His goal was to test his players. Could they play effectively with an advantage or a disadvantage? What were they prepared to do mentally and physically to deal with that advantage or disadvantage?

"Do you let up when you have an advantage? Do you give in to a disadvantage?" Knight asked. "There are a lot of excuses you can make when you have a disadvantage, and you can be easily satisfied when you have an advantage. It is a test of your concentration, a test of your toughness."

Jon Gruden's coaching philosophy is similar. "What was our team going to do when we were exhausted, getting beat, the crowd is so loud you can't hear yourself think, let alone hear the quarterback call an audible?" Gruden said. "That's when concentration is vital, when you are in the middle of a tough situation, under incredible pressure and stress. That's when you have to be tough."

Gruden's football teams would practice in that kind of crowd noise, pumped into practice over the sound system, which would eliminate his team's ability to hear each other, and force them to adjust and communicate nonverbally. They would have to read things out on the field, and read each other. That takes premier concentration. Gruden is a firm believer that a coach has to put his team, especially a young team, in those difficult and stressful situations.

"When we put in or designed a drill for our team," Gruden said, "we focused on two things: What do our players need to improve upon? And what happens most often in a game?"

Roy Williams remembers that under Dean Smith, every drill had a winner and a loser; every drill was competitive and there was a price to be paid by the loser. Through that structure, Smith reminded his players "of the importance of winning without ever stating the importance of winning. It was about competing," Williams said.

Attending a North Carolina basketball practice under Roy Williams is very much the same. In every drill, whether it is a simple shooting drill or a three-on-three defensive drill, there is something on the line, something to compete for. At the end of practice, there is accountability. For every drill they were on the losing team, or missed a benchmark, the players have to run. Through that very simple teaching method, the players are acclimated to perform in the same environment in which they will be asked to play: with something important on the line.

In anything important, there will be pressure. Everybody feels it, but the toughest competitors react positively to that pressure. Competitors want to be at their best under pressure, and by putting yourself in pressure situations as often as possible, you are acclimating yourself to that pressure, and the pressure will be less likely to get in the way of your performance. In time, you will learn to seek out pressure. That's where tough people operate.

That is where Indiana coach Tom Crean wants his team to live. Every day, Crean puts his team in pressure situations and conditions them to thrive under that pressure. Crean is an extraordinary basketball coach, and is one of the hardest-working and most prepared people I have ever met. He is driven, and he leaves no stone unturned in his preparation. Crean is also a voracious reader, and seeks out wisdom from the greats of every field. At Indiana, Crean inherited a difficult challenge—to rebuild a proud program—and it has not been easy. But his toughness helped him to thrive in an incredibly tough situation. I admire Tom Crean as much as any coach I know.

Crean believes that, in a fast-paced, high-energy game with great teams and players, there are going to be mistakes. But, Crean asks, are they mistakes of omission, mental mistakes? He doesn't mind an occasional mistake. He minds what he calls "hero" plays, where a player tries to do something outside of the team concept, or outside of what that player is capable of doing. Crean doesn't want hero plays, because hero plays don't win.

"We put our players in stressful situations all the time in practice, especially end-of-game situations," Crean said. "We put pressure on them, and we let them figure it out under great stress, together. Did we work to get and take the right shot? Did we do the tough things necessary to get the right shot?"

There was no more pressure or a more stressful situation than Indiana's game against number one Kentucky in Assembly Hall on December 10, 2011. Trailing 72–70, Indiana had the ball with 5.6 seconds remaining and no time-outs, and had to go the length of the floor to get up a game-tying or game-winning shot. After Cody Zeller set a great screen for Verdell Jones III, Christian Watford intelligently trailed the ball as Jones drove toward the baseline, and was able to step into a game-winning three-point attempt off of Jones's pass.

Watford drained it.

"Christian Watford took the right shot," Crean said. "And he took it the right way. He showed composure, didn't speed up, and he showed really good form on the shot. Whether it went in doesn't matter, because those shots will not always go in. But because our players took the tough steps necessary to get the right shot and made the right play, and did so under great stress, we had a chance to win."

Crean points out that when players are under pressure, they have to rely on their habits to kick in. When his players can be consistent under stress, he is pleased, because consistency is important to him. "To me, consistency leads to courage," Crean said.

For Knight, concentration goes directly to your level of mental toughness. "There are a lot of great physical specimens we've seen in basketball that were dumb players, that lacked concentration and mental toughness," Knight said. "If the mental were to even approach the physical in players like that, what truly great players they would be."

Knight has always said that there are many more mental mistakes in games than physical mistakes. "I always say, 'Dumb loses more games than smart wins.' That's about concentration, discipline, understanding the game and your impact on it. That's toughness."

Goals and Destinations

Mike Krzyzewski has always done an expert job of using simple concepts with his teams in order to make something complicated easier to grasp, whatever that task may be. A great example of his ability to simplify and frame an issue came from his 2001 team.

In 2001, Coach K had an outstanding team he believed was capable of winning the National Championship, and most observers agreed. His team featured starters Shane Battier, Carlos Boozer,

Mike Dunleavy, Jay Williams and Chris Duhon. I happened to be visiting Coach K on the day of Duke's first practice of the season, and he invited me to sit in on a meeting he was having with his team in the locker room before they took to the practice floor.

Standing before his team, Coach K asked a simple question: "What are our goals this year?"

One by one, the players responded. "Go unbeaten at home," one player said. Another said, "Win the ACC title." Another said, "Go to the Final Four." Yet another said, "Win the National Championship."

Then Coach K said, "Those are all really good things. But those are not goals. Those are destinations. Our goal has to be to get better and closer as a team every single day. If we keep those as our focused and cherished goals, we will reach our proper destination, whatever it may be."

Coach K's 2001 Duke team did reach a pretty good destination. That team won the National Championship that year, in part by concentrating on what was right in front of them.

A Season of Segments

Breaking things down to their simplest form is a great way to focus your concentration on what is right in front of you, on the present. When going "big picture," sometimes the picture is too big to act upon. Krzyzewski has always been great with such concepts, getting players to focus together, and he has always been good at keeping our horizons short. Entering my senior season, I had played on some outstanding teams that had been nationally ranked for the past two seasons, but did not navigate the NCAA Tournament very well. We lacked the singular focus needed to advance past the second round.

My senior season at Duke, in 1986, we had the potential to be a great team. Before the season started, the players got together and we looked at our schedule. We asked ourselves, "Which games on our schedule can we not win?" The answer was, "There isn't a game that we cannot win."

And we committed to each other to strive to win each game.

Coach K took it one step further by breaking the season down into segments. The first five games of the year were our first segment, and our goal was to be 5–0 for that five-game segment. When that was over, we moved on to the next segment, and did so for the rest of the season. We did not think of our season record; rather, we concentrated on the short term, the present, the record only for that segment. Nothing else mattered but that segment.

When we reached the NCAA Tournament, we had won a school-record thirty-two games and had won the Big Apple NIT title, the ACC regular season title and the ACC tournament title. And we were the number one–ranked team in the nation and the number one overall seed in the NCAA Tournament.

In 1986, the NCAA Tournament was in just the second year of its sixty-four-team format, and took place over three weeks. It could be quite difficult to navigate, and to concentrate only on your team's journey.

Before our first NCAA Tournament game that year, Coach K took a different approach with our team. He provided us with a condensed bracket of the NCAA Tournament, showing only our subregional at the Greensboro Coliseum. The bracket was a four-team tournament, with only our East Regional first- and second-round opponents.

Coach K told us to consider, just for a moment, the opposite side of the main bracket, which included thirty-two very good basketball teams.

And then he said, "Who cares what goes on over on that side of the bracket? Only one team is coming out of there, and we will play them Monday night for the National Championship." Whatever happened outside of our path should not concern us. Our task was to win a four-team minitournament in Greensboro, and then move on to the next thing.

We beat Mississippi Valley State and Old Dominion, and while we were concentrating on that, there were a lot of upsets around us. Highly rated teams like Syracuse, Oklahoma, Notre Dame and Indiana all were beaten in the first weekend of the NCAA Tournament.

When we got back to campus, we had another bracket for a four-team minitournament, this time the East Regional semifinal and regional final in the Meadowlands in New Jersey. With a short horizon and a goal we could easily wrap our heads around, we beat DePaul and David Robinson's Navy team to advance to the Final Four, which just happened to be another four-team tournament.

By breaking the vast NCAA Tournament down to its simplest terms, we were able to concentrate on what was right in front of us, and it seemed easier to digest. Like climbing a ladder, we were not thinking about the top while taking our initial steps. We were concentrating on each rung of the ladder, and taking things one simple step at a time.

In Dallas at the Final Four, we were able to beat number two Kansas to win our thirty-seventh game of the season, and set an NCAA record for wins in a single season. But we weren't able to finish it off with a win in the championship game on Monday night. We lost to Louisville, 72–69.

Many of the best coaches in basketball now routinely break games down into smaller segments, asking their teams to play in concentrated four-minute segments from TV time-out to TV time-out. Davidson coach Bob McKillop breaks his team's games down into rounds, like a boxing match. McKillop's rounds are four minutes in length, and he keeps score by round, telling his team that they won or lost a round, and keeping their horizons shorter and more focused.

Preparation is multifaceted. It is about hard work, but it is also about concentration, in planning and execution, and it is about how you frame things in your mind. The toughest people stay in the present, and concentrate fully on what is in front of them. Whether it is a single play in a game, a single step on a ladder, a practice or a work task, preparation and concentration are vital ingredients in toughness. The toughest people have the will to prepare and the will to concentrate. Those are skills, and can be improved like any other skill. So can your toughness.

CHAPTER 3

COURAGE

Everyone has to deal with fear and doubt. Yet I often hear commentary in sports indicating that some players are fearless. Nobody is fearless.

However, tough people face their fears and doubts head-on, and they overcome them so they can function at the highest level without that fear and doubt inhibiting their ability to perform at their best. Embracing fear and using it to push yourself to get better takes courage.

To me, courage isn't the absence of fear or doubt. Rather, courage is overcoming it. Everyone, in any endeavor, has moments of doubt, fears making mistakes or losing. But when you can overcome those fears and doubts, you can perform with a free mind, and get out of your own way.

Having been around team sports all of my life, I have learned that confidence and courage, the kind needed to play without fear or doubt, are most often derived from the strength of your group. Mike Krzyzewski has said, "You are not tough alone." Similarly, you are not courageous alone.

When your teammates and coaches truly believe in you, have your back and will pick you up should you make a mistake, you will derive great confidence and courage from that. And that requires trust and communication, both verbal and nonverbal.

While I was at Duke, I witnessed former teammate Mark Alarie exhibiting great courage on the basketball floor. Alarie was a nationally ranked recruit in high school, but because of an injury, he didn't get the acclaim some thought he deserved. Yet, in college, Alarie performed at the highest level early on in his career, which was not the norm at that time. Alarie was selected All-ACC as a sophomore in 1984. The other members of that first team were Michael Jordan, Sam Perkins, Mark Price and Lorenzo Charles. At the time I thought Alarie was unafraid and fearless. He wasn't.

Alarie said he was always afraid of failing, or being humiliated on the floor by not performing. He believes that fear motivated him to practice harder and prepare more diligently. "My fear was good. The positive joy of winning comes, in part, from the fear of failing. My fear of failing motivated me to practice and prepare to avoid failing," Alarie said.

But Alarie was quick to point out that he wasn't afraid of missing a shot or failing to complete a play. He took great care to separate fear of failing in the larger sense from fear of missing a shot in the game itself. For Alarie, his fear drove him to practice hard and earn confidence in his abilities. And when he got into the game, his concentration allowed him to perform the action without fear of missing or making a mistake. "When the action is here and now, when the game was being played, I wanted my mind fully on the action, and focused on it in a totally positive manner."

Alarie overcame his fear by training his mind to focus only on the positive when it was game time. His negative thoughts fueled his practice and motivated his preparation, but he wanted only positive thoughts when it was time to perform. "When you allow your mind to say, 'Don't miss,' I don't believe your mind can process the 'don't' part. It just visualizes the miss, and that tenses you and hinders you from performing." In any action, tension is the enemy of performance.

For basketball players, the test of your courage is a pressure free throw. During live game action, play is fast and furious, and there is little time to think. In game action, much of what happens is instinctive reacting. When there is a free throw, there is a break in the action, and there is time to think. That is where your mind can take you to places you would rather it not go.

Alarie wanted his mind focused on the positive, and only the positive. When he stepped up to a pressure free throw, Alarie's mind-set was, "I'm making this," which is vastly different from, "Don't miss." He told himself he'd prepared, he'd done this a million times, and he knew he could do it.

"Look, we never kidded ourselves," Alarie said. "We knew that pressure is real, unless you're a mindless idiot. It is how you respond to pressure situations that count. You have to be tough, and my preparation and routine made me tougher."

Alarie made it simple. He believed that his preparation was his ticket to success. His work earned him the confidence to step forward and take on the challenge, and do so without fearing the negative consequences of missing. "First, if you don't practice and prepare yourself, you have very little chance. Then the results are somewhat random," Alarie said. "But if you practice and prepare and still cannot perform, then fear has overtaken your ability to act. You have to push through that."

When taking a pressure free throw on the road, with a crowd going crazy, a national television audience, and your opponent trying to get into your head by saying, "Don't choke," as you step to the line, Alarie relied on his routine. "That's where my routine took over. I am mentally plugged into the game and aware, but I do the same thing I always do," Alarie said. "There's nothing to think about."

Alarie's routine was comforting to him. It was the same routine he used in practice, in games, or shooting in his backyard as a kid.

He would take the ball from the official, toe the line, take three dribbles and then eye the rim. As soon as he saw the rim, he shot it. He had a methodical, grooved and confident routine. He referred to it as a routine of confidence.

It is ironic that for Alarie and countless others who have played at the highest levels, when they were young and practicing in the backyard, they would imagine themselves shooting pressure free throws in a championship game. Then, in that championship game, they would rely upon the very same routine they grooved in the backyard.

Steve Kerr agrees with Alarie. Kerr played more than sixteen seasons in the NBA, despite the fact that he was barely six-three and, according to Kerr himself, "athletically challenged." In overcoming such challenges since high school, Kerr became the most accurate three-point shooter in a single season in NCAA history, and helped lead Arizona to the 1988 Final Four. Still, despite his success, Kerr's toughest struggles were with himself. He battled fear of failure from the beginning of his career to the end, and fought to overcome it.

For Kerr, the mental part of the game was of vital importance, and he had his own routine. "Before every game, I would watch a tape of me playing well, being in the groove, to give myself that positive feeling," Kerr said. "I wanted to fill my memory with good things so I could draw upon it."

Kerr had a free-throw routine similar to Alarie's, one that he had honed over years and years of practicing. He had shot thousands upon thousands of free throws taking a deep breath, then taking three dribbles and going into his shot motion. But Kerr didn't rely upon his routine only. He wanted his mind fully focused on the positive, and used a key to get his mind to the right place and not let fear or doubt have a chance to creep in.

After he performed an action perfectly, he used a trigger to stay positive and give him the best chance to perform. "In Houston early one season, I shot an absolutely perfect free throw," Kerr said. "After that, every free throw I took that year, I would say, 'Houston,' before I shot it. I wanted to put that picture in my head, that feeling."

Kerr believed he had to "trick his mind" because he thought it was just too easy to let his mind go to those "dark places" where negativity resides. "Why give yourself one other thing to overcome out there? You have to overcome your own clutter in your mind, and not add to it," he said.

In an odd way, I was comforted by the fact that Alarie and Kerr, two great shooters whom I mistakenly believed were fearless, were not fearless at all. They worked hard to overcome their fears, and showed great mental toughness to stay positive and not allow negative thoughts to get in the way of positive performance.

Curtis Strange is also a firm believer in routine, and when a golfer gets away from a honed routine, he cannot expect to perform at his best. The effectiveness of a routine in a high-pressure situation is a result of the work and time put into preparation, and of the mental toughness it takes to stick to that routine when your mind wants to speed up and take you out of it. "In golf, it is all about reps, repetitions," Strange said. "I practiced hard. My high school basketball coach told me the harder practice was, the easier the game would be to play, and the same is true of golf."

The more Strange worked and prepared mentally and physically, the less he feared the pressure moments. In fact, he came to want the pressure and to want to be on the game's biggest stage. Strange wasn't born to be on that stage. He earned his way onto it with his work, and with his mental toughness.

"If you prepare properly, you love the stage," Strange said. "The more I prepared behind the scenes, the more I wanted the pressure. I trained myself to want the pressure, and my preparation and routine helped my confidence. My routine started at home, with how I prepared for a tournament. It started long before I ever arrived at the tournament site. That takes discipline and preparation."

Strange was quick to point out to me that golf is not a game of reaction, like basketball or football. Contrary to what Alarie and

Kerr noted about basketball, the game-time action is about instinctive reactions, and there are far fewer opportunities to think and "get in your own way," whereas golf is a game of thinking, and can feel like the equivalent of five hours of pressure free throws.

Strange asked me to think about how much time it takes for the actual actions of putting the club to the ball in a round of tournament golf. How many seconds does each swing take? He roughly estimated that, in a five-hour round of golf, it takes under five minutes of actual time to hit the shots that make up your final score. "That's a lot of time to think before you act," Strange said. "And that's why you're ready for a rubber room if you're not mentally tough."

In a way, routine is part of your preparation. Preparation and work in your routine are the keys to confidence and courage in any sport or in any endeavor, and Jon Gruden believes that preparation is what allows a player to concentrate at the highest level. You cannot be tough without being confident, and you cannot be confident without working hard and preparing. "You have to be able to anticipate what is going to happen and react to what is happening," Gruden said. "There is no way you can concentrate and execute at the highest level without being totally prepared."

Gruden does not limit preparation to the physical act. For him, preparation is what provides the courage necessary to concentrate and to carry out the objective. "The way you study film, the way you take notes, the way you gather information and process it, the way you get the proper rest, what you eat," Gruden said. "All of that is critical to being fully prepared, which will allow you to concentrate and execute."

The coaches I have been around are not bothered by an occasional mistake. Rather, they are most disturbed by mental mistakes, or mistakes of omission. If a player gives his all, mentally and physically, and simply fails to complete an action, most coaches can accept that, as long as the same mistakes are not repeated.

But if a player makes a mental error or fails to do something he is supposed to do, that is when the likes of Bob Knight, Mike Krzyzewski, Tom Izzo, Bill Self and Tom Crean will hold that player fully accountable. For Crean, mental errors are from a lack of concentration, which is a lack of mental toughness.

Mistakes will happen in stressful situations, especially against a quality opponent. The aim is to minimize mistakes while still striving to execute, but not to be paralyzed by concern about a negative outcome. "I want my players to have the license to excel without the fear of making a mistake," Crean said. "We play through mistakes all the time in practice and games. We strive to make the right play."

Bill Self drives his team to eliminate mistakes too, but believes that the more important trait is to keep fighting through mistakes, with the focus on overcoming them and winning anyway. "I liken it to tennis," Self said. "You can lose more than half of the points played and still win the match. You have to understand what the most important points are, and be at your toughest at those points. You have to have your concentration and your effort at their highest levels at those points in the game. That's what tough players and tough teams do."

Failure is a part of competition. You can get over failure. But you should never forget the feeling, and you should never want to have that feeling again. The toughest players have the courage to acknowledge failure and take the necessary steps to learn from it and work not to repeat it.

Kerr, whose sixteen-year NBA career is directly attributable to his mental toughness, never really considered toughness early in his career. From the beginning, Kerr was battling himself, and always trying to overcome his self-doubt as a player.

"I didn't have a lot of confidence as a player. My whole NBA career, it was such a battle to compete, because I was at an athletic disadvantage," Kerr said. "There was a lot of self-doubt."

Like Alarie, Kerr was afraid of failure. "But the more work I put in, the more I prepared myself, the better foundation of belief I built," Kerr said. "I think you have to earn your confidence, earn your belief. You earn it through your work. I was able to battle my self-doubt by knowing I was working harder, that I was putting the effort in, and that I was as prepared as I could be."

Kerr built his confidence and belief in his abilities, and from that was able to compete with a free mind. And when he got positive results, he would examine exactly why he was successful and work to continue or duplicate what made him successful. But he was careful not to overanalyze every little detail. Kerr guarded against being "too self-aware" and "too self-conscious."

"I think you have to be self-aware to improve," Kerr said. "You have to understand your limitations or shortcomings to attack them, but you also have to overcome your limitations and forget them so you can go out and play. You have to achieve a positive mental state to perform."

Kerr agrees that everyone faces and must overcome the same fears and doubts. "It's not just me. I see Dwyane Wade, one of the best players in the world, struggling with self-doubt and anxiety," Kerr said. "He feels it too. I see LeBron James get nervous at the end of games sometimes. Toughness is about overcoming that anxiety we all feel and getting yourself to a place where you can compete and perform," Kerr said.

As a young coach, Mike Krzyzewski had a fear of failing and a fear of losing. He learned that he had to separate the two. "Fear of failure leads to losing," Krzyzewski said. "I hate to lose, but I can't fear the actions I take when I am taking them, or I am a culprit in the loss."

When Krzyzewski was a player, he recalls that he was often afraid of making a mistake at that very moment. For Krzyzewski, his hatred of losing more than his desire to win helped him achieve his best mental state. "I hate to lose. Hating to lose put me in a more positive direction," Krzyzewski said.

Tom Izzo welcomes fear, and thinks it is a healthy, natural feeling that can be a net positive. But the fear that drives him doesn't extend to the final result. "I think fear can be really good," Izzo said. "It helps keep you grounded, and it helps you prepare better. If I have thrown everything into preparing to compete, and I have thrown everything into the competition itself, I'm okay with the result. I really want to win, and I hate to lose, but I am not afraid to lose."

Kerr agrees with Izzo. "Fear of failure drives you to work harder to avoid failing," Kerr said. "But once the game starts, you have to put fear of failure totally out of your mind."

Living with the Consequences

Kerr finds it funny that so many people remember him as a "clutch player" because he hit some very high-profile shots in the NBA finals. He counts himself a bit lucky to have that distinction in the minds of so many. "People are really nice to remember and remind me of hitting a couple of key shots," Kerr said. "They'll say 'clutch' and I'll smile a little bit. Because I wasn't 'clutch' early in my career. I was nervous, and I missed a lot of big shots. I missed *a lot* of big shots."

For Kerr, a turning point was taking the focus off of the result, and deciding that he was willing to live with any result from the actions he took. "I had to free up my mind and say, 'Screw it; I don't care if I miss.' Fear of missing gets in the way of a lot of players," Kerr said.

Kerr cited Kobe Bryant and Michael Jordan, two of the most "clutch" performers of all time, as examples of players who want desperately to make the important shot, but are tough enough to accept the outcome, positive or negative. "That's really the key. You have to be willing to live with the result. You have to be tough enough to live with the result."

Kerr referenced a commercial that Michael Jordan appeared in many years ago that focused on all of the shots Jordan had missed in his career. "The point was, he fails all the time, but it doesn't stop him from taking the next one," Kerr said. "That mind-set was critical for me in my career. It was a breakthrough for me, a major hurdle I had to get over. I had to be willing to live with it, whatever the result, to accept it," Kerr said. "I trusted the process, I trusted the work I had put in, and I was willing to live with the results."

Accepting the consequences doesn't mean that failing doesn't bring hurt or disappointment. It means that you have the courage to accept the result without fear affecting your ability to perform, and that you are also willing to get up off the deck and try again. Kerr believes that a willingness to accept the consequences is the mental attitude that every player needs. "In a way, you have to not care, really," Kerr said. "You have to instinctively shoot and make your play, and live with the result. And it has never been harder to do than it is now. With blogs, social media, all of the noise—there's more noise than ever.

"If you allow it, your mind can get you pretty screwed up," Kerr said. Kerr strove not to allow his mind to negatively impact his performance. That was his mental toughness. It was earned, and it was something that he improved upon from the beginning of his career to the end.

Likewise, Curtis Strange has trained his mind to survive the pressure that comes with a career as a golf pro. "I think you have to play the game within the game, and play games in your mind," Curtis Strange said. "In golf, you fail more than you succeed. You have to train yourself to deal with losing every week. You cannot survive unless you want to play under the pressure again after you fail."

Krzyzewski uses the 2008 Olympics as a prime example of the difference between hating to lose and fearing it. When Krzyzewski was selected to be the head coach of the United States Olympic team comprised of NBA superstars, conventional wisdom posited that a "college coach" like Krzyzewski could not reach these top players. The approaches taken by Krzyzewski and his family differed greatly.

"My family was so fearful of us losing and failing to win the gold medal," Krzyzewski said. "They thought my legacy was on the line; they feared the criticism of a college coach with the pros, all that stuff."

Not Krzyzewski. He didn't want the result, whatever it might be, to affect the journey or the steps taken on that journey. "I wanted to be excited about what I was doing, what we were pursuing," Krzyzewski said. "My family was the opposite. If I had felt like that, we very well might have lost."

The United States hadn't won Olympic gold in men's basketball since the 2000 Sydney games, and USA Basketball had endured several years of embarrassment in international competition. Sports analysts opined that the United States was losing its position at the top of the historic basketball hierarchy. Finally, on August 24, 2008, the U.S. team coached by Coach K defeated Spain 118–107 to take home the gold medal.

When the buzzer sounded and the United States secured Olympic gold, Krzyzewski and his family had completely different reactions. "When we won, my first and only feeling was joy," Krzyzewski said. "It wasn't relief. The feeling my family had was relief, not joy. They feel great about it now, but they missed out on the initial joy of it. I think we control how we approach these things."

When Coach K talked about pursuing the gold medal while his family feared losing it, it had a familiar ring to me.

When I was an assistant coach under Krzyzewski, Duke began the 1991–92 season as the clear number one team in the nation and an overwhelming favorite to become the first team since UCLA in 1973 to win back-to-back National Championships. Krzyzewski's 1992 Duke team was already being referred to as "defending national champions" before its very first practice.

Krzyzewski would have none of it. Nobody outside his team defined his players or his team, defined its mission or framed its journey. Only Krzyzewski and his team did that.

In the very first team meeting before the start of the season, Krzyzewski told the team he didn't want to hear anyone use the term "defending" national champions.

"We aren't 'defending' anything," Krzyzewski said. "That trophy has already been won, and is displayed out in the lobby of Cameron. It doesn't need to be defended.

"We are pursuing this championship. We are not defending. We are pursuing. That is the job at hand."

Krzyzewski, like Alarie, Kerr and Strange in their careers, fills his mind with the positive, and takes steps to limit the outside influences from getting into his mind. In his preparation for a game, Krzyzewski tries to get away from every distraction that can make him feel in any way fearful or insecure.

Krzyzewski has had to adapt to a changing world, one in which there is more coverage than ever, and every game and moment is dissected. A game may be for a record, or against a team to which you have lost three straight games, or against a coach who has a better record than you. Those things can distract you from what is important: the game right in front of you. "We are judged so many ways now, by so many different people and media, it can be really distracting. I focus on the job at hand," Krzyzewski said. "The rest will take care of itself.

"It is better for me just to coach and put things into bigger contexts," Krzyzewski said. "If the game is for a record or a championship, that gets you in the wrong moment. I try to isolate each game so it is just that game only. That's not easy to do. You have to work at it."

In 2010, Krzyzewski had to make a strategic decision that, if it failed, would have been second-guessed forever. With just 3.6 seconds remaining in regulation play of the 2010 National Championship game against Butler in Indianapolis, Duke's Brian Zoubek hit the front end of two free throws to give the Blue Devils a two-point lead, 61–59. If Zoubek were to make his second free throw, Duke would have a three-point lead, and the best Butler could do would be to tie the game, 62–62, and send it to overtime. If Zoubek hit the second free throw, Duke couldn't lose.

Krzyzewski motioned to Zoubek to intentionally miss the second free throw.

Instead of a potential tie, that one decision brought losing into the equation for Duke. If Butler were to take and make a final shot, it would almost certainly be a three-point shot, and Duke could lose the game and the championship.

Duke had played the last five minutes of regulation with senior big men Brian Zoubek and Lance Thomas with four fouls each. Under normal circumstances, Krzyzewski's strategic decision would be for the shooter to try to make the free throws, and if up three points, his team could foul to eliminate the possibility of a game-tying three-point shot.

But with both foul trouble and momentum on the side of Butler, playing just a few miles from their campus, Krzyzewski was concerned a made free throw would give Butler the chance to set up an out-of-bounds play that could be better executed than a scramble play off of a missed free throw. By missing the second free throw on purpose, Krzyzewski believed Duke could set up its defense and the best that Butler could do was a difficult, desperation heave from half-court. He played the percentages and also followed his gut.

Krzyzewski did not feel Duke's chances to win were good in overtime. He felt the best chance to win was right then and there, with a missed free throw.

"I'm often asked about the strategy of that game," Krzyzewski said. "I'm asked if I was relieved when the heave by Butler didn't go in. The answer is no, I wasn't relieved. I was joyful we had won."

Krzyzewski followed his instincts, but not just on that final play. He followed his instincts the entire game. "People ask me if I would do the same thing again, and I say that I would do exactly the same thing. I would follow my instincts." That doesn't mean the strategic decision would be the same if he had to make the same decision again. Krzyzewski doesn't know exactly what he would do in a similar situation. He just believes that he would follow his instincts. His preparation allowed him to do that, and he was willing to live with the outcome.

"The key was, I made a decision, and I wasn't afraid of the outcome," Krzyzewski said. "I was willing to accept the consequences that go along with that decision."

And for Krzyzewski, his behavior shouldn't change because the decision was to be made at the end of the game. The fact that people call it "crunch time" makes no difference to Krzyzewski. To him, every play is important, and every play demands his full attention and concentration. Tom Crean sees that as a fundamental truth. "Crunch time is ongoing," Crean said. "It all matters. Every play matters."

To Krzyzewski, fear is greatest toward the end of any endeavor, but it is not more important. "The end is not more important than the beginning, but at the point of completion is when you can fear the most," Krzyzewski said. "The end is when you most often meet the forces that can stop you from completing the effort. You don't let those forces in, and you don't make it monumental. Completion is just the next step in the process.

"I look at it this way," Krzyzewski said. "If you're true to yourself the whole way, then why not at the end? But you have to be willing to accept what comes with falling short, because if you compete, you will fall short at times. Mental toughness is being able to accept what comes with winning and losing."

The name Mia Hamm is synonymous with women's soccer, and she is largely considered to be the finest player in the history of the sport. Hamm has scored more career goals in international competition than any other U.S. soccer player—male or female. She attended the University of North Carolina, where she led the team to four consecutive NCAA soccer titles. A World Cup champion and Olympic gold medalist, Hamm is America's most decorated soccer player.

Even Hamm, one of the all-time great athletes of her generation, has had to deal with self-doubt and fear of failure—just as Steve Kerr said. Her longtime friend and teammate Julie Foudy was incredulous that Hamm could ever be afraid or doubt herself. But Foudy saw an amazing vulnerability and humility in Hamm. That vulnerability did not limit Hamm, but instead helped her, according to Foudy. Hamm had the courage and toughness to show it, but also to let that natural fear drive her to greatness. Foudy called her drive, and the drive adopted by the team, a "wholesome discontent."

"She had that fear of failure that drove her," Foudy said. "It drove her to work harder, to put even more time in. That was her 'wholesome discontent.' Because of that, she was going to work on free kicks, corner kicks, her skill level, her fitness; she was going to put her time in.

"Her confidence didn't just come from her ability," Foudy said. "Her confidence came from the work she put in. That confidence was bought and paid for with her sweat. But when the game started, she went out and played without the fear that drove her."

Foudy and Hamm both remember teammate Joy Fawcett embracing fear of failure to drive her. Fawcett was one of the best soccer players in the world for more than a decade, yet she was always fearful she wouldn't make the team.

"She used to sweat, literally sweat, over whether she would be on the roster," Foudy said. "She didn't take it for granted." Fawcett wouldn't even allow her family to book travel for upcoming competitions like the Olympic Games until it was final that she had made the roster. "She worked like she hadn't accomplished anything," Foudy said. "Then she played with tremendous confidence because of the work she put in."

Foudy saw Fawcett's attitude as a fear of failure, but she felt it was also that Fawcett never viewed her place on the team or her level of performance as being a birthright. "She never felt entitled," Foudy said. "She gained her confidence and self-worth from her work and her preparation. She was totally invested."

"You cannot feel entitled and be tough," Crean echoed. "The

toughest players and people I have encountered are not content to rest upon what they have accomplished. Instead, like Fawcett, they strive to accomplish that next task as if it were the only task. Because for the truly tough, it is the only task."

As Boston Celtics assistant coach Kevin Eastman says, teams of entitlement don't win championships. Entitlement never wins championships. Investment wins championships.

It isn't just on the field that our toughness is tested. Some of my toughest challenges and battles with myself came in my first year of law school, when I had to confront my fear of failure with shaky confidence and belief. I was out of my element in law school, and in unfamiliar territory. I was intimidated, and I was scared. I had always been a decent student and a competitive athlete, but I had never been through anything like Duke Law School, and I had never been around such high-caliber and high-achieving students and such bright minds. I was afraid I was going to fail.

I had just finished playing three years of professional basketball overseas, so I was not a kid. But I felt like one during my first year, especially in class. I tried to hide it, but I was terrified.

In my early law school classes, my head was spinning. I didn't feel like I understood things, and I felt like I was always a step or two behind the other students. It seemed like everyone else knew the lingo, and talked like lawyers already. They seemed to get it. I was lost, and I was sure I was the only one.

My father didn't go to college or law school, but he is smarter than anyone I know with advanced degrees. My dad knew about work, and he knew about what it took to adapt and succeed in business. My dad is not only smart; he is the toughest person I have ever known.

When I was having doubts early in law school, I called home to check in. After I talked to my mom, she put my dad on the phone.

"Hi, Jay. How's school?" he asked.

"I'm still here, Dad, but I'm struggling," I admitted. "Everyone here seems to know this stuff already, and I am having a hard time keeping up. Dad, I don't think I can hack this."

He laughed. Then he said, "You sound like a new parent. All new parents talk about how their kid could walk when he was eighteen months or talk when he was only fourteen months. Who cares? They can all walk and talk when they're two years old.

"You don't get a prize for knowing it first," he said. "You get a diploma for knowing it at the end. You'll figure it out."

Then he said, "How many lawyers do you think there are out there?"

"I don't know. Hundreds of thousands, I guess," I said.

"And *you're* the one who can't do it? No way. Just concentrate on what's in front of you, and don't worry about what anybody else says or does. If you do your best, you'll do just fine."

That snapped me out of it. My dad was telling me to toughen up. He was telling me not to give up, not to give in, and not to settle for less from myself. He was telling me that my fear was getting the best of me, that I could do it, and that I would do it if I was willing to pay the price and concentrate on what was important. Concentration is a measure of toughness, and a skill that needs to be exercised to improve just like your fitness.

It was just another step on the ladder, and all I had to do was concentrate on what was important, on what was right in front of me, and I would do it.

And thanks to him, I did do it.

I found out later that my fear of failure was almost universal among my classmates. Our fears, like the fears of Mark Alarie, Mia Hamm, Steve Kerr, Joy Fawcett and Tom Izzo, were not a sign of weakness or a lack of courage. Our courage in overcoming those fears was a function of our toughness.

Toughness isn't an absence of fear. It is the courage to face it, to keep plugging, and to overcome it.

CHAPTER 4

COMMUNICATION

Communication is a vital element in true toughness, and it is a vital element in any good relationship. When communication is built on trust, true toughness can emerge. That lesson has been best illuminated for me through basketball.

I believe that basketball is the greatest game ever invented. It is the ultimate team sport, where each player on the floor must play both offense and defense in continuous action, without a break at or after conversion. Basketball is the ultimate "we first" or team-first endeavor, but it is one of the easiest games to degenerate into a "me first" or selfish endeavor. The selfless team player, the tough player, is a selfless communicator, on and off the court.

There is no aspect of basketball in which communication is more important than on the defensive end of the floor. Clearly there is an individual aspect to defense in basketball, but the team aspect is the most important and the most difficult for any player, young or experienced, to fully grasp and embrace.

In "man-to-man" defense, each player has an individual defensive assignment, an opposing player to guard. It is easy for each defensive player on the floor to take an individual view of the game and to have tunnel vision, unaware of what his or her teammates are up against. Many players step onto the floor with the mind-set that "my man" is not going to score.

But the toughest players play "team" man-to-man defense. Those players strive for their teams to play "five as one" on the defensive end, and take the collective view that it is "our defense" that is going to protect "our basket" and "we" are going to get a stop against the opposing offense, and do so together. A truly tough player plays the ball, not just his or her man.

Ask any successful coach or player: Communicating (or talking) on the floor, especially on defense, is critical to a team's success, and to any individual player's success within the framework of that team.

Talking on the floor is difficult and, to some players, seems unnatural. But when a player talks on defense, it is difficult if not impossible for that player not to be more engaged than he otherwise would be. The talking player is more likely to be down in a stance and ready, and more likely to be in the right position and prepared not only to cover his assignment, but to help a teammate and still recover.

Talk is essential to a winning team's confidence. Communicating is about connecting and being connected. It is about trust and commitment. On defense, when one teammate is guarding the player with the ball, it is important for all other teammates, or help defenders, to "play the ball" and talk to their teammate guarding the ball. That on-ball defender is your teammate, and he is on an island without the ability to see what is going on behind him. That teammate needs the confidence to pressure the ball without the fear of getting beaten off the dribble. It is the talk, the communication of his teammates that instills that confidence and trust.

If, as a help defender, you are talking to your teammate guarding the ball, you are letting him know that you are *there* and ready to help him, and that you are providing him with the confidence to defend, all-out, without concern for getting beaten. But if you are not talking to him, if you are silently into your own defensive assignment and not focused on your part in the whole, your teammate may give in to that fear that he is all alone on that island, and may back off to keep from getting beaten off the dribble. Then your entire defense is far less effective. The "me" of your defense diminishes the power of the "we" of your defense.

Your talk lets everyone know that you are not just concerned with guarding your man. Rather, it lets everyone know that you have their back, and you are totally engaged in collectively stopping your opponent. Your teammates must be able to trust completely that you are there to help them, and that you will be there without fail. Talking to your teammates positively reinforces that trust, and demonstrates your commitment to the mission of that possession: to stop the other team from scoring and secure the ball, and to do it together.

Early on in my playing career, I didn't know how to talk or communicate on a basketball court. I was a good defender in high school, but I was a good individual defender. I was not a good team defender who made it his mission to do whatever it took for my team to get a stop: to play the ball and see my man (rather than play my man without concern for the ball), talk to my teammates, and be there without fail to help my teammates should they get beaten.

The truth was, I needed to be tougher mentally on the floor for my teammates so they could do their jobs better. And so I needed to be more alert and more engaged. To do that, I needed to learn how to talk, and to internalize that being a good team defender was not about keeping my assignment from scoring, but making certain that *our team* kept *their team* from scoring.

In other words, I needed to internalize the attitude that was best expressed to me by a NASA engineer I had met.

Not long ago, I was traveling to a basketball clinic in Orlando, Florida, and was fortunate to sit next to a man named Daryl Woods on my flight. Woods is a NASA engineer who pointedly educated me on the significance of true teamwork and communication in his field. It is a lesson I have since shared with coaches and others, and one that struck a chord with me.

Woods is deputy manager of vehicle integration for the Space Launch System program at NASA, and he discussed the leadership or "coaching" challenges associated with his diverse team made up of NASA personnel and outside independent contractors, all of whom could easily get bogged down thinking only about their own specific element of a space launch.

Woods explained that, at the beginning of any project, the spacecraft or vehicle is the center of everything, and it is easy for everyone to see and focus together upon the big picture. "The vehicle has individual elements, engines and rocket boosters, for example," Woods said. "The mission is getting that vehicle to fly."

But as the project progresses, those responsible for each element of the vehicle can sometimes get what Woods calls "siloed" or "stovepiped." They put their heads down and focus totally on their own specific element, and can lose sight of the big picture—the vehicle. They are not intending to be selfish, but it can happen. "You have to provide your element, but you also have to keep the vehicle at the forefront," Woods said.

The communication challenge for Woods is to constantly remind and reinforce to his team that each specific element of the vehicle is not so important that it can fly by itself. But, Woods says, each element is so important that the vehicle cannot fly without it.

To get his point across, Woods used an auto racing analogy with his large, diverse team. "Every member of the pit crew has a specific role," Woods said. "The driver and crew chief are out front and get the public credit, but I showed film of what it looks like when the pit crew does things right, and what it looks like when they do things wrong."

When Woods showed his NASA team film of a NASCAR pit crew doing things incorrectly, it was quickly apparent to all how important each job, each element, is to the whole. "You have to have team norms," Woods said. "You have to play your position and understand what every other position does and how you fit within the team."

To further emphasize his point, Woods came up with a saying for his team: "Responsible to the element, accountable to the mission."

Wow.

When Woods shared that with me, I was floored. That simple NASA phrase summed up team play in basketball better than anything I had ever heard. On defense, a true team player, a tough player, needs to be *responsible* for his specific role and assignment, but *accountable* to the *mission*, which is to stop the opponent from scoring on the defensive end.

"It really is just like sports, and there is a common thread," Woods said. "If you are playing in a zone defense, you are responsible for an area and a matchup. If you mess up, you need to be accountable, and you need to play your position correctly, with the mission above all. If you don't, the team suffers."

This is by far the best summation of toughness through communication on a basketball floor. And it hit home with me, because early on in my basketball career, communication was difficult for me to fully embrace.

My freshman year playing for Mike Krzyzewski at Duke, in both practice and in games, I would often hear Coach K shouting at me, imploring me to talk. "You're not talking, Bilas!" Krzyzewski would often say. "You are totally into yourself. Quit being selfish! Talk!"

I thought to myself, *Selfish? Me?! I'm not selfish!* I mistakenly believed that I was busting my tail to guard "my man." What was Coach K talking about? While I may have believed that I was doing a great defensive job, the truth was, I wasn't.

I wasn't throwing myself into each defensive possession and committing myself to helping and being there 100 percent for my teammates. I was worried about *my* man, *my* defense, *my* role. Instead I should have been more concerned with *our* defense, and what I could do to help my teammates in our defense. Instead of being invested in the team's goals, I was all about me. I was dipping my toe in the water, instead of fully jumping in.

To be great defensively, all five defenders have to play together, "five as one," instead of just "five ones" out on the floor. And to be a great teammate, I had to demonstrate to my teammates that I was fully committed and trustworthy. That starts with communication, with talking. The more I talked, and the more I committed to talking, the better I played defensively and the more alert I was to what was happening beyond my own little sphere of responsibility.

As NASA engineer Daryl Woods would say, I was responsible to the element (guarding my man), and accountable to the mission (all five guys, together, stopping our opponent from scoring).

Communication is vital on every level of basketball, including and especially in the NBA. Grant Hill believes that the best teams and best players in the NBA communicate and talk the most. "Kevin Garnett won't shut up," Hill said. "The San Antonio Spurs talk; everybody on the team does it. And when the whole team talks, it is a very powerful and intimidating thing."

Hill said that talking on the floor may not be easy or natural, but it's an acquired skill that must be worked on and emphasized every day, every play. And it is absolutely necessary to keep each player involved and engaged, and to send a positive message to teammates that you are fully absorbed in the team's objectives. "People have asked me how I can talk and play at the same time," Hill said. "I always counter by asking, 'How can you not?'"

Effective communication is important not just on the floor, but off the floor as well. To be an effective communicator, a great teammate and tough player has to talk, but also has to be able to listen. Nobody ever learned anything while talking. You have to know how to listen, and you have to be aware of what to listen for. The best-communicating teams listen and act upon what they hear. And if you don't listen, how will you know whether your team or teammates need to be kicked in the backside or need to be hugged? How will you know whether you need to speak forcefully or gently?

How will you know whether your team needs to be driven to accomplish more, irritated to fight harder, or encouraged to pick up its confidence?

Perhaps the best teammate and best communicator I ever played with was Duke point guard Tommy Amaker. Though he was the floor leader of our team, he was not the biggest, the strongest or the most physically imposing player on, but he was the smartest and most aware. And I believe he was the best listener, and did the best job of observing, and processing what he observed into positive action.

Amaker had—and has—a special kind of toughness. As a coach, the qualities he values in a player today are the exact same qualities I saw him exhibit as a player. For Amaker the most valuable player and teammate you can have is the player who knows *his* game, and also knows *the* game. "The players that understand both, and where they fit into both, are the special players," Amaker said. From playing with him for so many years, I can state without reservation that Tommy Amaker was one of those special players he so covets now as a coach.

"One of my strengths as a player, and as a person, is that I know who I am," Amaker said. From the time he was very young, whether with coaches, teachers or his parents, Amaker classified himself as a "pleaser." "I wasn't just trying to be liked, but I was always trying to do what was expected of me by my team or my family," Amaker said. "I was always trying to make people around me better."

Amaker was a "secure" player. He always felt the best about his performance when he was able to facilitate his teammates' playing their game, and putting his team in a position to perform at the optimum level.

"I took pride in knowing what my teammates were going through, and what they needed. I wanted to know what mattered to them, what was important to them," Amaker said. "If it was important to them, it was important to me." And to understand what was important to his teammates, Amaker had to listen to them, observe, be aware of their personal situations, and be tough enough to put aside his own personal wants and needs and focus on his team instead.

Amaker had a special relationship with our star player and the captain of our 1986 Duke team, Johnny Dawkins, who to this day remains the most important player in the history of Duke basketball. Dawkins became Duke's all-time leading scorer with 2,556 points, and he led our 1986 team to the National Championship game and a record of 37–3, which was an NCAA record for wins in a single season until 2012. Dawkins was a two-time first team All-ACC performer in 1985 and 1986 as well as the school's first consensus two-time first team All-American. The 1986 Naismith National Player of the Year, Dawkins's number 24 was retired into the rafters of Cameron Indoor Stadium.

Amaker was very aware of Johnny's intensity and pride as a player and as a person. From 1983 to 1986, Dawkins had a very intense rivalry with Georgia Tech star Mark Price. Both were All-American guards, and were the two best guards in the ACC. In 1986, Duke and Georgia Tech played in the ACC Championship game, and Dawkins and Price were again matched up with each other, head-to-head. This time it was for a championship.

The game came down to the wire, and with Duke leading 66–65, Georgia Tech had an opportunity for a final shot. Predictably, Georgia Tech coach Bobby Cremins put the ball in Price's hands. And Price was being guarded by his rival, Dawkins. Georgia Tech went into a "1–4 low" set, with Price up top and his four teammates along the baseline. Cremins wanted Price to go one-on-one against Dawkins for the win, and for the ACC Championship.

As Price dribbled to the right, Amaker was guarding Georgia Tech guard Craig Neal in the right corner. Amaker had to "help and recover" toward Price, coming off of his man, Neal, to help Dawkins on Price's drive. Amaker's help defense caused Price to pass the ball to Neal. Then Amaker had to recover quickly to Neal to pressure the shot. In large measure because of Amaker's pressure,

Neal missed the shot. Duke then secured the rebound, and Mike Krzyzewski won the ACC title, his first championship of any kind as a head basketball coach.

Amaker's defense on that play was more than just a simple "help and recover" defensive play. Because Amaker was a selfless team defender, leader and an extraordinary listener, he was fully aware of what was going on with his team and each of his teammates. He was especially aware of what was going on with Dawkins.

Amaker knew the importance of that game to Dawkins, especially the matchup with Price, and especially that final play. Amaker wasn't going to let Price score, but more important, Amaker was not going to let Price score over Johnny Dawkins. "Maybe they would score over me, but Price was not going to score over Johnny. Period," Amaker said. "If it was over me, so be it."

Just after the game, while celebrating winning the ACC Championship on the floor of the Greensboro Coliseum, Amaker and Dawkins shared a moment. "Thanks, man," Dawkins said to Amaker. "That was big."

It was more than big. It was truly tough, and it was the measure of a great teammate. Tommy Amaker was a tough player, and his ability to communicate, listen and show empathy for his teammates made him even tougher.

Communication in basketball, or any endeavor, is about trust and honesty, and good communication requires toughness. To be a great communicator, you must be tough enough to say tough things to your teammates when it is necessary, and to hear tough things from your teammates when they believe it is necessary.

Jon Gruden believes it is his duty to challenge his players and staff. "I challenge them to accept and embrace the urgency of what we are doing," Gruden said. "If I stop pushing, if I stop demanding of you, if I stop getting on you, then I probably don't think you have very much to offer." Gruden tells his players that the time to be concerned is when he stops pushing and expecting more of you as a player.

Michigan State coach Tom Izzo constantly challenges his players, and sometimes outsiders don't understand how he gets them to respond so positively to such challenges. "People ask me all the time how I can get on my guys so hard," Izzo said. "I spend the time to build trust. I can challenge them to get better, to push themselves to be their best every day, and not to expect anything less of themselves, because they know I want what's best for them, and I want them to expect it of themselves."

I often heard former Wake Forest coach Skip Prosser quote Ralph Waldo Emerson on the issue of trust and holding each other accountable: "A true friend is somebody who can make us do what we can."

"I have always been taught that discipline is the greatest form of love you can show," Izzo said. "Part of discipline is accountability. What would we be as a team if we didn't hold each other accountable? I can't imagine it."

Those challenges in communication go far beyond sports. NASA engineer Daryl Woods faces difficult challenges and tough truths every day with his team. Doing such high-profile government work requires him to plan to a budget profile, when government appropriations change from year to year. Often NASA's fiscal requirements can change from what was budgeted in the prior year. When there are such budget cuts, funds have to be moved around for efficiency, and tough decisions have to be made.

"That's when I hear some very real concerns," Woods said. But Woods and his team have a mission, and the mission comes first. "It's about the mission. Sometimes I have to tell colleagues that their element is not on the critical path. That's not easy," Woods said. "It's not easy to hear or to say. But we prioritize things in a big-picture way, work through it; we unite and move on together. We keep working the problem, and we work toward accomplishing the mission."

Accomplishing the mission, at NASA, on the basketball floor, boardroom or football field requires a collective toughness, and that toughness is facilitated through great communication. When bad news is communicated, one has to be tough on both ends of that message.

"In our business, toughness is the ability to respond positively to any situation," Woods said. "Budget issues, technical problems, engineering challenges, you name it. You take emotion out of it without losing your passion and inspiration, and you apply discipline to work through it, to work through the problem, and do it together.

"You concentrate on the things you can control while still being aware of the things you can't control but [still] can affect your mission. That's toughness."

Toughness is about accountability, and tough players are willing to hold teammates accountable for the team's standards, without worrying that a player will take criticism or a command the wrong way. Similarly, there needs to be a level of trust that one will say what is necessary in the right tone, and with the right intentions. Teammates cannot fear hurt feelings, but have to trust that everyone is tough enough to accept that anything said is said in the best interests of the team's performance and development.

Kevin Eastman, assistant coach of the Boston Celtics, often says that players and coaches need to be acutely aware of how a message is delivered, and that any effective message is delivered with respect.

But communication, trust and toughness do not stop once the buzzer sounds. To be a great team, and great teammates, we all had the responsibility to communicate, to connect, and to understand the issues and responsibilities of each person on our team. We needed to be teammates on and off the floor, twenty-four/seven. That takes toughness. You have to be tough enough to handle your business, and to help those you rely upon and who rely upon you, to handle theirs.

Mia Hamm knew what it was like to be called out by her coach, and she knew how tough a player needed to be to handle it. Hamm told me a story of toughness and communication from a time she was taking part in a scrimmage. It was her first practice since coming back from an injury, an MCL tear. "I had worked really hard to come back, and it was the first time I stepped on the field," Hamm said. "I was taken down to the ground from behind on a play, and I wasn't happy about it."

Hamm got up slowly, and was annoyed that she had been taken down, especially when she was just coming off of an injury. Hamm's coach, Tony DiCicco, didn't care. He had a blunt assessment of the play, and of Hamm's reaction. "What's your problem?" DiCicco asked Hamm. "Look, if you don't want the contact, go play tennis. We're not going to play with cones around you. Get off the field!"

Hamm was stunned and, at first, a little hurt as she went to the sidelines. But after she thought about it, she quickly toughened up and fully understood. "He was basically saying, 'We're not lowering our intensity and standards to wait for you,'" Hamm said. "And he was absolutely right."

DiCicco was saying to Hamm that she needed to be mentally and physically ready to step onto the field and truly compete. "Sometimes you need to hear it that way," Hamm said. "It was an intense scrimmage, and Tony couldn't whisper in my ear and reason with me. He was just as intense as the situation."

When Christian Laettner was playing for Mike Krzyzewski at Duke from 1989 through 1992, Laettner was the National Player of the Year and most often a target for opposing defenses. And opposing defenses always tried to be extra physical with him.

One game, after he had been roughed up a bit, Laettner was fouled. After the contact and whistle, he recoiled and stared at the opposing player who had fouled him as if he had committed some sort of crime. Much like DiCicco did with Hamm, Coach K reacted right away.

"Christian! Are you too good to get fouled now?" Coach K said. "You're so good that defenses aren't going to play hard against you? Step to the line, and hit your free throws."

Laettner was about as mentally tough as you could get, and true to form, he snapped out of his minor funk and stepped to the line and knocked down his free throws. He was a headstrong player, but Laettner listened, and trusted in his coach and teammates enough that they could challenge him and he would respond positively.

Grant Hill agrees. "Christian Laettner was an incredibly tough player," Hill said. "He wanted to win and he always competed. He would fight you, literally." Hill still marvels at Laettner's ability to take the brunt of things from opposing crowds and players on the road, in part so his teammates wouldn't have to. "He would take incredible abuse and attention on the road, and he never backed down from it," Hill said. "He would knock down free throw after free throw on the road, and it never seemed like he would miss. I learned a lot from him about being tough. He was as tough a teammate as I have ever had."

In 1991, when I was an assistant coach on Mike Krzyzewski's staff, we were watching film of Laettner swishing two huge free throws late in Duke's upset of UNLV in the Final Four. Coach K turned to all of us and said, "Laettner will never choke. He may miss, but he will never choke."

Krzyzewski wasn't suggesting that Laettner couldn't miss, wouldn't miss or didn't care if he missed. Clearly he could miss, and clearly he cared. It was that he was willing to accept the consequences that came with making or missing those free throws, and he performed. He concentrated on making his free throws, rather than thinking about the fact that he didn't want to miss. There is a difference, and staying mentally tough is most difficult on the road, or when things are not going your way.

Grant Hill believes that toughness is really about the little things in communication, the details. "Are you tough enough to hold a teammate accountable to your team's standards?" Hill asks. "That can be uncomfortable, and requires toughness on both sides of the conversation, or the confrontation."

Hill said such confrontations can come on the floor, in the locker room or in the personal life of a teammate. "There are times when a teammate needs to be told that we need him to wake up, to compete," Hill said. "Or, 'You have a responsibility to take better care of yourself or to act the right way.' And you have to work at it and do it in a respectful way to build credibility and trust with your teammates."

Hill recalled that the first time he really felt challenged by a teammate was his freshman season at Duke, when he was called out by Laettner. It came in a preseason pickup game in Cameron Indoor Stadium. Laettner barked to Hill that he needed to drive the ball and get to the rim, but his tone and his explanation bewildered the inexperienced Hill. "Laettner said to me, 'Grant, you can't shoot! Drive the ball and get to the rim!'" He was communicating to Hill that if he was missing more shots than he was making, he needed to take the shots he could make, or work on being a better shooter.

Hill was stunned at first. "I didn't say anything," he said. "But as I thought about it, he was right." Hill believes it was best for him to have heard that directly from Laettner, rather than from Coach K. "When players are willing to hold each other accountable, I think it carries more weight and has more impact," Hill said. "And the coach doesn't have to be the only voice."

To Hill, the sooner a player learns such lessons in toughness, the better off that player will be. "Sometimes in the NBA, players have missed some steps in life," Hill said. "They may have left school early to be a pro and have not spent enough time in an environment where they are part of something bigger than themselves. They are not bad people, but have a 'me' mind-set, a selfish mind-set. A lot of them don't know how to handle being challenged and held accountable, and they get defensive about it."

In other words, some players, even in the NBA, have not internalized the "we" part of the game, instead of the "me" part of the game. That starts with communication.

Julie Foudy believes it is imperative to be able to have such confrontations and challenge each other, whether it is player-to-player or coach-to-player. "That is really hard for women," Foudy said.

"There is a feeling of not wanting to make the other person mad or hurt her feelings." But Foudy fights that feeling, and encourages young girls and women to seek out such challenges and to embrace them. They are a good thing. "Challenging each other, that's not a negative," Foudy said. "It's a positive, an incredible positive."

Foudy, along with Mia Hamm, was co-captain and a nine-year veteran of the U.S. women's soccer team. After retiring from the field in 2004, Foudy moved into broadcasting and is the primary color commentator for women's soccer telecasts on ESPN. She and Mia Hamm, along with Joy Fawcett, retired together after the 2004 Olympic Games, and the media labeled that date the end of the "golden era" of U.S. women's soccer. In 2007, Foudy and Hamm were inducted together into the National Soccer Hall of Fame. Their induction marked the first all-female class in history.

Today Foudy, a Stanford graduate, is an advocate for women's and children's rights and an outspoken critic of commercial working conditions. In 2006, Foudy and her husband, Ian Sawyers, launched the Julie Foudy Sports Leadership Academy, which weaves together sports and leadership for girls. The academy has received national and international attention for creating leaders both on and off the field.

Foudy believes that it can be harder for girls and women to confront each other in competitive settings due to antiquated social mores, and she continues to advocate that women and girls in sports should not shy away from such confrontation, but seek it out and strive to be tough enough to process it in a positive manner. To Foudy, confrontation among teammates, if handled respectfully, is healthy and good. It can make everybody better. "It could be a game, or it could just be a practice. There's no difference," Foudy said. "It gets heated. It's supposed to be heated. If you're competing, really competing, isn't it supposed to be heated?"

Foudy recalled intense arguments with teammates in practices and scrimmages over whether a ball was in or out. Foudy credits that spirit, and the collective toughness to handle it the right way, for her team's success and closeness. "We'd fight over it," she said. "When you're around people that embrace that, you will be better."

But, Foudy said, what you do after the competitive challenges is critical. "You have to push each other and challenge each other, but make sure you hug each other after," she said. "In a supportive and trusting environment, you can challenge each other. It is okay to go at it—you have to go at it—but you also have to be 'one group' after you go at it."

For Hamm, toughness is also about taking responsibility when you are wrong. During a match against Brazil in which Hamm and her U.S. National Team were not performing well, her coach subbed the superstar Hamm out of the game and onto the bench. That was something that rarely, if ever, happened to Hamm.

Her initial reaction was to be defensive and angry. "I disagreed in a big way," Hamm said. "I was livid about it, and I let him know it." As Hamm left the field and walked past DiCicco, she said to her coach, "What are you doing? I want to stay out there to help my teammates!" DiCicco snapped back, "You have a better chance of doing that sitting over there [on the bench]."

Following the loss, an angry and frustrated DiCicco informed the team that, while the next day was a scheduled day off and a beach day in Brazil, every player was required to watch the tape of that game. DiCicco told the team that since he had to suffer through watching the game live, the players should have to watch it too.

After watching the film, Hamm marched right to DiCicco's hotel room. When DiCicco answered the door, Hamm said, "About you taking me out of the game . . . what took you so long? You should have taken me out sooner. I was terrible. I'm so sorry."

Hamm, the star player, handled the challenge, and was tough enough to accept her shortcomings in the game and to grow from it. She heard and processed some tough, critical words from her coach, and she looked herself in the mirror and was honest with herself in evaluating her performance. Then she acted upon it in a positive manner. In short, she was coachable. She was tough enough not only to be held accountable, but to actually *be* accountable.

Great communication provides the foundation for coaches and players to be accountable to one another, and to trust one another. Great communication fosters better toughness. The better you communicate, including listening to others and yourself, the tougher you will be.

CHAPTER 5

PERSISTENCE

When I asked Mike Krzyzewski what element of toughness he felt was underemphasized, he had a quick and direct response: persistence. Persistence is your ability to keep going without giving up or giving in. If you can be persistent in your belief, preparation, communication, your willingness to endure, and all of the other elements of mental toughness, you will be tougher. Persistence is a mind-set.

As a player, Mark Alarie was an All-ACC and All-American at Duke, and while he was often quiet off the floor, he was an intense competitor on it. As I stated earlier, Alarie was one of the toughest players, both mentally and physically, I have ever been around in all my years around the game.

When Alarie and I were playing for Coach K at Duke, we annually ran the mile for time as a team. It was a measure of our fitness, but also of our toughness. Mark always ran a good time, and considerably better than my time, even though we had trained together and put in the same preparation. Our junior year, I put in extra preparation for the mile run, in part because I wanted to beat

Mark's time, and in part because I wanted to see how well I could do if I were better prepared.

For me, the extra preparation was a big commitment, because I dreaded distance running. In fact, I used to laugh about Bum Phillips's response to a reporter when he inquired about Earl Campbell's loafing during a Houston Oilers mile run. "When it's third and a mile, we don't go to Earl." That was the excuse I used for not wanting to do it, because basketball wasn't about distance running. You didn't have to be a champion miler to be a good basketball player. It was an excuse, or rationalization, for simply not being tough enough to endure it.

I trained for the mile by doing extra distance running, some of it around the Duke golf course. After all of that preparation, I ran my best time ever, and completed the mile in five minutes and forty seconds. It was my best time by a fair margin. Alarie, without having put in as much extra work as I had, clocked a 5:11-mile time. It seemed like Alarie was back in the locker room before I crossed the finish line.

Afterward, when I could breathe again, I asked Alarie how he did it, especially since I had prepared more for this one than he had. He said, "For me, the mile run is about how much pain I'm willing to endure."

Wow. I thought about it, and he was right. I always believed that I trained and worked just as hard as Alarie did, and maybe even harder for this one event, but there was a difference in mind-set. I trained to run the mile for my best time, *and* I trained to do it as comfortably as I could.

Alarie took a different approach. He trained not to do the same thing more comfortably, but to be more productive. He decided he was going to be in just as much pain and discomfort, but he was doing it to get more out of it. It was a great lesson for me on how to approach training, and what it was all about.

For me, it wasn't about working hard. I was a hard worker, and I knew it. It was about my mental approach to my work. I worked hard in the weight room and worked hard playing, but I did all of that with the goal of doing the same job with greater ease, and more comfortably.

Mine was the wrong approach. Alarie's was the right one, and the tougher one. When I worked out, it should not have been to do the same job more comfortably, but to improve my capacity, to be more productive in my time on the floor.

For Alarie, it was about resilience and persistence. "In my mind, whatever toughness I had was about my ability to pick myself up and keep going," he said. "It wasn't about optimism. It was wholly different. It was about perseverance."

Former NFL head coach Herman Edwards passionately echoed Alarie's approach. Edwards measures a player's toughness by the very last wind sprint in fitness training. Is that player going to run just fast enough to finish in the middle of the pack? "You know it's going to burn, and nobody's watching," Edwards said. "If you can push through and give that effort, do what it takes, to push through it, not just get through it, that's a mental disposition you don't want to play against. You don't want to play against those guys. They make it too hard on you." Edwards was talking about Alarie. I never saw him quit, and I never saw him give in.

Alarie grew up in Phoenix, Arizona, and was five years older than his brother, Chris. Chris was born with severe cerebral palsy, and was confined to a wheelchair his entire life. From a very early age, Mark would take Chris with him whenever he would play, whether it was a pickup basketball game, Wiffle ball or football in the street. That was Chris's playtime too, and Mark would roll Chris's chair to wherever he went to compete. Mark's game was Chris's game.

Having Chris sitting in his wheelchair watching him clearly had an impact on Mark. "There was never a time I thought I could give in, that I was too tired or it was too hard," Alarie said. "He couldn't even fall out of his chair, and I wasn't going to run downcourt because it was just too hard? No way."

Alarie knew he was the lucky brother, and whether that feeling created a sense of guilt or responsibility, it motivated Alarie to do more. Alarie's perspective made him feel like he had more in reserve than other players, and that he could always do more. "I would rather pass out or faint than give up in front of my brother," Alarie said.

"How many times have you seen a player collapse because of exhaustion? Never, really," Alarie said. "You can push through it. So I pushed through it. Because of my brother, I would not give in to fatigue, and I never let fatigue get the best of me." Even today, Alarie says that he would rather faint or pass out than quit.

For Mike Krzyzewski, like Alarie, quitting was not an option. Refusing to quit was ingrained in Krzyzewski through his family and West Point. "I was taught and conditioned not to quit," Krzyzewski said. "My family went to work every day, sick, tired, whatever. My mom, my dad, my brother . . . every day."

"And West Point was a toughness lab," Krzyzewski said. "They make you fail, and put you in incredible situations where you fall short. Everyone at West Point fails in a list of things, but failure is never a destination. There is always someone to pick you up, pat you on the back, kick you in the rear, whatever you need at that moment."

West Point taught Krzyzewski that he was not allowed to quit. He and his fellow cadets had the resources, both internal and external, to overcome. At West Point, Krzyzewski was taught that he was not isolated, even though he might have felt that way. He was taught to rely on and use his internal resources—what he is made of—and his external resources—the people around him supporting him and pushing him—to continue to fight through adversity. "You have to get them all in the fight," Krzyzewski said.

"When you are knocked down," he said, "you are conditioned that it's unacceptable where you are, and it becomes a habit to fight, and to fight through things."

Julie Foudy agrees. Persevering, getting up when you have been knocked down, is what true mental toughness represents to her. She likens her spirit to her kids' toy, an inflatable punching bag that pops back up when it is hit. "That's always what I wanted to be," Foudy said. "Knock me down, and I will pop right back up. That's where my toughness comes in. I will get back up."

Foudy wasn't the most skilled or the fastest player, but she was one of the toughest. "We used to joke that I was a lethal scorer from two feet and in," Foudy said. "But I wouldn't give up. I do think that is a common denominator in tough people. They don't quit. They don't stay down. They don't give up, and they don't give in."

Or, as Boston Celtics assistant coach Kevin Eastman often says, "Are you going to give up and give in, or are you going to get up and get in?"

Sage Steele: Persistence and Perspective

Sage Steele is one of the most recognizable sports anchors at ESPN, and her career in broadcasting has been on an upward trajectory for years, with seemingly no limit. Simply put, Sage Steele makes it look easy. But her career hasn't been easy. It has been tough and, correspondingly, she has had to be tough. To me, Steele is a great example of how persistence, perseverance and perspective are essential elements of toughness.

I appreciate Sage Steele's talent and ability. She has a perspective that not many people have. She is willing to pay the price to achieve, but she is also willing to make tough choices. In my judgment, Steele isn't necessarily striving to "have it all" or "do it all." She has made the choices that are right for her and her family, with great perspective, and has fought to achieve excellence in every area while maintaining the right balance.

Steele was born in Panama, the daughter of a soldier. Her father, Gary Steele, was the first African-American to play varsity football at West Point in 1966, and has been called one of the finest athletes in West Point history by both Bob Knight and Mike Krzyzewski. As a child of the military, Sage moved around often with her family, living all over the world before spending her final year of high school in Carmel, Indiana, and attending Indiana University in Bloomington. She thinks being an army brat really toughened her up.

"I had to learn to survive in new surroundings, with new people," Steele said. "I had to learn how to talk to anyone, how to walk into a new classroom with confidence and how to make new friends. That isn't always easy."

She didn't realize at the time that she was persevering through difficulties. It was just the way her life was, Steele said. "I was a sensitive child, hypersensitive, really," Steele said. "I was a pleaser. I was the first child, and my parents pounded into me the need to be tougher, that I couldn't let others affect me, change me or make me compromise my values."

Steele set her sights on a broadcasting career early in her life. "People may not believe this, but when I was in the eighth grade, I announced to my entire family that someday I was going to host *SportsCenter* on ESPN. It's crazy for me to even think about that," Steele said. Her first big break in broadcasting was in Indianapolis. She was offered her dream job at age twenty-four, but looking back, she realizes she wasn't completely prepared for it, and it could well have been a nightmare.

At the time, she was making $21,000 a year as the weekend sports anchor in a top-twenty-five market, and was the only woman anchoring sports in Indianapolis. Steele confessed, "I had no business being in a top-twenty-five market at that time. I was terrible."

At one point, she was having some trouble making ends meet and paying her bills, but she was too proud to ask her parents for money. She decided instead to work up the courage to go into her boss's office and ask for an advance on her contracted raise of $1,500 for the next year. She was scared to death.

Steele's boss in Indianapolis was a prominent and well-respected fixture in the television broadcasting industry, and the executive who "discovered" *Today* show legend Jane Pauley. Steele was nervous, but mustered up the guts to go in and ask him for an advance. He told her he would think about it and get back to her.

Two weeks later, he called her into his office. He told Steele, "I've talked to some people here, I've thought about it, and you don't deserve it. You're not worthy of it." Steele was devastated.

"I worked hard and, look, I knew I wasn't great and had a long way to go," Steele said. "But not worth it? I cried and cried, and I wanted to quit," Steele said. "But it also really pissed me off. In the end, it motivated me."

She called her parents, and her mother was partly mad at her boss, but also devastated for her daughter. Steele's father was calmer, and snapped her out of her despair by telling her she had a choice: She could give up and let this guy dictate her life, or she could get up and do something about it.

Steele's father challenged her and said she could do only so much crying, that she had to just "shut up and get to work." She knew she had to choose. Was she going to just accept what she was told, or was she going to fight? Steele sees that experience as a "toughness wake-up call."

"It really toughened me up," Steele said. "I had support at home to help me be tougher. My dad challenged me to be tougher, and I responded. I'm proud of that."

She went back to work, and she worked to get better and to prove herself to others.

Soon after that, Steele's agent got her an opportunity to interview for a job at a station in Tampa, an opportunity to jump from the twenty-fifth-largest television market to the thirteenth. But she needed to be released from her contract. "The woman who wasn't *worth it* needed a release," she said. Based upon that, she didn't anticipate gaining a release would be difficult.

Instead, her boss said no, he wouldn't give her the release. The person who told her she wasn't worth it was now telling her she couldn't leave a place where he said she wasn't wanted in the first place, Steele said. "That made my blood boil."

She went to the general manager of the station, and he agreed to release her from her existing contract. To be released, however, she had to pay back the moving expenses fronted to her when she first took the job. She had to pay the station $900.

"Believe me, I wanted to pay that nine hundred bucks in nickels and dimes, but I didn't," Steele said. "I chose the harder right over the easier wrong. My dad learned it from West Point, and made me memorize it." The motto comes from the Cadet Prayer of the United States Military Academy. The key part reads:

"Encourage us in our endeavor to live above the common level of life. Make us to choose the harder right instead of the easier wrong, and never to be content with a half-truth when the whole can be won. Endow us with courage that is born of loyalty to all that is noble and worthy, that scorns to compromise with vice and injustice and knows no fear when truth and right are in jeopardy."

That experience was a turning point for Steele, and something clicked with her. "I remind myself every day that I need to keep getting better, and to be an example. I needed to be ready, but I wasn't ready yet," Steele said. "But I was going to be ready from then on. I was going to be prepared, and I was going to tough out every situation. I was going to meet the challenge and own up to it, not shrink from it."

In the next nine years, Steele went from Tampa to the Washington, DC, area. She worked for Comcast SportsNet as the main sports anchor and beat reporter for the Baltimore Ravens. She turned down a job offer from ESPN in 2004 but ultimately accepted a second offer from the "Worldwide Leader in Sports" in 2007.

Yet, looking back, Steele feels her first day at ESPN was one of the lowest points of her professional career. "March sixteen, 2007, and I was assigned to do the six p.m. *SportsCenter.* You don't usually start there. You work your way up to that," she said. "But I started there."

Her first day at ESPN was the first day of the 2007 NCAA Tournament. On such a day, there is a lot going on and a lot to process. Game results and stories are breaking quickly, and the "rundown," the plan for the show, can go right out the window. "I was lost. And I was scared to death," Steele said. "I had no clue what was going on, and it seemed like nobody talked to me in my ear [the producer of the show will communicate during the show through Steele's earpiece] for the majority of the show."

Steele recalls saying a quick prayer, then proceeding to "stumble" all over herself. The broadcast was a disaster.

After that first day, Steele's confidence took a huge hit. "It took me a long time to shake that off. In fact, I was so shaken that I started some lame skin-care business on the side," she said. "I wanted to have something in case I didn't get renewed at ESPN. It was almost laughable."

But then she made the conscious choice to toughen up and fight back. "I got really mad at myself," Steele recalled. "I had allowed this to get into my head. So I made the conscious decision to move on. I moved on and concentrated only on improving, on getting better."

She accepted that she couldn't change the past, but she could impact her future with how hard she worked in the present and by getting better today. "Right here, right now," Steele said.

Next, Steele was assigned to the new "live" morning *SportsCenter* in 2008. "Every day I put my feet on the ground and asked myself, 'How tough are you?'" Steele said. "I decided, and it was a choice, that I wasn't going to settle for less. I was determined not to be satisfied. I was going to try harder today than I did yesterday, and keep doing that every day. I saw my parents do it, and damn it, I was going to do it too."

She heard the naysayers. Steele knew they said she was only

there for the sake of diversity, because she was an African-American woman. But she firmly believes it is up to her, and only her, to choose what influences affect her or bring her down. "I decided I wasn't going to allow anything to get in my way," Steele said. "Go ahead; say what you want. Nothing was going to bring me down. Nothing. I was going to fight through it.

"There aren't all that many women in this field, and even fewer African-American women," Steele said. "I understand the way things work. The naysayers may be right in that I was able to get this job because of diversity, numbers and demographics. But I also know that if you suck, they'll find someone else—and quick. You have to bring it every day."

Steele admits that it hurts when she hears that friends and co-workers may have said negative things about her. "It gets back to you," Steele said. "But I pick my battles. And one person I will not battle is me," Steele said. "I know the truth. I have a lot of pride in what I have been able to accomplish and overcome. And I am proud when I go home every night. I'll be damned if I am going to let others define me."

She is also very conscious of the example she is setting. "I really admire people like Robin Roberts, not only for what she has done and how good she is, but for how she's done it and who she is as a person and a professional," Steele said. "She has been such a fabulous role model for me and so many other women. I owe her, and I can't ever repay her. I owe her my best."

Steele attributes a lot of her success, and her ability to persevere and endure, to her perspective, which has been inspired by her husband, Jonathan Bailey. Her parents inspired her to be tougher, while her husband inspires her to be more unselfish.

For the last ten years, Bailey has been a stay-at-home dad while Steele made a name for herself on air. Staying at home wasn't easy for him, and it wasn't easy for Steele. Truthfully—and selfishly, she says—she wanted to be the one at home, the one to have dinner ready and to be all things to all people.

When they were first married and living in Washington, DC, Steele was working for Comcast SportsNet, and Bailey had a good job in IT training and consulting. But after having three children in four years, they knew they had some tough decisions to make that might not fit into their original plan.

"We agreed that no way would our family have a nanny or do the day care thing. We both wanted a parent in the home," she said.

"Honestly—I thought it would be me. We looked at all of the numbers, and I happened to make more money, and I had more future earning potential," Steele said. "So we decided Jonathan would stay home and I would work outside the home."

While the plan sounded very logical, Steele and Bailey were going against traditional roles, she said. They convinced themselves to embrace what was important to them and not worry about someone else's traditional feelings about their decisions.

Their emotions, too, were raw and rough. "The first day I drove away from home to go cover the Baltimore Ravens training camp, I could barely hold it together," Steele said. "Jonathan held our little girl's hand and waved it at me as I was driving away. When I got around the corner, I pulled over and I just lost it."

But Steele believes her husband has it far tougher than she does, and that his role was the major adjustment that made her career possible. At first, the two accepted their roles, but over time, they firmly embraced them. "We just decided that we would simply do our absolute best. Can we be there a hundred percent of the time? No. But we can give a hundred percent of ourselves in the time that we are there."

Steele said she doesn't beat herself up anymore when she misses one of her kids' events or an important time at home. "But," she said, "I own the moments when I am there. I own them."

So many of the people I work with at ESPN make it look easy, and few make it look easier than Sage Steele. However, it isn't easy. It is difficult. To make it at the highest level and excel, you have to be talented, and Sage Steele is certainly that. But you also have to be committed and tough. At first glance, Steele may not look tough, but she is. In my judgment, it is Steele's toughness that has set her apart. And an essential ingredient in her toughness is her persistence. I have learned a lot about toughness from her story.

Pushing Limits

Persistence is not just about pushing forward; it is about pushing through to reach a new height, exceeding a limit you thought you had. Everybody limits themselves in some way, whether it is to manage expectations and avoid disappointment, or to avoid the physical pain and discomfort that accompanies the reach for a new limit, a higher standard. It takes toughness to push your limits, to push through being tired, to push past muscle fatigue to muscle failure. Are you, individually and as a team, tough enough to push past what you think is a breaking point and reach a new height? Pushing your limits is a critical element of toughness.

Mia Hamm is quick to cite former teammate Michelle Akers as the toughest player she has ever been around. Akers suffered from chronic fatigue syndrome and finished every game and practice absolutely exhausted, often requiring intravenous fluids.

Akers understood playing in pain and fighting through real fatigue. And she taught Hamm and her teammates how to be true pros. "Michelle made soccer her life. It was twenty-four hours a day, seven days a week for her," Hamm said. "Part of that was because she wanted to, but part of that was because she had to. With her chronic fatigue, she constantly had to figure out what she needed to do to prepare herself and be at her best."

Akers had a nutritionist to squeeze every ounce of energy out of her body, and a strength and conditioning coach to teach her how to train efficiently when she had the energy. But the thing that really stuck out to Hamm about Akers's toughness was her willingness and persistence to study and perfect her craft.

Hamm joined the U.S. National Team straight from college, and at that point in her career, she couldn't imagine staying for an hour or two after practice to get extra work in. For Akers, that was the norm, and it made a profound impact on Hamm and her teammates.

"I would show up to training early, thinking I was this hard worker, and Akers would have already been there for over an hour," Julie Foudy said. "She's already drenched in sweat, back when we wore the gray old cotton T-shirts, and it would be drenched. She was out there banging balls, working."

Foudy knows that Akers had terrific natural talent and ability, but that wasn't the reason she was such a great player. "She was the first one out there and the last one to leave. *That's* why she was great," Foudy said. "That is mental toughness, discipline, commitment and wanting to win."

Akers not only controlled her fitness; she controlled and took complete ownership of her skill level, including working hard to make her nondominant foot just as good and capable as her dominant foot. "For most of us, it was just a given that your nondominant foot was not going to be as good," Hamm said. "But that wasn't good enough for Michelle."

Akers told Hamm she couldn't control the circumstances in a game that might require her to use her nondominant foot, and her left foot would have to make the play. In that situation, which Akers could not control or predict, she would have to rely on her skill level under pressure. That takes work. It wasn't just magically going to happen.

"Her attitude and toughness cannot help but rub off," Hamm said. "It's an investment. It's hard work. And it's worth it."

Hamm was always one of the very best athletes in her sport, but she felt she wasn't truly pushed until she reached the U.S. National Team. "Part of it is inside you, but I knew I wasn't tested," she said. "Being one of the best athletes, I could get away with stuff."

It was in fitness training that Hamm realized that she needed to do more than just get through it and survive it. She needed to commit to it fully to really improve. "It has to be twenty-four/seven—it just can't be when it's convenient for you or when you feel like it," Hamm said. "It isn't easy, and it isn't comfortable. But it is necessary."

During USA team training, Hamm and her teammates found and created their toughest competitions. "We worked so hard," Hamm said. "In a unique sense, the price we paid was there, in training. We could come back and rely upon our training in the games."

In 1995, Hamm's U.S. National Team was playing against the Chinese National Team when Michelle Akers, already playing with a damaged MCL, was drilled in the head with a corner kick. Her teammates were not surprised when Akers tried to play on one leg with concussion symptoms. But Akers could not perform to her usual level, and the U.S. team did not have her scoring and physical presence. Hamm and her teammates lost the game.

"We weren't tough enough to win," Hamm said. "We were scared, and none of us stepped up to take more responsibility without Michelle leading the way. We just weren't tough enough."

In 1996, Hamm and her teammates were going through grueling fitness training and had reached a point when they would either quit or push through a perceived barrier. "We were teetering on the edge," Hamm said. "It was at the point where it was so much easier to quit."

It was a breaking point, but it was also a turning point.

At that breaking point, teammate Carla Overbeck said something Hamm has never forgotten. "Norway is not fucking doing this right now!" Overbeck screamed. "They are not willing to pay this price!"

Overbeck's passionate statement of toughness pushed Hamm and her teammates through a barrier they had not approached or broken up to that point. Overbeck provided her team with a collective toughness, a pride and a confidence that could come only from accomplishment. That kind of accomplishment isn't just handed to you. You have to earn it.

"It isn't always easy being pushed to that edge," Hamm said. "Nothing is guaranteed, but if you get it, if you succeed after putting in all that effort, preparation and work, there is so much more pride and accomplishment than if it just dropped in your lap."

Overbeck made that profound impact because she had the courage to push herself and her team, and she trusted her teammates to respond. If she didn't say it, would it have been said at all? If she didn't challenge her teammates and herself at the crucial breaking point, would they have taken the easier path? The limit they pushed through together—when they could have broken—fueled these players into champions. And it was a remarkable example of true toughness in the face of adversity.

"That moment, when Carla said that, was exactly when I realized that fitness is largely mental," Foudy said, which echoed Alarie. "It becomes something you embrace. When Carla said that, we were like, 'Hell, yeah! You're right! We're going to work harder than anyone, and we're going to love it.'"

Before that moment, fitness training was something Foudy, Hamm and her teammates dreaded, and just tried to get through. After Overbeck's cry for collective toughness, fitness training was embraced, and the team reached new heights. "Then we loved it. We pushed each other, laughed together at ourselves at times, and realized that we weren't just surviving it; we were thriving in it," Foudy said.

Foudy believed she could do it because she had a teammate who would be driving her, encouraging her. "Every time, it might be a different player that was feeling great, having her best day, and they would drag everyone else with them," Foudy said. "It became a team thing, instead of a bunch of individuals trying to get through it."

Overbeck's toughness was contagious. Players would hit the finish line in fitness training, then immediately circle back and encourage the ones behind them to pick it up and keep going, keep pushing.

"It wasn't just 'my' fitness; it was 'our' fitness. Instead of a 'me' thing, it became a 'we' thing. You think that didn't make a positive impact?" Foudy said. "We won because of that kind of thing. That takes toughness, too, to think outside your own individual struggle and to help a teammate through hers."

Foudy then told me the same thing that Alarie told me many years before. "Your threshold is not what you think it is," she said. "You can do more; you can give more."

From Overbeck's statement of toughness, Foudy and her teammates began to ask, "Why is the sky the limit?" Now being persistent and pushing through limits was a collective expectation, and it was embraced by all. "It was a toughness, but with a vulnerability mixed in," Foudy said. "We weren't as good or as tough by ourselves, and we needed each other."

That is where the women's soccer team's saying of "wholesome discontent" came from. "It was the idea that pushing it was not good enough," Foudy said. "I do believe that the toughness factor on the mental side separates great from elite."

Tom Izzo couldn't agree more with Foudy. "Very few people are willing to do what it takes to do extraordinary things," Izzo said. "They talk about what they want. But to be the best, you have to pay the price to be the best. And you have to be willing to pay the price every day. It isn't easy, but it is absolutely worth it."

Grant Hill attributes much of his success and toughness to his willingness to work, and to push his limits. "When I was in college, we practiced so incredibly hard," he said. "I still apply it now. Not to pat myself on the back, but I practice harder than most of my teammates, so much so that they have to take me out of practice to preserve me. I don't think you can work that hard without being tough, and tough minded.

"And"—Hill laughed—"the harder I worked, the tougher I seemed to get. Funny how that works."

Hard work is not punishment. The toughest players go as hard as they can for as long as they can, and soon they increase their capacity to do more. And when you see nothing but hard work from your teammates, it raises your standard and your level of expectation for yourself. No coach can make you work as hard or want to work as hard as a tough teammate can. Coach-directed teams only go so far. The best and toughest teams reach their greatest heights because teammates feed off of each other, and are inspired to match or exceed the level they experience each day.

Under Bill Self, Kansas teams have become accustomed to working hard enough to reach players' limits, then operating at high levels under those conditions. "When our players have reached a point of exhaustion or deficit, I put them in tough situations where they have to band together and buy into a common goal," Self said. "They have to trust and believe at those points, and they really have to concentrate to be able to make winning plays and decisions. We drill it.

"Players need to be put through it almost every day," he said. "They need to be made to execute at game point, to hit a free throw with some pressure, to execute and concentrate when they're tired. That builds confidence. That builds togetherness. Then, when they leave a time-out in a tough situation, they leave knowing we are positively going to do this. They aren't just hoping we will.

"How can we expect players to care or believe unless they have gone through tough times together?" Self said. "As coaches, we have to put them through those tough times so they will know what to do when they get there."

Stepping Out of Your Comfort Zone

My mother was the most important person in my life when it came to helping me push my limits. That meant pushing myself, but it also meant stepping outside of my comfort zone and trying something different. It meant testing myself and rising to a different challenge.

From the time I was very small, my mother would not allow me to settle for less than my best effort. As a kid, I was unfocused and a little bit lazy. I was quick-tempered, and did not have the toughness to stick with things, to see them through and to finish what I started.

My mother saw what I was capable of, but also saw what I wasn't accomplishing, and she did not allow me to fool myself. She always told me that I was capable of more, and that I should expect more of myself. She believed in me, and felt that the only person who could stop me was, in fact, me.

Once, in a basketball tournament my team had won, I was named to the All-Tournament team, but was passed over for the tournament MVP award, which I selfishly thought I deserved and should have received. On the way home, I complained to my parents that I had been the best player; I should have gotten the ball more, and I should have been the MVP. After my incessant complaining, my mother had heard enough.

Without raising her voice, she politely told me, "Jay, you're a big boy. If you want the ball, go get it. If you want to be MVP, go prove it."

Boom.

In a soft voice, my mother made a huge impact on me. Without being an expert in the nuances of basketball, she was telling me that my attitude might be understandable, but it was not acceptable. And if I wanted to talk big, I needed to play big.

What she was really saying was, "Don't tell me; show me."

At that time, it was one thing to have your father tell you to toughen up and grow up, but when your sweet, demure mother tells you to toughen up, it makes a lasting impression.

I didn't really know it then, but my mother was one of the toughest people in my life.

My mom constantly put me in situations where I had to adjust to uncomfortable surroundings. She wanted me to be able to handle myself and shine in any situation.

When I was young, my mother put me into a ballroom dancing

course because she wanted me to be cultured and have the confidence and ability to handle myself in any situation.

The truth was, ballroom dancing was difficult. It required my complete concentration, and it was physically and mentally taxing. I went into it thinking it was for wimps. I left thinking I might not be able to handle it. I didn't know it at the time, and it sounds funny to say it even now, but ballroom dancing made me tougher.

After several classes, the dance instructor, Margaret Michael, wanted to put me and my older, teenage dance partner into a ballroom dancing competition. At first I was a bit embarrassed, and concerned that my friends would find out and make fun of me. I never told any of my friends or teammates I was taking part in ballroom dancing.

My partner and I won a couple of events at the dance competition, but I put the trophies out of view in my room, so as not to be seen by my friends. Whenever I complained, my mother would cheerfully tell me that I could handle it, and it would be good for me to try something different and master it.

Essentially, she was telling me to toughen up and deal with it, that I needed to embrace stepping out of my comfort zone and learn how to handle myself in any situation thrown at me.

She told me that life was going to throw more difficult challenges at me than a dance class, and that I didn't get to choose life's challenges. The only real choice was how I faced them and responded. She said that I had better learn to face up to whatever came my way. She told me she knew I could do it.

The only time my friends saw me dance was during a mandatory cotillion we had at school, in the eighth grade. The instructor taught us how to perform the waltz, and all of the eighth grade boys, myself included, acted like we didn't want to be there. When it was time to get out on the floor, it was easy for me, and I killed it.

One of my friends said, "Bilas, how are you doing this so well?"

"Because I'm an athlete, that's how," I responded, laughing.

"The lady just explained it. How can you *not* be doing this well?" I enjoyed that.

Toughness from Forensics

In addition to encouraging me to step outside my comfort zone in ballroom dancing, my mother encouraged me to take elective classes in public speaking and drama in high school. I resisted that too, because it wasn't what my any of my friends were doing, and it wasn't considered "cool."

But because of those courses, I got to know a drama teacher named Billy C. Creamer.

Mr. Creamer was one of the best coaches I ever had, and had a profound influence on me. While he didn't fit the stereotype of a tough guy, I soon found out he was really tough.

Once, Mr. Creamer and I talked about how what my peers said and thought impacted me, usually negatively. "How is it that you can get ninety-nine wonderful compliments," Mr. Creamer said, "and you internalize the one person who's critical of you?"

"What, you don't care what other people think?" I asked.

"No, I *care* very much what other people think," he said. "I don't *worry* about what other people think. None of us are above criticism, but we all have to decide whether that criticism is warranted, whether it is right. If it is, we can change it. But we can't change our principles or who we are."

That made an impact on me. I cared far too much about what others thought, and I worried about it.

Mr. Creamer cared about what was important to him, and the people who were important to him. He was creative and energetic, but he was also uncompromising on his principles and values.

And he was uncompromising in his belief in me.

Mr. Creamer taught Forensics, which was a debate and public speaking course. After I'd taken one of Mr. Creamer's classes, he asked me to join his forensics team and participate in a couple of local forensics competitions around Los Angeles.

In my first competition at Occidental College, Mr. Creamer entered me into an extemporaneous speaking competition and an impromptu speaking competition, a challenge he would throw my way at every competition after that. I was absolutely terrified, but I tried to play it off as disinterest so I could maintain my jock bravado.

Mr. Creamer did not care to hear me whine about a forensics competition, and he didn't care whether I wanted to do it or not. I was there, and I was going to do this and do it well. He saw right through my act, and knew I was worried about making a fool of myself. And he got a laugh out of seeing the big basketball player concerned about appearing before a few bespectacled judges, when I regularly faced tough physical competitors.

Mr. Creamer told me that I had no earthly idea of the power I had inside of me, and what heights I was capable of reaching. He found it odd that he believed in me more than I believed in myself. He was more passionate about our performances than any coach I had had up to that point.

In extemporaneous speaking, I was given a speech topic and thirty minutes to formulate a five- to seven-minute speech that I was to give, without notes, to a three-judge panel. Of course, having to formulate a coherent presentation in such a short period, and deliver that presentation before a group of people you didn't know, just sitting there staring at you, occasionally taking notes while you speak, was quite daunting to a teenager.

In impromptu speaking, I was provided a quote or a simple topic, and had to come up with a five-minute speech in just a few minutes of prep time. I had to deliver my presentation in front of a single judge, or sometimes a three-judge panel. To me, this competition was the scariest, but Mr. Creamer always emphasized that it was simply a hurdle to clear, and once I cleared it, no other public speaking hurdle I ever faced would faze me.

Right before the first competition, I told him that I felt like I was about to jump out of an airplane without a parachute.

Mr. Creamer looked at me and said, "No, you are about to soar. Don't tell me how tough the situation is; show me how tough you are facing the situation."

He then told me that he expected me to "go in there, look them in the eye and own the room." Mr. Creamer never really spoke about what not to do. Rather, he spoke of how to best present yourself and your points in a persuasive way.

He got me to believe in myself, that I would do this and do it well, and urged me to sell myself and my presentation to the panel.

"They'll not only buy it; they'll ask for seconds," he said.

The last thing Mr. Creamer said to me before I entered the room was, "Jay, you do not lack—ever." Mr. Creamer repeated that simple phrase to me a lot over my four years of high school.

Mr. Creamer preached the fundamentals of "pitch, pause, pace and power," but he also was tough on small details. He gave me a copy of Strunk and White's *Elements of Style* and told me he expected me to know it backward and forward, and use it in my speaking and writing.

If I ever said "um" when speaking, he would take out a dictionary and ask me where the word "um" was and what its definition was. When I told him it wasn't in the dictionary, he would say, "Then quit using it. There is nothing wrong with a pause. The pause is one of the most powerful things you can ever use. There is something wrong with 'um.' It doesn't exist. You sound like you are grasping for any stray thought in your head instead of having a firm grasp of the language."

Of all of the Ps Mr. Creamer preached to me, "pause" was the most important to him. He was constantly reminding me to pause. He would encourage me to pause to think, pause in a speech, pause to maintain composure, and pause to reflect.

Mr. Creamer also preached preparation, and the confidence that comes from it. "When you are fully prepared," Creamer said, "you will be fully confident. And when you are fully prepared and fully confident, you will be able to perform consistently at the highest level."

Or, as Tommy Amaker says, "What is confidence? Hard work plus success equals confidence. You don't just get confidence. You have to earn it."

After going through those competitions, and experiencing both success and failure, I was never again intimidated or frightened by having to speak or appear in public. Whether I am in a courtroom or in front of a television camera, I still get nervous from time to time, but nothing has ever seemed as difficult as standing before those three judge panels.

Because of my mother and Mr. Creamer, I had already put myself in uncomfortable situations, and had become comfortable being uncomfortable. I understood the importance of preparation, and I had earned my confidence in my ability to handle myself in almost any situation.

It wasn't how tough the tough situation was; it was how tough I was in that situation. I had been pushed and challenged, and I knew I could handle it.

Toughness Onstage

My senior year of high school, Mr. Creamer asked me to audition for the lead role in a play he was directing, Lillian Hellman's *Watch on the Rhine*. The play, set during World War II in Washington, DC, was a high-level piece for a high school cast.

My first reaction was to decline the opportunity. I was worried that I might embarrass myself, and I saw his offer as an opportunity for me to look foolish if I couldn't meet the challenge. The truth is, I didn't believe I could do it; I thought that it was over my head. Then it occurred to me that I had to audition for the part, and might not even get it. I asked Mr. Creamer whether he thought I could land the part if I auditioned.

"Considering that I am the director and have final say on the cast, I would feel fairly confident that if you audition, you will get the part," he said. "But if you miss one rehearsal, you shall wish I had chosen someone else."

For five weeks, we had some really difficult and grueling three-hour rehearsals until we were fully prepared to perform the play, and perform it well.

During the long rehearsals, Mr. Creamer was demanding of me about the level of my performance, especially my level of concentration. He once said, "I don't know anything about basketball, but I do know this: In this performance, you do not have an opponent trying to stop you from doing what you are supposed to do, being where you are supposed to be, and being fully engaged in each scene," he said. "You owe this entire production your highest level of concentration and your best performance. Until you decide to provide it, and give to the scene instead of taking from it, this will not be the best production it can be. Decide, and decide now."

Mr. Creamer was challenging me to be a better teammate.

Mr. Creamer demanded that, instead of just waiting for my time to speak and give my lines, I should give to my cast mates, and throw myself into their performances as well as my own. He wanted me to "give" by listening and engaging in the scene, and to make our production better by helping make my cast mates' performances better. And he held me accountable. If I was going to rehearse, I should rehearse to the best of my ability from start to finish, not just when I felt like it.

Our high school performance of *Watch on the Rhine* won some acclaim and some awards. I was recognized for my performance with the Bank of America Drama Award for Best Actor. Later, Mr. Creamer wrote to me and told me that *Watch on the Rhine* was his best work in twenty-five years of directing, and thanked me.

The truth is, I was recognized with that Drama Award because of Billy Creamer. I was actually a bit embarrassed by the award when I was selected, because I considered myself a jock who simply went out for the play, but I was also proud of it. I had done something I wasn't sure I could do, I worked hard at it, and I did it well. And I did it with a group of people I had never worked with before, and we formed a good team.

But, perhaps because I had struggled with recognition issues with my high school basketball coach, it didn't seem right to me that I should receive an award over other more experienced actors.

Mr. Creamer didn't want to hear it. "Nobody else deserves this award more than do you. You earned it, and you will accept it with appropriate pride," he told me. "You put yourself out there, you worked as hard as, if not harder than, anyone else, and you nailed the lead in this production. I expected this from you. This is yours."

Mr. Creamer was a director and a drama teacher, but he was also a great coach. And he believed in his people and held them to high standards. As a result, I believed in him, and I believed in myself too.

I didn't realize it then, but two of the toughest people in my life were my mom and Mr. Creamer. Both were demanding without ever being demeaning, and both showed up every day and were committed to making me better. Whatever success I have had in law and broadcasting, I attribute to my mother and Mr. Creamer. Nobody did more to prepare me, and to toughen me up.

The Payoff of Stepping Out of My Comfort Zone

During the summer of 1988, I was home in Los Angeles after playing my second season of professional basketball in Italy. The summer before, on the advice of a friend, I had auditioned for a national television commercial for Minolta cameras, and got the part. I was playing a basketball player, so it wasn't much of an acting stretch.

Through my role in the commercial, I was able to join the Screen Actors Guild, and I learned I could make money acting in more commercials. I got a theatrical agent, and he sent me on periodic auditions, and I was able to get a couple more commercials and print ads. It seemed like easy money, and it was fun.

One day that summer, I received a phone call from my theatrical agent, Joe Kolkowitz of Sports Casting. Kolkowitz asked me if I had ever done any acting work.

"Well, I was in the school play," I said. "But I'm not sure I would call myself an actor."

Later, when I recounted that story to him, Billy Creamer said, "You were right. You weren't an actor. You were an award-winning actor!"

My agent told me that there was an audition for an action picture starring Dolph Lundgren, and producers were looking for bigger, athletic actors for the film. "Let's do this," Kolkowitz said. "Why don't you go to the audition and see if you like the process? If you do, I can send you out on more of them."

I went on the audition and drove to an office building in West Hollywood. When I arrived, there were several actors sitting in the waiting room, and it was clear to me by how they carried themselves that they were experienced pros.

For a moment, I felt badly out of place. Every other audition I was on prior to that was for athletes, not actors. I was totally out of my element, and I could feel it. My goal quickly became not to make a fool of myself.

As each actor went in and out of the audition room, I could see through the open door that they had to stand before a group of four or five people, auditioning for them in a simple, antiseptic office environment. I got a pit in my stomach.

Then something clicked in my mind. I had felt this way before. I had been here before. I knew this situation.

I thought about the forensics competitions I had attended with Billy Creamer. I thought about the play I was in that he directed.

Was this any more difficult, challenging or tougher than appearing before a three-judge panel, being judged on an impromptu speech? Was this tougher than his play, which was totally out of my element at the time?

No way. This was a layup by comparison. I had done tougher things than this, and I could handle this. As Mr. Creamer told me, I did not lack, ever.

With that realization, I immediately became more confident, and I became competitive. I wasn't going into the audition so as not to embarrass myself. I walked in there to get the part, even though I had no idea what it was!

When my name was called, and mispronounced, I walked into the room and tried to, as Billy Creamer mentored, own it.

There was no chitchat, and very little was said. I was given a page or two of dialogue from the script. I was told I would be reading the part of an alien police officer, and I was asked to read it several different ways. I wasn't trying to "get the part." That would have focused me on the end result. Instead I was trying to play the part they gave me, which was the task at hand. If I did that, the rest would take care of itself. The rest was out of my control. I did exactly what they asked, and I did it to the best of my ability.

When I was finished, one woman coldly said, "Okay, thank you. We'll be in touch."

I wasn't sure how they liked what I did, but I knew I had held my own. I had faced a situation that was far outside of my comfort zone, and I handled it well. Whether I got the part was irrelevant to how I performed in that room. I walked in without the part, and I walked out without the part. But I handled the situation in between well. That was all I could expect and control, and that mind-set made it easier to concentrate fully on the job in front of me.

I got a callback for another audition. Simply doing the job helped me get another chance to get the job. I would have to do it all over again, and I had to keep plugging, to keep concentrating on the task. I needed to persistently and consistently do the job.

After a few more callbacks and subsequent auditions, all with the mind-set of simply doing the job in front of me, I was awarded the part of the alien cop in a film called *Dark Angel*, which was later changed to *I Come in Peace*. It still plays on late-night television, and I am reminded often that people still see it.

Working on that film was a wonderful experience, but it never would have happened without my mom encouraging me to step out of my comfort zone and do some things that made me uncomfortable, and Billy Creamer pushing me to push my limits in forensics and drama. Through stepping out of my comfort zone, pushing my limits, and persistently sticking with it audition after audition, I was able to achieve something I never thought I could achieve. Similarly, much of what I have been able to do in law and broadcasting I attribute to the toughness I gained from stepping out of my comfort zone in areas I never would have imagined would make me tougher and prepared for almost anything.

A Different Court

In my job as a trial lawyer, I took great pride in being prepared for every eventuality. I never wanted to be surprised, and I wanted to be so thoroughly prepared that I could react to anything that happened without having to think about it.

I had a plan, and I mapped out exactly what would or could happen based upon every known fact or document or other piece of evidence. But if things didn't go according to plan, I wanted to be able to react and come up with the right answer. That can be done only with meticulous preparation and concentration.

When I prepared a cross-examination of a witness, I crafted every question with a direction in mind and to elicit a certain response, even if it was an untruthful or unexpected response. I didn't care whether a witness told the truth or lied, because a lie was just as revealing as the truth. Being prepared for both the truth and a lie allowed me to do something really important: listen.

Instead of my being consumed by what question I would ask next, my preparation allowed me to listen and think about the witness's testimony, process it and react quickly and decisively upon each response. I wanted to be in control of every step of the examination, and I wanted the witness to know I was in control too.

I would prepare a cross-examination where the specific answer would take me down a certain path. If the answer was different than expected, I was also prepared to go down that alternative path in advance.

In emphasizing the importance of preparation, former Wake Forest coach Skip Prosser used to say, "No Pearl Harbors." Prosser didn't want any surprises, and wanted to be thoroughly prepared for anything that could possibly come his or his team's way.

Perhaps the most nerve-racking experience of my law career was arguing a case before the United States Fourth Circuit Court of Appeals in Richmond, Virginia. The Fourth Circuit is one step below the United States Supreme Court, and can be very intimidating.

When I argued my first case before a three-judge panel at the Fourth Circuit, I was unsettled, to say the least. It was a case I had won at trial, and it was about a complicated issue of trademark and copyright law. I sought out advice from other lawyers I knew who had appeared before the court, and I had prepared myself and my argument as thoroughly as I could.

I thought I was ready, but I was scared. This was totally different from anything I had ever done before, and I wasn't sure I was up to it. I had doubts.

Arguing an appeal is different from a trial. The lawyer has only a certain amount of time to make the oral argument, and cannot expect to speak uninterrupted. The justices can, and often do, interrupt to ask questions, and can take the argument in any direction they like.

When the first question comes at you from the bench, it can be jarring, and it can throw you off. You have to answer the justices' questions, however long that might take, then get back on track and continue your argument. And you had better be able to think on your feet and make adjustments.

What if I didn't have the answer? That scared me more than anything, the idea of standing up before three learned judges and not having the answer to a question asked of me.

On the day of the oral argument, I thought I was ready to go. Mine was the second argument on the court's docket. As I sat in the gallery waiting for my case to be called, the case before mine was being argued.

It was not going well for one of the lawyers. He was being peppered with questions from the justices, he was sweating and it was uncomfortable. I sat there, and I was getting nervous just watching. I felt like a gladiator waiting his turn, about to go into the arena and get mauled after the guy before me got dragged off.

Then I thought back to the forensics competitions with Billy Creamer. I thought about the acting auditions I had been through. And it settled me down.

I kept telling myself that I had been here before, and I had handled this same type of situation, and handled it well. And I told myself that I did not lack, ever.

I also thought about something a caddy said to me earlier that summer as we stepped up to a long, treacherous par-three on a difficult golf course.

As I stepped onto the tee of that difficult hole, I said to the caddy, "This is a really tough hole."

"Not today it's not," he replied. "And not for you."

That one simple response was brilliant, and the perfect positive mind-set. I have thought about that response a lot since that day. And I thought about it before I argued before the Fourth Circuit. The Court of Appeals is tough, but not today, and not for me.

Predictably, I was also peppered with questions during my argument, and I concentrated, fought and worked my way through them. I don't know how others viewed my performance, but I was still standing at the end, and thought I did pretty well.

After the argument, the Fourth Circuit does a really neat thing. The justices come down from the bench and shake hands with the lawyers.

One of the justices shook my hand, told me he was a Maryland grad and said, "This court is quite different from a basketball court, isn't it?"

"Yes, Your Honor, it certainly is," I replied.

But the truth was, I didn't find it any tougher than the high school forensics competitions. And for that, I was very grateful. I was prepared; I had been through tough situations before, and that confidence in myself helped me.

Forensics and drama made me tougher. Go figure. And they helped set me up for my future in law and in broadcasting. Without those experiences teaching me the value of persistence, of sticking with it when you are outside of your comfort zone, I'm not sure I would have been able to succeed.

CHAPTER 6

NEXT PLAY

In my time playing for and coaching under Mike Krzyzewski, there was one concept that stood out above all others, one that I continue to use every single day, in almost every facet of my life. In fact, I not only say it to myself, I will often say it out loud.

Next play.

The concept of "next play" is so ingrained in my thinking that I cannot pinpoint exactly how the lesson was conveyed to me by Coach K, or exactly when I internalized the concept. In fact, Krzyzewski can't recall exactly when he learned it either, but he is certain it was introduced to him at West Point. "It just made great sense to me, and I incorporated it into everything I do, and with all of my teams," Krzyzewski said.

Coach K taught us early on that basketball is a fast-paced, continuous game in which there are no built-in natural breaks in the action like there are in baseball and football. In basketball, players must convert from offense to defense (and vice versa) at almost any moment, and convert with speed and alertness. In basketball, every player on the floor is required to play offense and defense, and to do so without a break.

Because the game is so fast paced and converts so quickly, it requires extraordinary concentration. Coach K's use of the concept of "next play" is really a prompt to focus players on the present, rather than dwelling upon what just happened. It's a prompt to concentrate on what's truly important—the next play in the game.

When something happened in the game, positive or negative, we were conditioned by Coach K to immediately move on to the next play without concern over what had just taken place. If we committed a turnover or made a costly mistake, he did not want us to react to the error. If we lingered on the past play, perhaps we would miss an opportunity to get a stop or a steal or otherwise impact the game in a positive manner. Essentially, by not moving on to the next play immediately, we would be compounding that mistake, either by making another or by missing an opportunity to make a great play. Failing to move on to the next play was itself a mistake, because it took focus and concentration off of the current moment, the only point in time that we could do something positive to impact the game.

If we just reacted to the mistake by throwing up our hands, shaking our heads or cursing our failure, we would be making a bigger error—one of omission.

For Krzyzewski, it is one of the best concepts in his coaching paradigm, and in his life. "By moving on to the next play, concentrating and trying to move to the next thing, you have a better chance to be your best at that moment," Krzyzewski said. "You have to be tough enough to move on, whether the last play was good or crappy. It takes real mental toughness."

Krzyzewski has used next play as a term of art. To Bob Knight, Krzyzewski's coach and mentor, the concept is another way of emphasizing concentration and its vital importance to any endeavor, especially basketball. "I wanted my players to move on from a mistake," Knight said, "but not without a clear understanding that, when we've screwed up, let's not do it again." For Krzyzewski, next play helps players and coaches let go of fear. "Next play is the absence of fear of failure," Krzyzewski said. "You have moved on."

Kansas coach Bill Self may not use the exact terminology as Krzyzewski, but shares the same view. "I want my players to have a short memory on the court," Self said. "I don't want them remembering their screwups; I want them moving on to make another positive play."

For Mark Alarie, the concept of next play helped him to forget the negative plays during a game. "I really needed to let bad plays go," Alarie said. "I hated dwelling on my mistakes, and wanted a positive image in my mind. That's why I hated getting yelled at so much, and I hated watching film of myself screwing up."

Alarie uses the concept of "next play" as a trigger to erase the negative and focus on the positive and move on. In fact, Alarie was careful to separate the analytical from the emotional, and he took steps not to allow negative images in his memory bank.

"When corrective steps need to be taken, like technique or something analytical, I am fine with watching film of negative play. But I wanted to see the good stuff, watching myself successful. That makes you feel good for a reason, and inspires you," Alarie said.

Alarie believes that all players need confidence and a positive mind-set for competition, whether it is practice or a game. Alarie would purposely ignore any negative image that could get stuck in his mind and inhibit his ability to perform on the floor. However, it is not that Alarie ignored failure altogether. He was always open to addressing any failure, analyzing why it occurred, and taking the necessary steps to avoid repeating it in the future. But he steadfastly refused to dwell on failure. Alarie used failure to drive him to prepare, relied upon his routine and used the next-play philosophy to free him up to perform without negativity getting in his way.

Alarie was especially attentive to negative messages when his coaches were upset or trying to motivate through negative reinforcement, which all coaches do at certain times. "I never told him this, but when Coach K would show film of me playing poorly, I tried not to watch it, and I would zone out," Alarie said. "It didn't help me commit good plays to my memory bank for me to draw upon as positive. I don't want a memory bank of negatives. Next play really helped me with that, although he probably didn't intend for it to work quite that way."

Soccer star Julie Foudy can relate. She and her team went through certain periods when the coaching staff showed film of negative outcomes, attempting to motivate through negative reinforcement rather than analytically teaching and correcting. "I caught myself in a game thinking, 'Oh, shit, that's going to be on the tape tomorrow,'" Foudy said. "That was so stupid."

Thinking about the mistake, and whether it would be shown during a team film session, took Foudy out of the moment, and affected her concentration. Foudy wanted only one thought in her head at one time, and it was up to her to manage the images in her mind. "I have to choose the positive thought and put it in there. Go to my 'happy place,'" Foudy said. "But I was in control of the thought I put in my head, nobody else. And I was in charge of moving on and concentrating on the next play."

A few years ago, a college basketball coach was kind enough to allow me to sit in on a film session he was having with his team. The coach showed his players game film of other teams, both college and professional, to demonstrate how they handled key game situations. The coach would set up the situation, and then critique the players and coach, and list what he expected of his players in similar situations.

After the film session, I asked the coach why he had used game film of other teams, instead of using his team. "My players aren't tough enough to handle it," he said. "If I show our guys making mistakes, even though it is just to correct the mistakes and not to call any individuals out, they will retreat back into a shell. I could lose them."

I was blown away by that. There is a difference, and perhaps a fine line, between an analytical approach to improvement and beating up your team with negativity and negative images. But, there is no question in my mind that today's culture has allowed too many of our young people get away with not being accountable. Every player, especially every tough player, has to be held responsible for mistakes and correcting those mistakes, and has to be tough enough to handle constructive criticism that is respectfully provided. In other words, every player has to be tough enough to be coached, and allow himself or herself to be coached.

The concept of next play applies to positive plays, not just mistakes. When a great play is made, you still need to say, "Next play," and move on without dwelling on that great play. That great play was in the past too, and it is imperative to move on right away to put yourself in the best position to make and complete the next play. At the end of each play or action, the most important play is the next play.

One former Krzyzewski player who constantly makes use of the concept is Grant Hill. "I say, 'Next play,' all the time. And I mean all the time," Hill said. "My teammates hear that from me constantly. It is such a little thing, just two words, but it is such a big thing." Hill uses "next play" to refocus himself and his teammates, and to move on and stay in the moment.

"If you don't move on to the next play, mentally and physically, you're just lingering in the past," Hill said. "And you're cheating yourself and your teammates. Next play is a very real form of mental toughness."

Staying in the moment really means concentrating on what is right in front of you, without concern for what is in the past or future. I most often hear "stay in the moment" or "live in the present" in golf. For any golfer, whether professional or amateur, the most important shot is the shot right in front of you, or the next shot. Whether you hit your tee shot in the fairway or hook it into the woods, the hole isn't over. Celebrating a great shot or getting angry over a poor shot does not do anything to help your next shot. Once that tee shot is executed, you have to accept the result and turn your attention and total concentration to the next shot.

Both golfer Curtis Strange and North Carolina basketball coach Roy Williams use golf as an example of the importance of the next-play mentality. "No concept is more important in golf, and next play is the equivalent to the next shot," Strange said. "We golfers have time to dwell on things, too much time. Those who are tough have the ability to let the last shot go and concentrate on the next shot. This shot." Williams believes that next play helps one concentrate on the process, not just the result.

For Strange, it helps him put his disappointment, frustration and anger aside. "I get as mad as anyone," Strange said. "But the next shot is the most important shot of my life. That has to happen every single time. Every single time." Strange says that golfers have to have a short memory, which he calls a "Teflon memory," a memory in which nothing negative can stick.

Similarly, Jon Gruden preaches "one snap at a time" in football. "If the last play was good, forget about it and get ready for the next snap," Gruden said. "And if the last play was poorly executed or led to a bad result, forget about it and get ready for the next snap. Then hit, finish and make a play."

Like Bill Self, Gruden wants his players to have short-term memories, and for the memory to end with the last play. "That goes for failure and success," Gruden said. "If you fail, you lose confidence. You're going to face bigger, better players that are going to be kicking your ass from time to time. You have to snap out of it right away and trust you'll be in a better situation on this snap."

Gruden expects struggles, and will help his players overcome them by calling a different play or running a different scheme to put his players in a better position to be successful. But when there are struggles—and they are inevitable—Gruden expects toughness. "You have to be mentally tough enough to put that behind you right away, and play the next snap," Gruden said. "One snap at a time."

But Gruden believes that being mentally tough doesn't just

mean the response to adversity. "I think dealing with success is harder," Gruden said. "Whether it is complacency from having a big lead, getting loose with details because you have won and experienced success, or making mistakes, getting penalties, missing blocks, or fumbling from a lack of concentration due to complacency, it all comes down to toughness and staying in the here and now. Don't fool yourself," Gruden said. "You can be victimized by both failure and success."

Whether I am working in my role as a broadcaster, lawyer, husband, father or weekend golfer, I am constantly saying to myself, "Next play." It has become a tremendous help to get me quickly focused and concentrated on the next thing. "Next play" helps me move forward in a positive direction and anticipate performing the next action to the best of my ability by putting the last action in the past, where it belongs. Instead of staying angry or self-satisfied about the last play—neither of which leads to positive outcomes for the next play—those two simple words focus my concentration and improve my chances to be successful. "Next play" eliminates excuses. No matter the result of the last play, I am moving on and I meet the next play with equanimity.

"It is an incredible thought and phrase, when you really think about it," Amaker said. "It has been so meaningful in my life. I have been faced with so many different situations as a player, coach, and person where 'next play' would immediately come to mind and focus me on what was important instead of dwelling on what was already done.

"If we win, next play," Amaker said. "If we lose, next play."

A few years ago, I was on the sidelines broadcasting a Notre Dame basketball game. Mike Brey, one of Coach K's former assistants, is head coach for the Fighting Irish. Notre Dame lost at the buzzer, and as I looked over to Brey, I could clearly see him purse his lips, slap his hands together and say, "Next play." He never dropped his head, but simply walked over to the victorious coach and shook his hand.

In saying, "Next play," Brey wasn't diminishing or dismissing the loss. Rather, he was focusing his mind to move on to the next thing, which was leading his team, and putting his players in the best position to be successful going forward. How would his team respond to the loss? And what did they need from him to be successful in their next outing? "Next play" doesn't mean Brey doesn't carefully evaluate the game to determine exactly what his Irish did right and did wrong, or that he and his team weren't accountable. It simply and powerfully signals that the focus is on how to get better now, rather than living in or dwelling on the past.

"Most of the time, there will be a next play," Krzyzewski said. "You play it out, then do it again, then again, then again. Then it becomes a habit. And habits lead to true consistency. That is what is really good about 'next play.'"

For Foudy, consistency is the mark of excellence, but it is more than that. "I think it is the mark of toughness too," she said. "Whether there are two people watching or two million, are you going to be tough enough to stay in the present and execute?"

For Krzyzewski, "next play" not only leads to consistency; it leads to composure too, because when you take the next-play mentality, you are firmly in the present and prepared to make the most important play: this play.

The ultimate next play was Christian Laettner's winning shot against Kentucky in the 1992 Elite Eight. I was fortunate to be a Duke assistant coach in that game, which was arguably the greatest college basketball game ever played.

Late in the overtime period, Kentucky's Sean Woods drove the lane and hit a running one-handed shot over Laettner to put Kentucky ahead 103–102 with just 2.1 seconds remaining.

It was a stunning moment. When Woods's shot banked in and Coach K called a time-out, I have to admit that my first thought was that we had lost. The chances of going the length of the floor in 2.1 seconds seemed remote. And it turns out I wasn't alone in that thinking. My fellow assistants Tommy Amaker and Mike Brey had similar thoughts going through their heads, as did both Bobby Hurley and Grant Hill.

It was a tough situation, and the players' body language confirmed it as they walked back to the bench. The players had their heads down and did not have a look of confidence on their faces. They were dwelling on the last play, and how devastating it was to our chances to win.

But Coach K had moved on to the next play. It was yet another great lesson. The perfect pass made by Grant Hill and great catch and composed final shot by Christian Laettner were obviously vital, but what provided the opportunity to make that final play was the mental toughness gained from concentrating on the next play. Coach K got his team focused and ready for the next play rather than lingering on the last play, which was a punch in the stomach. If they did not embrace moving on to the next play and believe they would do it, then it would be guaranteed that they had no real chance of winning.

"I marveled at Christian Laettner," said two-time U.S. Open champion golfer Curtis Strange. "What he did in that Kentucky game was rare. But without that positive belief that he could do it, that he would do it, he could never do it. You have to stay positive in the moment. Those who do will always be more successful than those who don't. That takes real toughness to stay positive on the stage when things seem to have turned against you."

Strange remembers watching that game, and credits Coach K's mental preparation of his team, in that moment and throughout the season, believing that it led to a certain calmness where things happened in slow motion. "The measure of your toughness is when you have the courage to pull off the shot and keep your concentration when things aren't going well," Strange said.

Strange and Krzyzewski both believe that, ultimately, toughness won that game—the mental toughness to move on to the next play, the toughness to believe, and the toughness to show the resiliency to come back, perform in the moment, the toughness to accept the consequences attendant to winning and losing.

And even after the game, it took toughness to move on to the next play from that iconic and magnificent game. Those players had to turn their full attention to preparing for the Final Four and winning a second straight National Championship. While most everyone associated with Duke wanted to dwell and linger in the glow of that game, Duke needed to show the toughness necessary to focus on the next thing, and to move on both physically and mentally.

When Sean Woods hit the shot with 2.1 seconds, which was a negative result for Duke, it was "next play." When Laettner hit the shot at the buzzer to win the game, after a short celebration, it was "next play." Whether you are playing in a game, executing a task in your job, or climbing a ladder, truly tough people concentrate on the next play, the next task, or the next rung. And when the game is over, win or lose, you evaluate the performance, clearly define where mistakes were made, and unite on a journey to correct those mistakes and make the next practice about getting better as an individual and as a team. For me, the concept of next play has helped me focus my concentration on what is truly important, and it has made me tougher.

CHAPTER 7

COMMITMENT

My father taught me everything I needed to know about commitment. He owned his own business, and he showed up for work every single day. It takes toughness to show up every day, but he didn't stop at just showing up. My father was committed to his work, and he embraced it. When he had a job to do, he never shied away from doing it, and he never put it off until later. When there was something to be done, he did it right the first time.

To me, former teammate and Harvard coach Tommy Amaker summed it up best. He values the toughness it takes to show up every day. But Amaker believes people who are truly tough don't *just* show up, but are totally "into it" when they show up. Those are the people who are truly committed.

Amaker has a saying: "Don't mistake routine for commitment." Just showing up is not enough. A player must show up fully committed and prepared to compete and perform at his or her highest level. Commitment is a vital and necessary ingredient for toughness.

Toughness over Talent

Talent is important. You have to have some talent to be successful in any endeavor. But talent is simply not enough. The number of highly talented people who fail in any field would be too long to count. Nobody can make it on talent alone. But when you combine talent with toughness, you have a winner in anything.

I played professional basketball in Italy for two seasons, and I loved living and working in Europe. I was drafted by the NBA's Dallas Mavericks in 1986, and after attending rookie camp and playing in the NBA Summer League, I opted to take a guaranteed contract to play in Europe before final training camp started and final cuts would be made. If I had stayed for training camp and stuck on the Dallas roster, which was a big "if," I was probably destined to be a towel-waving bench warmer in the NBA. I was smaller than average for an NBA power forward, but made up for that with far less quickness and athleticism for an NBA small forward!

I was a classic tweener who was capable of finding a roster spot in the NBA, but would probably have had a tough time hanging on to it for long.

My agent was Larry Fleisher, who is in the Naismith Basketball Hall of Fame. He got me a job playing pro basketball in Italy, which was probably "my level." I was a star-caliber player in the Italian A2 League, and one of the league's top scorers. It was fun to break out from being a role player and be a star-caliber player again, and I really enjoyed it.

I played for a team called Citrosil Verona in Verona, Italy. The club was owned by two brothers, Mario and Giuseppe Vicenzi, who also owned a popular and profitable cookie company in Italy, Vicenzi Biscotti. At that time in my life and basketball career, Italy was the perfect fit. I had spent my college career as a "role player" who supported star performers like Dawkins and Alarie, and Italy provided me the opportunity to be a star player again. But with that came greater responsibility. No longer was I playing in the shadows of star players expected to be the top producers; I was expected to be the top producer. It was a role I really enjoyed and embraced, and I played well.

In the late 1980s, the Italian professional league was considered the best place to play in the world outside of the NBA. While there were exceptions with certain teams in leagues in other countries, the level of play and the pay were the best in Italy. There were some outstanding players in the Italian league at that time, including Bob McAdoo, Drazen Dalipagic, Oscar Schmidt, George Gervin, Mitchell Anderson, and Joe Bryant, Kobe Bryant's father. Italian league games were very physical and intense and could get rowdy, especially in the stands. Fans would throw things onto the floor, including coins, which was pretty unpleasant if you got hit by one. At most arenas, the benches were covered with Plexiglas, like dugouts in baseball.

By far the most difficult and challenging part of playing in Italy was the road games. Crowds were fanatical and at times threatening, and you couldn't help but feel that the officiating was different on the road, more favorable to the home team.

The truth is, it was on the road that you found out just how tough you were, individually and collectively. I had played in some very difficult environments in college, but nothing like what I faced in Italy. Some of those arenas could scare you.

In my rookie year in Italy, I played in a road game against Liberti Firenze, an Italian pro team in Florence. In that game, I was matched up against perhaps the toughest player I had ever suited up against. His name was John Ebeling.

When people ask me who was the toughest player I ever played against, I think they expect to hear Michael Jordan, Ralph Sampson, Len Bias or Mark Price. Few have heard of Ebeling, especially when compared to the others. The truth is, I had never heard of Ebeling before I played against him that night in Florence.

Ebeling played college basketball at Florida Southern, where he was a Division II All-American, and then went on to have a long, productive career in Italy. He was not the type of player who would grab headlines. The crowd didn't chant his name. He didn't look like much. He didn't stand out as being especially big, strong or athletic. He was just tough. And he was respected because he was one of the toughest players in the league.

When I played against Ebeling, I wasn't worried he was going to elbow me, beat me up physically or dunk on me. I was worried he was going to outwork me, outscrap me, outfight me, outhustle me, and outcompete me.

And he did.

Ebeling played his ass off on every play. He didn't run the floor; he sprinted the floor, and he did it on every possession. He didn't just box out, turn and wait for the ball to come to him; he hit you first—hard—and pursued the ball as if every shot were a missed shot and his life depended upon securing possession of the rebound.

He never said a word and never did anything dirty. He was just mentally tough, which led to his physical toughness. Ebeling was committed to playing hard on every play. He was relentless and kept coming after you. It's really hard to play against relentless. It is really hard to beat relentless.

Ebeling made everything difficult for his opponent. He was no fun to play against. In fact, I dreaded playing against him.

But after playing against him, I wanted to play just like him.

Ebeling taught and reinforced for me a tremendous lesson. I played against many players with superior talent to John Ebeling's. But when I think of the players whom I hated to play against, his name always pops to the top of the list. Playing against superior talent didn't really worry me. What worried me was playing against a guy who would outwork me, and never quit or give me a break.

I could never match the talent of a Jordan, Sampson, Bias or Price. But nothing stopped me from playing as hard and as tough as Ebeling did. I remember him not because he had the ability to do something I couldn't do, but because he had the will, commitment, discipline and persistence to do what I could do, but didn't do as consistently because it was so damn hard.

That is what is truly amazing about sports, especially basketball. The players I most respected were not necessarily the most talented or gifted. They were the ones who, irrespective of talent, were the hardest to play against. They were the ones who played their tails off on every play and made it hard for me to play.

I appreciate talent. I respect and admire toughness. And that's why I respected and admired John Ebeling.

The Measure of Toughness: The "50-50 Ball"

Every coach values players who excel in the moments of truth, the points in games when you have to be tough. Indiana coach Tom Crean is no exception. And he purposely prepares his team for those moments every day in practice.

Crean knows he can't expect his players to excel without practicing and preparing for those moments of truth. So he intentionally puts his players in tough situations in practice where they are at a crossroads, where they can go one way or the other. During those portions of practice, he may stop and ask, "What are we going to do? Who are we in this moment? How tough are we going to be?"

For any coach, including Crean, perhaps the most important measure of his team's toughness is the "50-50" ball, the loose ball that is up for grabs and both teams have an equal chance to get possession. Those extra possessions can be, and often are, the difference between winning and losing.

When Crean sees that his team has the mental capacity to get 50-50 balls, then he knows they are ready for their best competition. It is not a physical standard. To Crean, it is purely a measure of his team's mental toughness and awareness. Crean believes that measure matters, and matters in a big way. He charts 50-50 balls as a valued statistic, and he takes it very seriously.

The commitment to securing possession of loose balls is within a team's and player's own control. It is not about being quicker and stronger; it is about being mentally alert. It is about being engaged. It is about being aware on the court. It is about being tough.

Crean measures mental toughness by the awareness of his players. Awareness on the court, including self-awareness, is vitally important to Crean, but he also believes that awareness goes hand in hand with communication and vision. How can a player talk and see what is going on, and be in a position to impact the game, if he doesn't have great concentration and awareness? "A player cannot be tough without being aware," Crean said.

Kansas coach Bill Self agrees, and defines his team's toughness by similar standards. To Self, toughness is a mind-set, individually and collectively. "I don't know if you can be truly tough for all forty minutes of every game. But you can be tough at the most important parts of the game," Self said. "Not going after a loose ball, or pursuing every ball with both hands. That defines your toughness."

Both Crean and Self are staunch believers of Philadelphia 76ers coach Doug Collins's philosophy of getting 70 percent of "50-50 balls" as an ideal measure of a team's overall toughness. The philosophy is straightforward: Going after loose balls gives a team extra possessions in a game. Everything Self does in Kansas is based upon that mind-set of being committed to gaining extra possessions. Offensively, Kansas wants to get at least one good shot on every possession. A good shot is a high-percentage, open shot—the shot you want rather than the shot the defense wants you to take—and more than one shot per possession means that your team gets offensive rebounds, which are usually the highest-percentage shots you can get. Defensively, Kansas wants to limit opponents to one or fewer "challenged" shots on every possession. A challenged shot is a shot taken by the opponent that is closely guarded, pressured with a hand up on the shooter. With all five defenders rebounding the miss, the best defensive possessions allow only challenged shot, if any shot at all.

To Self, a team's mind-set, its commitment to doing what it

takes to be successful, is a measure of its toughness. "The rest is just strategy to fit your personnel," Self said. "You can't compromise your principles and give up the easy basket, or give up anything easy. That mind-set is who you are. We are unwilling to compromise on that, and our players believe in it."

Self believes that if his team gets 50-50 balls, it is limiting its opponent's chances to score. If the other team can't score, Self's team can't lose. That is the mind-set he drills into his players every single day. It is a simple message of collective toughness.

When Roy Williams was coaching at Kansas, a chip in the wood floor in Allen Field House served as a constant reminder of the toughness (and the importance of 50-50 balls) he wanted for his Jayhawk team. Against archrival Missouri, Kansas star Raef LaFrentz dived on a loose ball to save it from going out-of-bounds. LaFrentz saved the ball and Kansas kept possession, but in doing so, he hit his face so hard on the floor he knocked a chip of wood out of the floor—with his teeth. "It did a number on his teeth too," Williams said.

In later years, whenever the Kansas maintenance staff would resurface or revarnish the Allen Field House floor, Williams refused to let that chip be repaired. He wanted it as a monument to toughness, and to show the chip to his players to demonstrate what true toughness really is, how hard you have to pursue a loose ball. "That chip was something else," he said, "and I wanted it to teach toughness to the players who followed."

For me, a 50-50 ball was a turning point in my understanding of what toughness really meant. Early on in my college career, we played a road game at California. I was an eighteen-year-old freshman, and Duke's starting center, playing in my home state. My parents and friends were in the stands, and I had a lot going on in my head before and during that game.

I wanted to play my best, and I wanted to win, but I didn't realize that at that time, I just wasn't tough enough to do either.

In the second half, there was a loose ball, a 50-50 ball, right in front of the Duke bench. If a photograph had been taken at the exact moment the ball became loose, anyone examining that photo would have determined that I should be the player who secured possession of the ball. The truth is, it wasn't a 50-50 ball. It was a 75-25 ball, and I was the closest player to it, and I was the player who should have secured it.

I didn't get possession of the ball.

Instead of diving on the floor for it, I bent over at the waist to pick it up like I was picking a daisy on a walk through the park. As I reached to grab the ball, a Cal player dived onto the floor, knocked the ball away, and Cal scored an "easy basket" in transition.

Coach K was livid. I was stunned. And we ultimately lost the game.

Coach K not only let me have it right then and there, but he made a special point of examining that play when we watched the film as a team. Coach K ran the play back and forth, over and over again. And he told me the truth about what the play signaled about me.

He said if I had really wanted that ball, and wanted to win, I would've dived onto the floor for it. I would have put my body on the line, hit the deck, and fought for that ball, instead of just casually bending over for it.

The truth was, Coach K said, it just wasn't that important to me, and if that was the only time he had ever seen me play, then he would've assumed I wasn't tough enough to play for him. Those words weren't easy for me to hear, especially in front of the entire team.

But he was absolutely right.

From that moment on, knowing that I needed to be tougher, I made it a priority to dive on the floor for the ball. Was I always the toughest player, and did I get every loose ball after that? Truthfully, no, I didn't. But I strove to be tougher, and I worked to be tougher, and I was tougher. Toughness is a skill, and it needs to be emphasized, prioritized and valued.

Coach K's running the film of that play over and over was a powerful message. But he sent other powerful messages too. When I did the tough things that were expected of me, he noticed it, acknowledged it and reinforced its importance. Toughness was important, so doing something truly tough should excite you. He would run the film back and forth when I took a key charge too, or when I made a positive play that required some courage or fearlessness.

And when Coach K or my teammates got excited about a tough play, like a charge or a rebound in traffic, it made all of us more determined to be tougher, and to do it again. We were building a culture of toughness, and Coach K made it "cool" to join in and be a part of it.

Grant Hill came to believe that taking a charge was the best measure of true toughness. In basketball, a "charge" is an offensive foul where the defensive player establishes legal guarding position in front of the offensive player, and the offensive player runs him over. It is like a catcher establishing position in front of home plate, and the runner having to knock the catcher over to get to it. Taking a charge takes alertness as a defender, but it takes courage too.

"My wife gets on me sometimes about being forty years old and still taking charges," Hill said. First and foremost in his mind is the physical part of taking a charge that exudes toughness. A player is sacrificing his body for the team, putting his body on the line. Second, a charge is a really big play and is deflating for the other team.

To take a charge, a player must be mentally alert, fully engaged, and willing to help his teammates. Taking a charge is perhaps the ultimate unselfish play and the ultimate tough play in basketball. "I promise you," Hill said, "that most of the biggest, toughest-looking guys in the NBA, the ones considered the stereotypical tough guys, aren't tough enough to stand in there and take one. In fact, they are the ones that run from taking one."

Commitment to Doing What It Takes

In my life, my level of commitment is important. Being committed, or being "in with both feet," means that I will keep going when it is difficult, and I won't give in. That's what it means to be truly committed and truly tough.

When I was a young kid, my mother gave me a job to do. She wanted to put new contact paper on the floor of the cabinet underneath the sink in my sisters' bathroom. First she wanted me to take the old paper up, and then put down the new, flower-patterned paper she had chosen.

It sounded like an easy job, a layup. I soon found out that it wasn't.

Whoever put the original contact paper down used an adhesive that *really* worked! I thought I would need a sandblaster to get that contact paper off of the cabinet floor, if I could ever get it off at all.

I used a putty knife and tried to pull the old paper up off of the wood, but it was incredibly slow and tedious work. To me it seemed impossible, and it seemed like it wasn't worth the effort it took. I gave it a go and got three-quarters of the contact paper up, but just I couldn't get all of it up.

So I made the executive decision that, since it was just under the bathroom sink and nobody would ever see it or even care, I would simply put the new paper over the exposed wood and the patches of old paper that I couldn't take up. As far as I was concerned, the problem was solved and the job was done.

The truth was, I had quit. I simply gave up. It just wasn't important enough to me to do the job right. I wasn't committed to it. I wasn't tough enough. I just didn't know it.

Later that night, having moved on, I walked past my sisters' bathroom and saw my dad underneath the sink, sweating, working to get the old paper up from the wood. He was just finishing up after having taken up the contact paper I had put down, and having painstakingly gotten every single shred of that old paper off of the cabinet floor that I hadn't gotten up. He was just about to put down the new contact paper that my mother asked me to put down.

"Dad, what are you doing?" I asked, even though I knew exactly what he was doing.

"I'm just finishing up."

"Why?" I asked. "Nobody is ever going to see that paper under the sink. That isn't important."

My dad was very matter-of-fact in his response. He wasn't at all upset, but he made a clear point.

"It's important to your mom," my dad said.

With those few words—but more important, his clear actions—my father was telling me that if you're going to do a job, you commit to doing it right the first time, or you just have to do it again. That wasn't my dad's job to do. It was my job. I just wasn't committed enough to doing that job, and doing it right. I wasn't tough enough to finish it.

Because I lacked commitment, my dad had to do it for me, and do it after he had spent a full day at work. The job was important to the person who asked me to do that job—my mom—and in accepting it, I should have treated it as just as important. I simply wasn't tough enough.

I don't ever think I'll forget that flower-print contact paper.

Doris Burke: Always Keep Plugging

I work with some great people and tremendous basketball minds at ESPN. Of all the people I have worked with, there is nobody I respect and admire more than Doris Burke. She is a remarkable and selfless teammate.

Burke grew up in New Jersey, and began playing basketball in the second grade. Around that time, she also realized that she had but one person she could rely upon: herself.

"I had a very difficult childhood," Burke said. "I knew very early on in my life I needed to be self-reliant. I needed to be able to rely upon me. I decided when I was around eleven years old that I was on my own, and it was up to me, and only me, to take care of and to protect me."

For Burke, the question was whether she could indeed rely upon herself in tough times. She ingrained in herself the need to make sure she showed up every single day, fully prepared to do her part. She believed that nobody else would do it for her.

Doris accepted a basketball scholarship to Providence College and played point guard for the Friars in the rugged Big East. Her freshman year, the team went 19–7. It was a good year, and she enjoyed it. She was learning, and playing well. Her first year was what she had hoped for.

Her sophomore year was not as successful, and doubt crept in. "We were 14–14, and I was absolutely miserable," Burke said. "The losing was hard to take, and it wore on me. As the year was winding down, I was worn down mentally, and totally worn out by the losing."

Burke found the adversity, the losing, had affected her desire to improve, to strive to be excellent. The summer between her sophomore and junior years, she struggled to push herself to get better, and she wasn't sure she wanted to devote the time basketball required. "It hit me that I had a choice. I could wallow in self-pity and accept it, or I could fight. I chose to fight," she said.

"That summer was a bridge in my career, and my life, really," Burke said. "I could give in to complacency, or I could rise to the challenge and meet it. I chose the latter. And it is a choice we all have to make."

Following a coaching change, Burke's hard work began to pay off and she was named All–Big East, and All–Big East Tournament, and Providence won the Big East regular season championship. That season marked a turning point for Burke. She saw it as a real test of her toughness and her team's toughness.

Following her graduation from Providence, Burke was only the fifth woman to be inducted into the Providence College Athletic Hall of Fame.

Her broadcasting career started out modestly. Burke did color commentary for the Providence women's games on radio. "We had virtually no listeners. There were times when the play-by-play guy didn't show up to the games," she said. "When that happened—and it happened more than just a little bit—I would have to call the game by myself over a telephone line. It was difficult, and I probably wasn't very good."

But that attitude of self-reliance and mental toughness has carried forward into Burke's adult life, and into her career. Whether the response to her work is skeptical or supportive, she does her job. Her goal at all times is to meet a certain job to a certain standard in her work, and she tries like crazy to meet that standard every time.

In the years since, Burke has gone from doing obscure games on the radio to being the first woman to do color analysis for the NBA's New York Knicks. She is the lead analyst for ESPN's women's college basketball and WNBA coverage, and serves as an analyst for ESPN's Men's College Basketball and NBA coverage.

Doris Burke has done things that no broadcaster has ever done before. She provides expert commentary for four different and distinct sports: the NBA, the WNBA, men's college basketball and women's college basketball. She is a "first" in so many different areas, and is the only person in the broadcast industry, man or woman, shouldering such a daunting load.

She knows she's had some assignments no other woman has ever had, and for that she's called a pioneer. "I'm not a pioneer," Burke said. "I've experienced no resistance. I just have skeptics. Those are not the same things.

"I'm here, and that is significant. But I know how I got here too," Burke said. "A lot of really strong, tough women came before me, like Jackie MacMullan and Robin Roberts, and they had real resistance. They had to fight the fights so I could accomplish some 'firsts' in basketball."

I have had the honor of working with Doris Burke many times. She is a professional in every sense of the word, has an unrivaled work ethic, and she is an unselfish, remarkable teammate. I would put her basketball knowledge and acumen up against anyone's in the game.

And in my judgment, she may very well be the toughest person in sports broadcasting.

Burke has heard the near constant chatter of those who doubt her credentials simply because she is a woman, or are not comfortable with hearing a woman as the voice of authority on a broadcast of men's basketball.

She's heard the criticism and viewers asking, "What does she know? She's never played or coached in the NBA," and Burke admits they are right on the latter point. "I never did play or coach in the NBA. But I study the game, and I know the game."

Burke treats praise and criticism the same. When people are supportive and welcoming, or when people are critical and object to having a woman calling an NBA play-off game or a men's college basketball game, Burke strives to meet those two perspectives with equanimity. She has learned to stay away from social media, and she learned that lesson the hard way. "There are just too many negative outlooks out there," she said, "and I refuse to participate in that. Actually, I refuse to participate in the positive or the negative response. It should not, and does not, affect how I do my job and the enjoyment of my job."

She says she just puts her head down, prepares meticulously and calls it like she sees it.

Broadcasting is a subjective business. Two people can have opposite opinions on the exact same thing. Those differences in opinion are fine to Burke, but she declines to participate in the drama that goes with them. She knows there is constant chatter regarding a woman in this job, considered by some to be a man's job. It comes with the territory, Burke says, and she accepts that fact. She does not, however, accept the truth of the assertion.

"My colleagues have been supportive, by and large," Burke said. "I have heard of one who ripped me, saying that I had no business doing NBA games. There's nothing I can do about that, and I don't worry about it.

"Look, I'm aware of the jobs I have had; I know my bosses have taken into account that I am a woman. I'm okay with that," Burke said. "My gender has helped me get in this chair. But I have stayed in this chair, and I keep getting assigned to it. You have to be able to do the job for that."

She feels pressure in her position, but her love of basketball overrides the pressure. "Basketball is in my blood. It is my passion. I go to games, and it doesn't matter who is playing. If they are lacing 'em up and tipping it, I'm going to be there," Burke said. "Doing men's college basketball, it took me a long time to relax and enjoy the game. It seemed like a test each time I was on the sidelines—a test to see if I belonged there."

She says the game is now fun for her again, and that is a victory for her, because she started playing the game precisely because it was fun. She has always enjoyed it, and why shouldn't she enjoy it now in her current role? She has been immersed in this game since she was seven years old. "Relax and enjoy it," Burke tells herself. "I know that there will always be people who hear my voice and automatically object when they hear a woman. But I'm much more comfortable now doing NBA and college basketball games. I feel a level of performance pressure, but I don't feel pressure as to whether I belong. I know I belong. That knowledge and my preparation have helped me enjoy the games more."

In the end, she knows the measure of her work is not the criticism on message boards or Twitter. The true measure is the work her bosses at ESPN assign to her. "They know the work I do, and I can best judge the job I am doing by the work assigned to me. When it is assigned, I do each assignment to the best of my ability," Burke said.

For Burke, immersing herself in the game is the saving grace. "I love basketball. Whatever anyone says about me, positive or negative, it cannot affect my love for and appreciation of this game," Burke said. "I don't love the game more when I am complimented, and I don't love it less when I am criticized. I love this game unconditionally."

The game has always been her comfort zone, and she believes the game truly saved her life. "Basketball provided me with an education and my career. I owe everything to this game," Burke said. "I love it. I absolutely love it."

She sees herself as a plugger, and she just keeps plugging. "Do your job, and shut everything else out. Does that take a tough mental approach? Sure it does," Burke said.

Despite her years around sports, she says she still doesn't value on-court toughness the same way she values real-life toughness. "Because of what I endured growing up, being tough on the floor paled in comparison with real toughness off the court."

Burke says the toughest person she knows is her sister, Helen. Years ago, Helen delivered a special-needs child, three months premature. The baby spent six months in the hospital, and when Helen brought her child home, her husband walked out. "He left the same night she brought the baby home," Burke said.

"Helen went on welfare, she and the baby moved in with our parents, and she had only a high school diploma," Burke said. She stocked shelves in a grocery store and put herself through two years of community college, then got her undergraduate degree. Eventually, she graduated magna cum laude from Rutgers Law School. Helen is now a practicing attorney in Florida. "With all she has been through and overcome, how can I possibly be concerned with a few critics? She is the toughest person I know, and it is not even close," Burke said.

"Look, my life has not been easy, and it has not been neat," Burke said. "People will let you down, and things can get tough. You have to figure it out. You just have to be tougher. But as hard as things have been, it has taught me so much. I've learned, and I have become better for the hard times."

I have had some great teammates in my life, but none better than Doris Burke. Doris inspires me to be better and tougher. In my profession, there is not a single person who better exhibits the elements of toughness set forth in this book. Burke does things nobody else in broadcasting does: She changes roles from game to game, assignment to assignment, and she never complains. She embraces her role, does her job, and does it to a level of excellence.

Doris will go from a sideline reporter on an NBA game one night, to the lead color commentator on a women's college basketball game, to the sideline reporter on a men's college basketball game, to the lead color commentator on an NBA game, to the lead color commentator on a men's college basketball game. That would make the head of a normal pro spin. Yet Doris Burke handles it with grace and ease, and never lets the role changes or preparation challenges become an issue. I know of no other person in our industry carrying such a challenging load, yet making it look so seamless and easy.

It is not seamless and easy. It is daunting and difficult. Doris Burke makes it look easy because she is prepared, committed, persistent, self-aware, embraces her role and is courageous enough to self-evaluate. But, more than anything, she keeps plugging. That takes commitment.

Doris Burke makes it look easy because she is tough. She is one of the toughest people I know.

Adapt and Overcome

Sacrifice and commitment are often referenced in sports, and I talk about those concepts quite a bit. The truth is, I have never truly committed to anything in my life that comes close to comparing to the commitment of our men and women in the United States

Armed Forces. To me, that is the highest level of commitment to selfless service, and the greatest of all sacrifices.

That realization didn't really hit home with me until I had the honor of visiting the Middle East as a part of Operation Hardwood, an event run by the USO in which college coaches visited military camps to coach servicemen. I was one of the coaches on two separate trips, Operation Hardwood I and II in 2005 and 2006.

Among my fellow Operation Hardwood coaches were Tom Izzo, Tubby Smith, Gary Williams, Rick Barnes, Mark Gottfried, Kelvin Sampson, Bobby Lutz, Bobby Cremins, Dave Odom and Mike Jarvis. We each had a team from a different camp or base in Kuwait or Iraq during Operation Iraqi Freedom, and our teams competed against each other in a tournament at Camp Arifjan.

To paraphrase Mike Krzyzewski's statement about West Point and toughness, Camp Arifjan was a laboratory for commitment. My perspective and understanding of commitment and its true meaning deepened on my trips to Camp Arifjan.

During the summer in the Middle East, temperatures can reach 120 or 130 degrees, and the conditions are beyond challenging. Yet in such conditions, our soldiers work, fight and, in this case, compete on the basketball court every day, and do so with amazing toughness, discipline and courage. Their commitment was unmistakable throughout the process.

On our very first day, as we entered Camp Arifjan, there was a simple sign that read: "Adapt and overcome."

We found out later that no matter the situation or the hardship faced, every committed soldier was expected to adapt to it, and find a way to overcome it. Failure was not an option.

The "adapt and overcome" philosophy was about one thing above all else: toughness. And in my judgment, the toughness necessary to adapt and overcome was born of commitment. No matter the situation, a soldier was expected to use all available resources—internal and external—to adapt to the situation, work the problem, and overcome any obstacle to complete the mission.

The first day our group was at Camp Arifjan, each coach was introduced to the team he would coach for the week. There was a gym with a concrete floor, and conditions were Spartan. But relative to the conditions in Iraq and Afghanistan, the Camp Arifjan gym was the equivalent of Madison Square Garden for any soldier in the Middle East. It was by far the best facility among our bases there.

The soldiers on each team were of differing skill and experience levels, but they were all similar in their level of competitiveness. I was amazed. The soldiers, each of whom had life-and-death responsibilities as soon as they stepped outside of that gym, were totally committed in mind and body to the task in front of them: to play basketball.

And each soldier played hard for the soldier next to him or her. The level of commitment to the endeavor and to teammates was so clear. You could feel it.

Each team had an hour's practice to put in an offense and some simple out-of-bounds plays, and to get a feel for what the coach wanted. Together the coaches decided that each team would take up one half of the court for its practice so two teams could practice at the same time.

In the second group, South Carolina coach Dave Odom floated an idea. He suggested that instead of practicing half-court, we should just have the two teams scrimmage each other, and the coaches of the two teams could stop things periodically and teach and make corrections on the fly. It was a really good idea, and we went with it.

As the first group scrimmage went on, we all noticed something unmistakable and incredibly impressive. The soldiers were playing and competing "all-out" and holding nothing back. They were physical, diving for loose balls on the concrete floor, yet when someone got fouled or knocked down, he or she just got up and got back into the fray. Not a cross word was said, not a brow furrowed, and not one form of weakness was shown.

Former Oklahoma and Indiana coach Kelvin Sampson pointed

out that there were no referees out there, yet not one player even looked for a foul. They just played right through it. "With my college guys, we might have had a fight or someone moaning about getting fouled," Sampson said.

It was truly amazing. Every single coach remarked that he wished his team could be there to see it. It was a lesson in how to compete, fight and concentrate on the task at hand.

On the penultimate day of my first trip to Camp Arifjan, a few of the soldiers took us on a tour of the base. As we drove past an area that warehoused heavy equipment, we noticed a bank of flagpoles with different-colored flags, and asked a young enlisted man what those colored flags meant.

He told us those flags represented heat orders, which let soldiers know exactly how long and under what conditions they could work outside. He went on to tell us that the most severe heat order, a black flag, meant the soldiers were limited to working outside "ten minutes on, fifty minutes off." That meant that soldiers were allowed to work only ten minutes per hour outside, with the other fifty minutes per each hour in a tent or indoors.

One of the coaches asked the soldier how they get their work done in such conditions. The answer floored us all.

He responded in a humble, matter-of-fact fashion, but I will never forget his answer. He said that, when faced with such conditions, his unit finds a way around those orders. "Our job is to 'make mission,' sir," he said. "We have brothers and sisters dying in Iraq, and they don't get fifty minutes off every hour just because it's hot. So we don't take fifty minutes off. We make mission."

We all fell silent, in awe of the commitment to the task at hand, and the commitment to comrades, to teammates. I have not encountered such commitment in my life. I have had it easy, and I have had it easy because of the commitment shown by our soldiers.

That same trip, then Alabama and current North Carolina State coach Mark Gottfried and I were walking from the mess to the gym when we passed two young women walking back to their barracks after having worked out in the weight room. One of the young women was wearing an Auburn shirt. As the coach at Alabama, Mark stopped the woman to ask her whether she was from Alabama.

These young women looked like they should be walking from their dorm room to the library on campus, or to a football game. They were not more than twenty or twenty-one years old. When we asked them what they did in the army, one told us she drove a HET truck and the other said she was a gunner.

Those two young women, by themselves, operated a heavy equipment transport vehicle that transported tanks and other heavy equipment in and out of Iraq. They told us they had just returned from Iraq after having their HET truck disabled when an insurgent's bullet went through the engine block.

"It was a lucky shot," one of them said. "Even if the insurgent had been aiming there, it would be highly unlikely to get that result." We asked what they did when the HET truck was disabled, what action they took.

"We were taking fire, and just hunkered down, protected the vehicle, and waited for reinforcements to arrive. We're not just going to leave it there," she said. "We waited overnight until another transport arrived and we were able to get it out safely."

Gottfried and I were blown away by how matter-of-fact these two young soldiers were about their duties, and the incredible difficulty of their dangerous jobs. And as we were parting, we were so impressed by what they said to us.

They thanked us for being there. We simply couldn't believe it, and we told them so. I said that it was the two of us who should be profusely thanking the two of them, and we did. Then one of them said, "We have to be here. You don't." Gottfried and I could not believe how committed and courageous those two soldiers were. In our time there, we found out that they were the rule rather than the exception.

The United States Armed Forces are, without question, the best team in the world. And, as I learned at Camp Arifjan, the toughest team in the world too. From my time around the military, I believe that toughness is built on a foundation of commitment—to the mission, and to each other. That level of commitment is unapproachable by me in my daily life, but I will still strive to reach it. I owe those soldiers at least that.

To me, commitment is perhaps the most important building block in any foundation of true toughness. From commitment, that devotion to the team, the family and the endeavor, flows so many positives. It may be measured in "50-50 balls," the work you're willing to put in to support a comrade, or the will to keep plugging through adversity, but you can't be truly tough without being truly committed.

CHAPTER 8

ACCEPTANCE

When I played basketball for Coach K at Duke, I was referred to as a "role player." For many people, that label is one of limitation, indicative of certain things that perhaps I couldn't do or wasn't allowed to do. The term "role player" is often seen as restrictive, and can be taken as an insult.

The truth is, I'm proud to have been a role player on my team. But there is no question that being a role player can be limiting, if you allow it to be. And I allowed it to be.

Let me begin with one clear and unmistakable statement on roles and role players. Every player on a team is a role player, and every player on a team should strive to excel at what I consider to be the most important role of all: the role of being a great teammate.

Every player should strive to be a great teammate, on and off the floor. In today's society of specialization within a sport, I believe that has been lost in our culture of "individual work" and "personal training." How, if at all, do we teach our young athletes to be great teammates?

Think about it. In participating in youth sports, did anyone really teach you exactly what it means to be a great teammate and what that entails, or was it something learned over time by being involved with some great teammates? Was being a great teammate something affirmatively taught, or was it like the United States Supreme Court's definition of obscenity: You can't define it, but you know it when you see it?

In youth basketball today, almost every young player of any means has individual instruction from a personal coach outside of the team. With so much attention and time devoted to individual work, what emerges is an individual whose focus is on himself, rather than a team player who has worked hard to be better individually so that he can be more productive for the benefit of the team.

The truth is, this phenomenon isn't new. It is just more pronounced now than it was years ago. And I fear that it is getting more pronounced as time passes.

When I came out of high school and chose to attend Duke, I arrived as a prep all-star ranked among the top-forty high school players in the nation. I was regarded as one of the two or three best players in the entire state of California, and was one of the prized recruits in Coach K's first number one–ranked recruiting class in the nation, along with Johnny Dawkins, Mark Alarie, and David Henderson. That group formed the nucleus of a team that would be together for four straight years and would play almost every minute of every game together. I came to Duke with confidence, and I expected to be a starter and an impact player right away.

But I found out quickly that I wasn't the best player, and that defined roles needed to be established for our team to be successful. Dawkins was the leading scorer and the team's superstar. Alarie was the second-leading scorer and a star player as well. Henderson was the third-leading scorer and the team's emotional leader. I was next on the scoring list, but I was valued more as a rebounder, defender and enforcer. I was the "piano carrier" to the virtuosos Dawkins, Alarie and Henderson, and referred to by my coach as an "offensive lineman" who did the dirty work without any of the credit. Tommy

Amaker was our point guard, floor leader and our best individual defender.

As determined by our skill level, our play, and by the coaching decisions of Coach K, each of us was required to play a specific and defined role for our team to be at its best. If we were each concerned about our individual standing within the team, outside recognition or our individual statistics, we would surely hinder what we could and would be as a team.

The truth was, and still is, that no role on that team was any more important than any other role. While some of us were recognized as stars and headline-grabbing scorers, others of us were considered "background singers" in supporting roles. But we all needed to be stars in our roles for our team to be truly successful. And we all needed to be great teammates to accept and embrace our roles.

Accepting and embracing a role is really about the selfless willingness to sacrifice. It is about the willingness to invest your personal wants and needs into the success of the whole. It is about discipline in your approach, and about complete and total commitment to the success of the team.

There is an emotional component to such sacrifice and investment in your team. In order to throw yourself completely into your role, you have to accept that you are second to the team, and your individual success is tied to your team's success. Any great teammate and great role player has to take more pride in the team than he does in his own individual wants and needs. Great teammates have to fight the urge to be selfish, and throw themselves into the team. That is not easy to do. It requires commitment and toughness to accept.

Boston Celtics coach Doc Rivers believes that a player's role may not be exactly what he wants to do, but it is exactly what the team needs him to do in order for them to win a championship. Rivers advocates being a star in your role. "When individual success is tied to team success, you have a chance to be special," Rivers said.

Embracing a role may be the most difficult aspect of team sports, according to former NFL coach Jon Gruden. Nobody keeps statistics for roles on championship teams, Gruden asserts, and there is no statistic for a back-side block or diving out-of-bounds to save a loose ball, or setting a screen. Acceptance and embracing of roles, and the celebration of them, has to be valued and emphasized within the team, because it will not necessarily be celebrated outside of the team.

"There's no award for the player on the scout team that simulates LeBron James or Adrian Peterson in practice, and does it to help you win," Gruden said. To make up for that lack of public recognition, Gruden emphasizes the "behind-the-scenes heroes" in his successful, winning operations. He points out the people in the building who sacrifice themselves and make the unseen commitment to help his teams win. And he makes sure that those who are publicly recognized understand that they cannot successfully fulfill their roles as stars without the work of the behind-the-scenes heroes.

"Accepting roles," Gruden said, "is about a 'big-picture environment,' and it takes maturity to accept it, to be convinced to buy in fully. No matter how big or small your role, it is important. It may not be glamorous, but it's a necessity for us to win a championship."

If you are a reserve, part of your charge is to push the starters to their limit, and to challenge them every single day in practice. In other words, your charge is to compete, and not to allow the starters to settle in or settle for less. That way the starters will get better, stronger, tougher and more prepared to fight with you to beat an opponent, and you, as a reserve, will continue to get better too. As a reserve, you must be prepared for your opportunity to play. The truth is, you never know when that opportunity will come your way. Nobody does.

Gruden was the youngest head coach ever to win a Super Bowl when he led the Tampa Bay Buccaneers to victory in Super Bowl 2002 during his first year with the team. His motto for the 2002 season was, "Pound the rock," a reference to never giving up. Gruden even went so far as to display a large chunk of granite in the locker room that season.

When Gruden was coaching the Raiders a few years back, he dreaded the games against the Vikings. "The biggest concern, the one that kept me up at night, was blocking John Randle," he said. "This guy was the baddest defensive lineman in the league, nearly unblockable."

The Raiders had a young rookie named Rod Coleman, who was a fifth-round draft choice from East Carolina University. Gruden just couldn't find a home for Coleman, and didn't know where to play the guy. "He was barely on the roster," Gruden said.

Coach Al Davis suggested to Gruden that they should put Coleman over the guard and use him as their own "John Randle" against their All-Pro guard, Steve Wisniewski. They told Coleman to be Wisniewski's worst nightmare, to go right at him every play, every single snap. They motivated him to play a role that wasn't easy to play, but was needed to prepare their team to win.

"Coleman took that role and totally embraced it," Gruden said. "And guess what? He became an All-Pro defensive tackle himself. That role he accepted of being John Randle for us, I really believe that was a launching pad for a great career. None of us foresaw that at the time, but here was this obscure rookie player that took the opportunity to help the team, and he helped himself."

Very few rookies, freshmen or other inexperienced players can step in and do the job right away, Gruden said. Rookies have to play on special teams, the scout team, and in the backup role. They have to be tough enough to take a limited role and turn it into a bigger role. At some point, most of them figure out they just have to do it.

Gruden is the son of a coach, Jim Gruden, who was an assistant coach to Dan Devine at Notre Dame and an NFL assistant coach with the Tampa Bay Buccaneers. Football was in his blood. "Watching my dad every day," Gruden said, "I knew football wasn't a nine-to-five job."

As son of an assistant coach, Gruden could have attended Notre Dame free of tuition. But he wanted to play ball, and wasn't good enough to play for the Irish, so he worked his way through high school and earned a spot on the roster of University of Dayton to play quarterback.

"Only one quarterback can play. It's not like basketball, where there are two guards at once," Gruden said. "I wasn't that good of a football player. I broke my neck as a junior in high school, and I think I showed some toughness in simply coming back from that to play again."

At Dayton, Gruden was what he calls a "ham and egg" quarterback. He lettered three years, but all he wanted was to have the starting position. "I put so much pressure on myself to win the job, I probably cost myself the chance to win the job," he said. "I would talk to myself on the way back to the dorm; you name it."

But he kept at it. Looking back, he knew he was willing to do anything to help the team. He ran the scout team, he served as the holder on extra points, and he mopped up in spot duty at the end of games. His senior year, he won Dayton's prestigious Zulli trophy for leadership. To this day, Gruden says that award is the most meaningful one he's ever received.

But Gruden still regrets not winning the starting quarterback job. He wishes he could go back and compete for it again. "But I got better because of it," he said. "Life isn't easy, but you never quit. Never. I may not have been the best, but I can always give my best. That's how you demonstrate toughness."

Gruden was fueled by his challenges as a college quarterback, and channeled his regrets into the next phase of his football life. In 1990, Gruden earned a spot on the San Francisco 49ers coaching staff under Bill Walsh and quickly ascended the ranks of NFL coaching. After serving as head coach of the Oakland Raiders, Gruden replaced the fired Tony Dungy as head coach of the Tampa Bay Buccaneers and ultimately guided the Bucs to a win over the Raiders in the Super Bowl.

One of the coaches Gruden admires most is Michigan State's Tom Izzo. Among Izzo's favorite phrases is, "Players play, but tough players win." To accept and embrace a role, you have to be a tough player. And to accept and embrace a role without allowing that role to limit you, you have to be especially tough.

Of course, working hard is a hallmark of toughness and of a great teammate. Hard work is not punishment. Hard work is the price of admission for the opportunity to reach a standard of sustained excellence. No player has ever achieved sustained excellence without hard work. The toughest players go as hard as they can for as long as they can, and soon improve and increase their capacity to do more. And when you see nothing but hard work from your teammates, it raises your standards and your level of expectation of yourself. No coach can make you work as hard or want to work as hard as a tough teammate can. Coach-directed teams go only so far. The best and toughest teams reach their greatest heights because teammates feed off of each other, and are inspired to match or exceed the level they experience each day.

But hard work is not enough. A great teammate has to first be committed to the team, and willing to sacrifice his individual goals for the good of the team. That sacrifice has to be balanced with the understanding on the part of every member of that team that acceptance of a role does not diminish or limit that player, and that role is not necessarily permanent. Truthfully, I did not fully grasp that as a player. While Jon Gruden regrets not achieving the starting quarterback position when he was in college, I regret that I allowed my status as a role player to limit my development, and to limit what I was able to bring, and brought, to the team.

That failure was nobody's fault but my own. I needed to be mentally tougher in my approach. If I had been, I would have been better, and I could have made my team better.

A great role player and a tough player must determine what he would sacrifice to win. *What task is too small? What role is beneath me? Is there anything I am not willing to do for this team to win, or for this team to operate at its highest level?* To be a great role player and a tough player, you have to embrace that championship teams are "we" driven and not "me" driven. I believe I had that as a player. I was willing to sacrifice, and I did. But the mistake that I made is conflating the acceptance of my role with the acceptance of the idea that I could not break out of that role to do more.

Former NFL defensive back and head coach Herm Edwards understands. He believes that every player has the opportunity to improve his station, but it is on the player to do it and nobody else. "Your role can be defined, and you don't have to like it, but if you are limited by it, that's on you," Edwards said. "You can have a defined role, but you cannot let that role define you. You can elevate yourself beyond that role. If you can't, guess what? That may just be who you are and you have to accept it. If you don't accept it, you'll never get where you need to be. You'll always feel slighted or mistreated."

The truth is, I limited my development and production by becoming comfortable in my role. I embraced it, but I allowed myself to get comfortable in that role and saw it as all I could accomplish. That was a failure on my part. That's on me.

Instead of putting in the extra work to be able to do more than my current role called for, I worked mostly on only what my role called for, and in a way cemented myself into that role. It wasn't until later, after I had become a professional and had taken on other responsibilities, that it became clear to me that I had been capable of much more, but had allowed myself to settle for less, to settle for only my role.

Don't get me wrong: I was good, and I was productive in my role. In my four years at Duke, I was a four-year starter, scored more than a thousand career points and grabbed 692 rebounds while shooting more than 55 percent from the field. I did well, and one could argue quite well, considering I played with the exact same lineup for four straight years, and played with the highest-scoring class in NCAA history. But the truth is, I know that I could have done more, not for my individual ego, but for my team.

Kansas coach Bill Self also assigns players to the roles he expects them to play, but he is careful never to take away or limit their games.

He encourages them in what he wants them to do, but he tries to avoid telling them what not to do. "Your role is different from your value," he said, "and there are so many times that players have to be able to break out of their roles. A role shouldn't be a limitation."

Boston Celtics head coach Doc Rivers said, "Every player has to believe his role is the most important role on the team. We cannot win without each player executing his role to the best of his ability."

Bob Knight never really used the term "role" or "role player" with his teams. He didn't want to say that each player had a narrowly defined role, but he did say that shooters shoot, passers pass, and everybody defends and rebounds. And that each guy on the team has the same role: to do whatever is necessary to help the team win.

Still, a coach must be conscious of the contributions players can make. "I never really referred to it as a role or role acceptance," Knight said. "I wanted the best shooters to get the most shots, and the best passers to be in position to make passes."

Knight often put responsibility for the outcome of the game on the shoulders of a player to do a fundamental task. He would sometimes put great responsibility on a player to box out, or to keep someone from penetrating. "I would tell that player he has four other guys counting on him to keep him off the glass, or we cannot win," he said. "I would put a critical element of the game in the hands of individual players, and let them know their part in the game was vital to our ability to win. I'd put more pressure on them than you would normally."

Soccer great Mia Hamm had special respect for her teammates who embraced their roles but didn't limit their identities to those roles. "We can't all be stars," Hamm said. "Teams don't work that way. But how do you handle your role? Do you sit on your hands, bitch and complain? Do you undermine a teammate or the team?"

Hamm emphasized that a player's role is to do whatever it takes to help the team win, and that nobody ever really knows what her role will be at any given time. "Your role can change at any moment," Hamm said. "Are you prepared for what the game will throw at you?"

To illustrate that point, Hamm told a story about Tiffany Roberts, a teammate whom Hamm remembers as a great team player with extraordinary energy. "She is an incredible human being," Hamm said. In the 1996 Olympics, Roberts had not played a single minute heading into the semifinal against Norway, and nobody could have expected her to play in that game. Prior to the game, the coaching staff made a tactical decision to start Roberts, for the sole purpose of guarding—or "marking"—Norway's best player, Hege Riise.

Roberts's assignment was to shut Riise down, to mark her all over the field and follow her absolutely everywhere. "Tiffany was asked to mark her totally out of the game," Hamm said. Roberts shut down Riise, and the U.S. team beat Norway and moved on to play China for the gold medal.

Tiffany Roberts did not play a single minute in the gold-medal game. "She didn't question. She didn't complain," Hamm said. "She just did her job and helped us win. Amazing."

Teammate Julie Foudy knew Tiffany Roberts would do anything to help the team win, even if it wasn't in a role she wanted. "Never once did she make it a team issue. Never once," Foudy said. "She was on a yo-yo string and never said a word about it. She just played and did whatever job was in front of her at that moment."

Foudy says people who complain about lack of game time or what they're asked to do for the team bring down the entire group. "Think about this: All of our teams that won championships, every one of them," Foudy said, "whether a gold medal in the Olympics or winning the World Cup, we had a complete group, from regulars to deep bench. We had people like Tiffany Roberts. That's not a coincidence."

Hamm emphasized that it is not about the minutes you play, but about how you play those minutes. When starters have role players encouraging them in times of adversity, and challenging them with everything they have every single day in practice, the team has a strong core and can be an always improving team.

Accepting a role on a team takes a special kind of selflessness and toughness on the court and the field. Those are the players who help their teammates succeed and—ultimately—help their teams win.

It's easy to be selfish as a player, and often few people really see the selfishness. In basketball, are you tough enough to close out to a shooter, even though it leaves you vulnerable to letting your man get the rebound? Are you tough enough to rotate on defense, to help your teammate out? And are you willing to get there *and* take the charge?

Many players are unwilling to be that selfless. Many of them have long athletic careers, but they shortchange their teammates, and they shortchange the game.

Embrace Being Number One

Whether is it acceptance of a role or the public view of your team, mental toughness and concentration on what is truly important are the key. To me, that is demonstrated in how different teams, coaches and players address rankings. Every competitor says he or she has the "goal" or dream of being number one, of being the best. Yet so often we hear of coaches and players wanting to be the underdog, or wanting to sneak up on an opponent. The truth is, many want to be number one at the end, but don't want to have to live with the burden of expectations, of living every day as number one and wearing that bull's-eye.

Coach K was never like that. He knew that we had no control over exactly where we were ranked, that other people voted on such things, and it was out of our control. But, he decided, if someone was handing out rankings, we wanted to be number one. Why not?

Coach K conditioned us to embrace the challenge and responsibility of being number one and warned us that we would see the best shot from every opponent. When playing as a number one–

ranked team, you face a more focused, enthusiastic and determined opponent that is playing at its highest level. When you beat a team when you are ranked number one, you know you have beaten your opponent at its very best. And that is especially true when playing on the road as a number one–ranked team. Nobody "mails it in" against number one on their home turf.

Being ranked number one comes with a responsibility to be prepared for that special effort against you. If you do not go after your opponent with vigor from the opening tip, it emboldens your opponent, giving them a belief they can win, and makes them even harder to play against and beat. That is where mental toughness comes in. When toughness and competitiveness meet, the truly great teams and players excel. It is a mental challenge, and it is exactly the arena in which Tom Izzo's mantra is required: "Players play, but tough players win."

The toughest teams are the most "together" teams. In basketball, you can often tell how tough a team is when there is a dead ball or a stop in the action. When the whistle blows, do the five players come together, or do they move off in five different directions? Are they connected and communicating, or are they five individuals? When one of them goes down on the floor, are the other four there to pick him up? Those are signs of collective toughness and togetherness. The toughest teams are not just made up of great players, but of "great teammates." And anyone who has ever been on a truly great team will tell you that the individual who fully sacrifices for the success of the team gets far more individual rewards than if that player had been selfish, and looking out only for himself.

The Toughness of "Together"

Coach K once asked our team to do a simple thing. He asked us to attach the word "together" to every sentence we used. We were not just going to play hard; we were going to play hard together. We were not just going to defend; we were going to defend together. We were not just going to win; we were going to win together. Adding "together" to everything we did and said provided emphasis that we were a part of something bigger than ourselves. And it made us tougher. Really, it was a way to condition us to understand and accept that we were a part of something bigger than ourselves. We each had a role, but we were not on a totem pole that was vertical, with a recognized top and bottom rung. Our totem pole was horizontal, with no role more important on our team than any other.

Larry Brown, the Hall of Fame coach who won an NCAA championship with Kansas and an NBA championship with the Detroit Pistons, once said that very few players have been members of a team. They have been *on* a team, but have not been *members* of a team. By committing to doing everything together, especially the tough things, and for taking responsibility not just for ourselves but for others, we were committing to being contributing members of a successful team.

Nobody does tough things alone. Nobody.

Of course, when that is said, individual sports immediately come to mind. Does that mean that Michael Phelps was not tough alone? What about tennis star Roger Federer? How about a boxer or marathoner with no teammates to rely upon?

Every competitor has a support team, whether it is a coach, a trainer or a family. Michael Phelps has won medals in team relays, and has coaches, trainers and family who have been supporting him for years. He has not been tough alone. The same goes for Federer, or any boxer with a trainer and those in his "corner." They have not been tough alone. Nobody is tough alone. We all have to embrace toughness and, as Coach K says, get all of our resources and support in the fight.

I always get back to basketball as the best example of what it takes to be tough together, in large measure because I believe basketball is the ultimate team sport. To get a good shot in basketball, you have to work hard, individually and collectively. An "easy" shot usually comes from having worked your tail off to get it. Easy shots are hard to get, and very few players can get an easy shot by themselves. It takes a team working together to get a great shot. And it is not your shot or my shot—it is *our* shot.

Basketball is an interesting and beautiful game because it requires incredible timing and teamwork, and it requires incredible effort under stress. Basketball, however, also requires a certain level of relaxation. In basketball, tension and fear are the enemies of performance.

We have explored the truisms that toughness is a skill that can be learned and improved, and that it is also contagious. Being around tough and tough-minded people can and will make everyone else around them tougher.

A player's role is so much more than just the position he or she plays, and the intricacies and requirements of that position. The role of every single player on any team is to be a great teammate. A great teammate is committed. A great teammate is selfless. And a great teammate is tough. When those qualities are personified by every player on the team, great teams can emerge. The contagious nature of toughness, of commitment, takes that team to the highest level.

Mark Alarie believes that being around tough people made him tougher. "And, maybe more importantly, it made me *want* to be tougher. Being around David Henderson made me tougher. Being around Coach K made me tougher, no question," Alarie said.

But, Alarie said, it works the other way too. If you have a player on your team who loafs, it will allow others to loaf. And that will ultimately bring down your team's overall level of commitment. If everybody fails to work as hard as they can or as hard as they should, it can and will drag down the group little by little. Alarie believes that the best of us fall prey to that lowering of standards. It can infect everyone on the team, and the team itself.

"Then, before you know it, you're not as tough," Alarie said. "Then you've got a losing team, and everybody looks around and asks what the hell happened. You have to value being tough, and emphasize it with the right people willing to commit to it." When you see mental toughness every day, you are more likely to join in.

Toughness is a vital part of every player's role. Toughness is of vital importance to Tom Crean, and it is an important element that each player on his team must accept as a part of his or her role. Crean doesn't value just talking about commitment, but showing it through extra work. "Commitment is not just doing what is required. It is extra," he said. "Commitment is extra time, extra work. Do you come in and do the extra work?"

Everybody on the team knows who has that commitment to be a great teammate, to sacrifice, to work, and to embrace doing what it takes to win, Crean said, and they know who doesn't have it. He believes it's his job to let every member of his team know about the "gap" between the truly committed and those who lag behind. "Everyone must be committed," he said, "and you need an awareness of who is working and who is not. That way, you can challenge others to work harder, to push their limits and the limits of the team."

For Crean, it's not hard to figure out. The better players spend the majority of their time working and encouraging others to work. That is not a coincidence. There is a causal connection between work and success, between sacrifice and success, and between acceptance and commitment to your role and the team's success. Great teams are made up of great teammates who accept roles, embrace constructive criticism and coaching, and accept the challenge of expectations.

You're Not Tough Alone, and You Don't Win or Lose Alone

While we were not tough alone, one thing Coach K never allowed was for us to "lose alone." In any game, win or loss, there are things that are done or not done that would win or lose a game if it were the last play. And when our team won or lost, we examined our mistakes in a positive way to correct them. But when we lost, no player was allowed to think that it was his fault alone. To believe that would be to also believe a player could be solely responsible for winning a game, and no matter how bright our stars, no single player ever won a game for Duke alone. We won and we lost as a team, and there were no exceptions to that rather simple, straightforward principle.

However, that does not mean we were not held individually accountable for the execution of our particular jobs or roles, or the importance of individual contributions to our collective success. Coach K simply did not allow us to to approach things in an individual way. To some, that sounds corny. But when you believe in each other and in what you are doing together, it is powerful. And it is a collective toughness.

It wasn't that we weren't allowed to feel bad about losing or be angry about what we did or didn't do that led to the loss. We were. But we were not allowed to be selfish about it. We were conditioned to channel our negative feelings into positive action that would help us win, and not let it negatively affect us going forward. As NASA engineer Daryl Woods said, we were each responsible for our element, but accountable to the team.

Toughness isn't just about you, but about being tough enough to step outside of your own self-interest and help a teammate. Are you tough enough to help a teammate, even if you are competing against that teammate for playing time or a bigger role on the team? That is where team interest intersects with self-interest, and the importance of "we" has to be greater than the importance of "me." As Mia Hamm pointed out, not everyone on the team can be the star. Are you willing to accept and execute your role, but prepared to break out of it when necessary? Are you going to sit on the bench and root for a teammate to screw up so that you can go in and play? Or are you going to support that teammate, while at the same time being prepared to go in when needed? There is a difference.

It is easy to be selfish. It takes toughness to sacrifice and be a true member of a team.

In 1986, I was a senior in college, and started preseason practice as a three-year starter on a national title-contending team. I was just coming off of knee surgery the prior spring, and instead of spending the summer rehabilitating my knee, I chose to play for the United States National Select Team, which I considered a once-in-a-lifetime opportunity to represent my country. I was not going to let knee surgery stop me from wearing USA across my chest and playing USA Basketball.

That October, I started practice at less than 100 percent physically. And I was competing for a starting job with the number one recruit in the nation, Danny Ferry. After several weeks of preseason practice, Coach K and the team orthopedic surgeon, Frank Bassett, determined that I should not play any further until my knee improved significantly. I missed the first six games of the season and, as a result, after being a starter every year of my Duke career, I came back into the fold as a reserve, a position I had never had at Duke, or in my career to that point.

The truth is, Danny Ferry may have beaten me out even if I had been healthy. He was clearly the better long-term prospect, and the only reason I might have been the better fit as the starter was because I was stronger and more experienced at that moment. The job, for me or for Danny, was to fill a role around our star players, Johnny Dawkins and Mark Alarie. Danny was clearly going to be a superstar in the future, but there was no way he could be a star that year, with those roles ably filled by Dawkins and Alarie.

Whenever a player is injured and on the sidelines, unable to play or practice, there is a significant risk that he can feel isolated and pull back from the team, that he feels less of a contributing member of the team.

That was my issue.

I tried desperately not to let that happen. And I had a choice to make in my relationship with Danny. He was a great, young, soon-to-be star, but I was the older, more mature player. Even though we were competing for the same job and the same minutes, and even though one of my main goals was to get my job back when I was healthy, I needed to support Danny.

When I did return, Danny and I split time for several games, and I was named the starter again. That wasn't easy for me, and it certainly wasn't easy for Danny. But we each had to be tough enough to put the team first, to choose to help and support each other. And we needed to be tough enough to accept Coach K's ultimate decision, then be strong enough to unite and move on, and to fight together to help our team win.

That is an important and essential form of toughness. When competing for playing time, it does no good to hope your teammate fails so you can play. A great teammate does everything he or she can do to make sure a teammate is in the best position to be successful, then tries like hell to beat that teammate out at his or her best. There is nothing wrong with competing and being a competitor. But rooting against a teammate is the absence of true competitiveness, and the absence of toughness.

Think about it. Are you the type of teammate, classmate or colleague who roots or hopes for a teammate to struggle so that you can benefit? Or are you helping and encouraging that teammate, but prepared for your opportunity? Accepting your role as a great teammate sets up all other elements of toughness. Accepting your role as a great teammate is all about your attitude and approach. It is about being a true competitor. It is about being truly tough.

Accountability for Others

Great teammates are accountable not just for themselves, but for their fellow teammates. When I was in my first full year practicing law as a litigation associate, I had a lesson in what it means to be a true teammate, and to accept accountability for a teammate. My first big courtroom experience was in a simple motion hearing before a federal judge. It wasn't going to make any headlines, but it was really big for me.

I was nervous, and I had worked hard to prepare. I thought I was ready. The morning of the hearing, a fellow litigation associate, Tamara Kettner, came into my office and sat down. Tamara had been practicing law for a few years already, and she had far more experience than I had.

"Ready?" she said.

"Yeah, I think so," I said. "I think I have my argument and all of my evidence down pretty well."

Then she hit me with a question I could not answer.

"Do you know where to sit?"

I hadn't the slightest idea. I hadn't even considered it.

Tamara then walked me through every practical detail I needed to know that was not in my civil procedure books or taught in law school. She told me when to arrive, where to sit, what to expect, what to look for, how to conduct myself, how to present exhibits to the court, and exactly what this particular judge liked and expected from counsel in a motion hearing.

In short, she put me at ease on the small details that could easily have derailed my hearing. Because of Tamara, I would not have to worry about details I had not considered, because she considered them for me.

The hearing was my responsibility, but Tamara took on the responsibility of helping me to prepare. And she remembered that she didn't know where to sit in her first hearing, and how much better she would have felt if she did. She was a tremendous teammate who thought beyond herself, and accepted accountability for her fellow teammates. To me, that is true toughness.

I had an understanding of accountability for teammates, but I did not really take it beyond sports in my mind. I should have. Because what Tamara Kettner did for me, I'd learned years earlier under Coach K; I just hadn't applied it to other areas of my life.

The most unadulterated lesson in accepting accountability for others came not on the floor, but on the team bus. Every coach I know values punctuality. In my freshman season at Duke, Coach K told all of us we had to be on the bus, ready to depart for a road trip at eight a.m., sharp.

My roommate and I packed the night before, each set an alarm, and got to the bus on time. But as the clock hit eight a.m., two of my teammates, Johnny Dawkins and Mark Alarie, who were room-mates that first year, were nowhere to be found. Johnny and Mark were in a dorm room right down the stairs from mine, yet I had no idea where they were.

One of my coaches asked whether we knew where Mark and Johnny were. My roommate and I both said no. Then the coach asked a question I could not answer. "Why not? Did either of you bother to check on them, or plan to come over to the bus together?"

The truth was, we hadn't even considered it.

Getting up and to the bus on time was not just an individual re-sponsibility; it was a collective one. As a teammate, I needed to check on Mark and Johnny, and I should have done that. It would have been so easy to stop by their room on the way, or give them a quick call and tell them we would meet down in front of the dorm. Instead it was every man for himself. From that time on, we always made sure to check on each other, whether at home or on the road, and to make sure we were all on the same page and the same clock. It was easy once we accepted and embraced that as a part of our roles as great teammates, and it made us a better, more aware team.

Accepting responsibility for your actions is a common theme on a great team. A great teammate, however, takes care of himself, but also reaches out to take care of others as well. That is an important form of leadership, and an important aspect of being a member of a team and not just on a team.

It is also an important form of toughness.

It is my obligation and responsibility to my team to take care of myself, get the proper rest, eat right, take care of my off-court obligations so that those issues do not affect me on the court, and to allow me to be fully prepared and fully engaged to give whatever I have to the team.

And if I understood that one of my teammates was not taking care of himself or his obligations, I had the important responsibility of bringing that to his attention and encouraging him to do the right thing. If I had a teammate in trouble, I had to help him navigate that trouble in an honorable fashion.

Coach K told me once about the simple honor code when he was a cadet at West Point. It read, "A cadet will not lie, cheat or steal, or tolerate those who do." Coach K said the first part of the honor code wasn't the difficult part; it was the last part. To Coach K, it didn't mandate turning in a fellow cadet who was doing wrong, but an obligation to confront a fellow cadet who would violate the honor code, and deal with it in the best possible manner. To Coach K, the second part required true toughness.

It is easy to focus only on what you have to do. The toughest people do their jobs completely, and they help their teammates do their jobs too.

Acceptance of Your Responsibility and Accountability to the Team

Your responsibility to the team doesn't end when you walk out of practice and step into your daily off-court life. Part of a great teammate's responsibility is to say no to things that can ultimately affect the team in a negative way. When preparing for the NCAA Tournament, I remember Coach K telling the team about one of the most important words they would need to use in successfully navigating the tournament: no.

Coach K told the players this was a special opportunity, and it was their opportunity. And he gave them permission to be selfish with it. He told them they were going to need to say no to people, including their families. It was their responsibility to get their rest, get where they needed to be on time, and prepare themselves physically and mentally to play. He told them there would be time to spend with family, but it was important to remember that family and friends were really there to watch them go through this experience, not to be with them every step of the way. They were there to support them.

Coach K believed it was important to prioritize things, and important for the players to be empowered to say no.

Bob Knight agrees. "The word 'no' might be the most important word in the English language," Bob Knight said. "'No' is a really important word, and it is a word used by tough people."

Knight believes that use of the word "no" requires great toughness, and its use is the responsibility of a great teammate. Whether it is peer pressure or trying to please everyone, tough people have the ability to say no. The vast majority of people don't want to upset or let down others, and too many bend to what others want to hear. To Knight, the vast majority of people simply aren't tough enough to say no.

Then Knight said something so simple and profound, it floored me. "'Yes' causes a hell of a lot of more problems for people than 'no' does."

Knight is right. In saying no, you may miss an opportunity, but you won't get yourself into trouble. Trouble follows yes, not no.

As a player, that concept made sense to me. I understood that I had a responsibility to be "selfish" with our basketball opportunities, for myself and my team. I felt like I got it.

But in my personal life off the court, I didn't accept and embrace that concept as I should have. Clearly I didn't really get it. Fortunately, a great teammate educated me on what was truly important.

In my current job as a sports broadcaster, I travel a great deal. For me, every game is an away game, and from the start of basketball season to the end, I am often away from home four or five days a week. With such an extensive travel schedule, it is not surprising that I would miss many of my son's ball games, my daughter's art shows or my wife's art gallery openings. But, as Hyman Roth said in *The Godfather*, "This is the business we've chosen." I accepted it. I make sacrifices, and so does my family. And I thought I was being tough in the way I was handling it.

In addition to my in-season travel, I am often asked to appear and speak at different charity functions, basketball clinics and other events. Invariably these events require travel and overnight stays, and take me away from home. When I am asked to do something by a friend or colleague, my first reaction is always to say yes. I have always tried my best to accommodate my friends and colleagues, like most people do. But when I say yes to such events, it is remarkable how quickly a calendar can get filled up.

I have the best and most understanding wife on the planet. My wife, Wendy, is a professional artist with a degree from Duke and an MBA from Wake Forest Business School, and she is a remarkable mother to our two children. She has her priorities in order and, more than anyone else I know, is comfortable in her own skin. She is incredibly smart, and she is the communications hub of our family. And while she is not one to give unsolicited advice, her words carry great weight with me.

A couple of years ago, I had accepted several invitations to speak and appear at events around the country, and it seemed like the entire month was filling up. And Wendy wanted to talk about my overstuffed calendar. She wasn't upset or angry as she showed me that I had scheduled myself over several of my son's ball games as well as a day that fathers were invited to attend my daughter's school. She just wanted to alert me that I should consider "our" schedule instead of just "my" schedule, and that I should prioritize what I thought was truly important rather than trying to be all things to all people.

"I'm really proud that you are in such demand, because it's indicative of what a great job you do. And I love the fact that you do everything you can to help people who ask you for help," Wendy said. "But I want you to remember something. When you say yes to someone else, you are saying no to us."

Boom.

What an idiot I was. Here I am, having spent my whole life around team sports and thinking I understood team dynamics, and I was neglecting the most important team, my wife and kids. I was fooling myself into believing I was being tough in the way I was handling things.

I foolishly believed that I was *missing* those family events. Instead I was *missing from* those family events. There is a difference. I wasn't tough enough to say no.

Fortunately, my wife was tough enough to tell me I needed to wake up and accept my role as part of our team, and that I needed to be tough enough to say no. Really, I needed to be tough enough to do what was right, and what was truly important to me.

I needed to be tough enough to say no to others, so that I could say yes to my family.

Whether a teammate on a sports team, a colleague at your place of work, or a member of a family, we are all members of teams, and we all have specific roles and responsibilities to our teams. To be truly tough, we all have to accept and embrace our roles, and not allow ourselves to be limited by them. Rather, we can and should be empowered by the acceptance of our roles, and committed and accountable to being a great teammate on all of our teams. That requires toughness, individually and collectively, and the toughness exhibited by great teammates makes others want to join in and be a part of it.

CHAPTER 9

RESILIENCE

The ability to come back, to fight adversity or difficulties, is a measure of true toughness. Every athlete and every person has to face difficulties, and to address them honestly and head-on, and to overcome them takes resilience, a major part of toughness. In a way, I learned that the hard way.

When I arrived at Duke in 1982 to play for Coach K, I was six-seven-and-a-half and weighed 220 pounds. When he was recruiting me, I asked Coach K whether he would have me play the center position, as most other coaches told me I would have to do if I went to Duke. Coach K was honest and direct with me. He told me yes, I would likely have to play center for a year until he could recruit a true center so I could move back to my more natural forward position.

That never happened.

A position in basketball, especially playing for Coach K, really comes down to what type of player you will be asked to defend or to guard. For four years at Duke, I was the starting center, which made me one of the smallest centers, if not the smallest, in the ACC.

Routinely I had to guard opposing centers who were six-ten all the way to seven-foot-four. I guarded (or attempted to guard) Clemson's Horace Grant, North Carolina's Brad Daugherty, and Virginia's National Player of the Year, Ralph Sampson. From a size standpoint, I was outmatched.

After my sophomore season, it became clear to me that I was going to be playing the center position for my entire college career. I knew I wasn't going to get any taller, so I figured that I had to get stronger to give me the best chance to compete more successfully against bigger players.

During the summer between my sophomore and junior years, I fully dedicated myself to getting stronger. But I didn't work to get a little stronger; I worked to get significantly stronger. I was not going be pushed around. I decided that I was going to start pushing other people around.

But I did more than get stronger. I chose to commit and to stay committed to my plan to get stronger. I committed to truly accepting and embracing my role, and I committed to pushing my limits in the weight room. And I committed to pushing through and playing through pain. I was going to be disciplined, and I was going to be tough.

One element I left out of my commitment, though, was to be smart.

I believed that I was showing toughness, and I was. But toughness is not just pushing yourself and running through brick walls. Toughness is also about being smart and aware, and taking charge of your health. Toughness is speaking up when things are not right. That takes true toughness too. I just didn't know it then.

Between my sophomore and junior seasons, I spent my summer at home in Los Angeles, and I got to work in the weight room, doing whatever it took to get stronger. I had a plan, and I stuck to it. At the same time I was working in the weight room, I was also spending time rehabilitating my knee to be fully healthy for the next season. During my sophomore season, I had problems with that left knee, and was told by the doctors and trainers that the best remedy was physical therapy and rest.

Every day, I went to a small, sweaty muscle gym near my parents' home called Barlow's Gym. It was owned by a teacher at my high school, and it was populated primarily by bodybuilders, Los Angeles police officers, and California Highway Patrol officers. I went to Barlow's every morning, early. And every morning, my father came with me to spot me and push me. After I finished my workout, my dad would leave the gym and go to work.

My first real workout in this new regimen was incredibly difficult for me. I lifted to muscle failure on every set, and I pressed more weight in that one workout than I had ever lifted in my life. It was grueling. After hitting muscle failure in the very last set, I did not feel right.

My dad went off to work, and I "maintained" until I could get myself into the tiny locker room in the back of the gym. The truth is, I barely made it into the locker room. I felt faint, dizzy and nauseous. I threw up, and then I couldn't stand up.

After a period of time lying on the nasty locker room floor, a bodybuilder and neighbor of my parents named Jim Fite came into the locker room.

"You okay?"

"Yeah, I'm fine, thanks," I said, lying through my teeth. I had no idea how long it would take me to even stand up again. I just wanted to be left alone.

"Do you know what just happened?" Fite said. "You just hit a new level. You pushed yourself past where you had ever been, and you reached a new one. Get used to it. This needs to be a good feeling for you. You just took yourself to failure, and that's success."

What? I had never felt this bad in my life. Was this what success felt like? As the day wore on, I started to feel better, but I was still gassed. I didn't doubt whether I could really do this; I doubted whether I really wanted to do this. Did I really want to do what it took to get significantly stronger?

The next day, I went back to Barlow's, and I did a different workout using different muscle groups. My dad was there again to help me, and I didn't want to give in or fail in front of my dad. Just having him there inspired me to push harder, because I didn't want to fall short in his eyes. I pushed myself to work just as hard as I did the day before, all the way to muscle failure, on every set. And again, I barely made it into that little locker room for a repeat performance of the day before.

But this time I felt better about it. It didn't shake me. This time I took myself there voluntarily. Each day after that, I worked just as hard. My father was there every set and every rep, encouraging me. And the bodybuilders and cops did the same. And every day I felt better and I made visible gains.

In addition to my workouts, I spent a couple of days a week at the Kerlan-Jobe Orthopaedic Clinic in Los Angeles, doing rehabilitation and therapy on my left knee. I heeded every diagnosis and did whatever the doctors told me to do, and I rested it exactly the way I was told. But I continued to work out at Barlow's, and any extra time I would have normally been on the basketball floor, I spent in the weight room.

I got stronger and stronger, and I got bigger and bigger. And because of the work I had put in, I became more confident.

When practice started in October of 1984, I was a totally different player. I returned to campus a solid and sturdy 240 pounds, and it was mostly upper-body muscle. Almost immediately my teammates started calling me "Arnold," for Arnold Schwarzenegger, and there were rumors and jokes floating around that I had to be on steroids to get that big and strong over the summer.

On the floor, I was more active, more aggressive and more productive. And I got off to a great start to the season. In the first six games of the year, I averaged more than thirteen points, shot 68 percent from the floor. But the pain in my left knee was getting worse and worse. And it was affecting everything, including how I was able to prepare to play, both mentally and physically.

Tough or Foolish?

Throughout my basketball career, I never knew whether it was called a high or a low pain threshold, but I knew I could play through a good deal of pain. Before I got to college, I never missed any time on the practice floor or in games. But I never really had to deal with constant, chronic pain.

During my sophomore year, the pain in my left knee became constant. In fact, my freshman season was my only healthy season at Duke. I played the rest of my college career with a significant knee problem, and it was something I dealt with every day. It started to become an issue during a summertime foreign tour of France after my freshman year. My left knee hurt so badly that playing and sitting down for long stretches became really painful. The pain was localized above my left kneecap, and it would not go away.

But I could still play through it, and I didn't complain about it. The doctors at Duke Medical Center told me that it was a condition called "patellar tendinitis" that was common among athletes. I was given anti-inflammatory medication, but I was told that rest, treatment and stretching were the best I could do. I was also told that this condition affected a lot of high-profile athletes, and they played with it and through it.

Of course, I figured if they could do it, I certainly could do it. Pain had never affected me before. I was tough enough to handle it and overcome it.

Grant Hill said that some players are incapable of playing through pain, and simply not tough enough. "Some guys, if they tell them they could be out up to four weeks, they're out for four weeks," Hill said. "Other guys take the mind-set to work and rehab to get back as soon as possible."

I played on that knee throughout my sophomore year, and I gobbled up anti-inflammatory medications like they were M&M's. Daily doses of Indocin and Clinoril were mainstays in my routine.

The pain could be intense at times, on and off the floor, and it was always with me. I could not sit in a car for long stretches of time, and I could not sit in class or through a movie without getting up and straightening and stretching my left leg.

The commitment to my workout program made me bigger and stronger than ever before, but I was carrying more weight than was natural for my frame. That had an impact on my knee, but I thought I was toughing it out. I spent time in the training room to rehab my knee, and I took prescribed anti-inflammatory drugs.

Even with the great start I had gotten off to in my junior year, the pain kept getting worse. I'm certain my coaches and teammates had an understanding that I was dealing with some pain, but I'm equally certain they had no idea how much pain. I occasionally talked to our trainer and to our team orthopedic surgeon about it, but for the most part, I kept it to myself.

Why? Because I thought I was tough. I was told other players played with this condition, and I didn't want to be seen as a complainer. If others played through it, so could I. I played through it and kept my mouth shut because I thought that's what tough players do.

My father never missed a day of work, and he never once complained. I knew I wasn't as tough as my father, but I knew I was strong enough to deal with and overcome pain that any other player could deal with. I took care of my responsibilities to rehab my injury, but I played, and I dealt with it.

It was my problem, and no one else's.

As my junior season wore on, the pain became almost unbearable. I had to adjust everything I did in order to keep playing. I knew something was really wrong, but I kept playing. And I kept my mouth shut about it. On two occasions I got shot up with cortisone prior to games. The shots didn't work at all.

Toward the end of my junior year, we were playing in the NCAA Tournament, and we had a practice the day before we were to meet Boston College in a second-round game in Houston, Texas.

The pain in my knee was really intense, and my first order of business was to get through practice. I was trying to be careful not to do anything that would set me back for the game the next day. That meant I had to pick my spots a bit.

We did a drill called the "Two-Man Passing Drill" in which pairs of players went up and down each side of the floor executing different kinds of passes. I was doing the drill with Johnny Dawkins, who was, in my estimation, the most important player in Duke basketball history, and an intense competitor and hard worker. He never settled for less from himself.

The very last part of "Two-Man Passing" is a full-court "baseball" pass from one player to the other, and Johnny was throwing the pass. He threw a long pass too far out in front of me, and the ball was heading straight out-of-bounds. To get that ball, I would have to sprint and come to an abrupt, complete stop on the baseline just to save it. Saving that ball meant I would suffer a jolt of pain through my knee that would not only affect me right then, but might set me back for the next day in our NCAA Tournament game.

So I decided to let the ball go.

Johnny and Coach K were both livid, and they got all over me for not going after that ball. Of course, it crossed my mind that I could tell them—and the whole team—that it was all I could do to get through practice, and that the price to be paid for going after that ball was going to be paid exclusively by me, not by them. But I didn't.

It was my issue, and I had to deal with it. And I had to take what came with it, including having others think I wasn't doing my job. I knew what the deal was. I could take it. I thought I was being tough.

The next day against Boston College, I scored fifteen points and grabbed thirteen rebounds and was named the CBS Player of the Game. I was also in the worst pain I had ever experienced as a player. But far worse than that was the fact that we lost the game by a single point, and our 1985 season was over.

Late in that season, I knew that I had too big a problem to

simply tough it out and continue to play through the pain. Around that time, I remember telling my roommate, Mark Alarie, that I must be the biggest wimp in basketball, because I just couldn't handle playing with this anymore. He said that if it was that bad, I needed to raise some hell about it. So I did.

Our team orthopedic surgeon, Dr. Frank Bassett, listened to me and said that after the season we should cut into that knee and take a look. Bassett was one of the finest orthopedic surgeons in the country and played football for Bear Bryant at Kentucky. He was a huge supporter of mine, and I trusted him. But what I didn't realize was that Bassett and all of our people had been listening all along. I wasn't saying anything. The reason nothing had been done until then wasn't the fault of the medical staff or the coaching staff; it was mine and mine alone.

Dr. Bassett scheduled a surgical procedure at Duke Medical Center, and when he cut into my knee, he told me that I had a small hole, approaching the size of a dime, in my patellar tendon. He told me he was amazed I could play on that knee, and that I could do so without complaint.

At first I thought Dr. Bassett was confirming how tough and hard-nosed I was. I felt proud when he said that. But looking back on it, I feel stupid, and he was really confirming just how stupid I was. I wasn't smart enough, or tough enough, to handle my injury the right way.

Nobody knew my body or the kind of pain I was dealing with better than I did. I knew from early on that I had a big problem, but, for the most part, I just kept my mouth shut and played through it. I figured the "tough players" play through pain and deal with it on their own, but I was wrong.

If I had spoken up earlier, and raised a little more hell about what I was going through, I could have had that surgery a year earlier, and perhaps the problem would not have been so severe. But I wasn't tough enough.

I was stupid.

The tough players don't take no for an answer, and are tough enough to ask tough questions of their doctors and trainers, and tough enough to make certain that they properly take care of their business. I didn't do that. I could have played without pain if I had pushed harder, and I could have been a better and more effective player if I had handled that better. That was nobody's fault but mine.

After the surgery, Dr. Bassett told me it would probably be a year before my knee felt the same again. There would be some pain going forward, but it would not be nearly as severe and would improve over time. I did what I was supposed to do to rehab my knee, but soon after the surgery, I was faced with a choice.

I was chosen to play for the 1985 United States National Select Team.

I had always wanted to play for USA Basketball, to wear USA across my chest, and now the opportunity to play for USA Basketball came right after my knee surgery. I didn't want to pass up that opportunity. I wanted to play.

I cannot say I regret playing, because I don't. But clearly it wasn't the *best* thing for me. The truth is, I wasn't tough enough or mature enough to do the best thing for me. I had played in pain before, and I knew I could play in some additional pain to do something I had always wanted to do: play for the U.S. National Team. Plus, at that time, I hadn't yet processed that I wasn't tough enough to do what was best.

I was about to make the same mistake again.

The USA team doctor who conducted my physical told me he was reluctant to clear me, and he said playing would, in all likelihood, set my rehab back. I told him that if he didn't think I would do further damage to my knee, I wanted to play. I told him that if I was going to have to play in pain anyway, and if it would take a year for it to be completely right again, what was the harm? The doctor saw my desire to play, and he cleared me.

But my coach didn't. I was playing for Purdue coach Gene Keady, and he told me flat-out that he wasn't going to take me overseas unless I was 100 percent. I told him I was. I went through every practice and every exhibition game without saying a word about my knee, and I never even acknowledged that it was an issue.

Well, it was an issue. My knee wasn't strong, and I was in pain. But the pain wasn't as severe as the pain I had become accustomed to in prior years, so I didn't worry too much about it. I thought I was tough, and I thought I could handle it.

When we were finished training in Los Angeles, and the night before we went overseas, Keady asked me how I felt. I told him I was 100 percent ready to play, even though that wasn't true. I just wanted to play.

Of course, playing set my recovery back. I played for more than a month on that knee without time to properly rehab it. As a result, I wasn't prepared physically to start the next season. I missed the first six games of my senior season, probably because I played for the National Team. If I had been tough enough to do what was best for me, instead of what I wanted to do, perhaps I would have played my entire senior year, perhaps I would have played pain-free, and perhaps I would have been more effective. I made a choice, but I did so without really being tough enough or mature enough to make the right choice.

I felt like I was being tough, and taking one for the team by playing on an injured knee. But I wasn't. I wasn't smart enough to listen to my body, and to discuss my injury honestly with the medical staff.

As I get older, and health becomes a bigger issue, I think about how foolish I was at that time. When I go to the doctor today, I am not timid. I ask questions, even if they are tough questions. I am totally honest with my doctor so I can get the best care. I don't ignore problems; I let the doctor know about whatever is going on. To me, that is the tougher approach.

Grant Hill summed up the issue very well. "I used to think, 'I can play through this injury. I'm tough. This is nothing,'" he said. "Well, that's not toughness. That's foolishness."

Bingo. I was just being foolish.

Toughness isn't just playing through pain but also being informed, and being tough enough to make the right decision, to know your body, and to take ownership in taking care of your body. I wasn't being tough. I was being foolish. And I paid a price for it. That might be okay if it were just me, but I believe my team paid a price for it too.

Grant Hill: A Model in Overcoming Adversity

Grant Hill's basketball career has been marked by versatility, longevity and triumph. His statistics at Duke reveal his remarkable range of talent. In four years, he averaged 14.9 points and 6.0 rebounds per game, while hitting 53 percent of his shots and 70 percent of his free throws. He went from a player whom Christian Laettner ordered not to shoot to a good three-point shooter. Hill left Duke ranked in the top ten of all time in scoring, rebounding and assists, steals, and blocked shots.

Upon Hill's arrival at Duke in 1990, the high school All-American was instantly an integral part of Coach K's team. He led the team to three NCAA title games and back-to-back NCAA championships, received the Iba Award as the nation's top defensive player and ACC Player of the Year, and was a unanimous first team All-American selection.

Grant was a Lottery selection of the Detroit Pistons in 1994, and quickly became one of the NBA's best players. In his first two seasons, Hill led all NBA players in All-Star votes and was a member of the 1996 Olympic gold medal–winning Dream Team in Atlanta.

Hill's NBA career was sidetracked by an ankle injury that required multiple surgeries between 2000 and 2004. After his last ankle surgery, Hill was hit with a life-threatening staph infection that caused a 104.5-degree fever and convulsions. His wife, R & B singer Tamia, rushed him to the hospital. The infection hospitalized him for a week and required him to endure six months of the strongest IV antibiotics available to rid his body of the bacteria.

In late 2000, Grant Hill was recovering from ankle surgery, but he knew something just wasn't right. On the court, Hill wasn't having the success to which he had become accustomed, and which had been a given. "Guys I had been *killing*—I mean guys I had been scoring forty points on—were all of a sudden killing *me*," Hill said. Because of his injuries, Hill lost confidence in his body, and in his ability to stay healthy. That loss of confidence in his body, something that had never let him down before, affected his overall confidence level.

"I lost confidence in my *game*," Hill said. "In my ability to play."

Fear and doubt were constant companions for Hill, as were the question marks about his ability to overcome his injuries and play basketball again. "Would I trust my body? Will it let me down again?" Hill said. "There was doubt that I could come back and still be effective, let alone be the player I was before."

Those years were loaded with fear and worry for Hill, but he highlighted that they were rewarding years too. During his recovery and comeback, Hill learned about himself, and gained perspective that helped him get back onto the court. "Looking back, I realized how much I had overcome to come back," Hill said. "I proved to myself that I was tough—mentally and physically." That realization gave Hill a new and special brand of self-confidence.

"For Grant, it was three and a half years of struggle to overcome the injury and the self-doubt that comes with injury," Krzyzewski said. "Along the way, he conquered internal demons. Others helped him conquer things externally and helped him get back to being a great player again."

Krzyzewski believes that Hill's value system, his principles and who he is as a person, helped fuel him to come back. "I believe Grant needed to look at himself. His motivation was that he 'owed' it," Krzyzewski said. "He would not accept a free meal. He is simply one of the most principled people I've ever known. He's the most unselfish person I've ever known."

To Krzyzewski, Hill's value system was the foundation of his toughness, and led him to come back. "He could not fathom making that much money without feeling he was somehow letting people down. He just would not accept something for nothing," Krzyzewski said. "I think he actually felt guilty about getting injured, and it motivated him to do all he did to come back."

Krzyzewski believes it was okay for Hill to get angry and to channel that anger into his recovery and into his healing. "The struggle for Grant was internal. He needed to acknowledge that he was stronger than his injuries and sickness," Krzyzewski said. "As a player, he needed somebody to help him get what was inside of him out."

Coming back from multiple surgeries and a staph infection that threatened his life, Grant Hill felt like he had overcome the biggest obstacles of his career and his life. "I had to dig deep to overcome the injuries, and all that came with them," Hill said. "I'm proud of the toughness I found inside myself, and that I showed. I am prouder of that than any basketball accomplishment."

When I talked extensively with Grant about his struggles to overcome his injuries and to come back, I couldn't help but notice his near constant use of the words "overcome" and "adapt," the words used by the United States Army that made such a profound impact upon me and my fellow coaches when visiting Camp Arifjan in the Middle East.

"Adapt and overcome."

Hill emphasized that overcoming his injuries was only part of the challenge. He had to adapt to a completely new way to play, and a new way to be effective. "I had to be tough enough to accept that I was not the same player as I was before, but I could still be effective," Hill said. "That I am still good, that I am still competitive and still have the ego of a good player."

Hill struggled to get back to who he was as a player. "It was emotional, and required mental toughness to face it and overcome it," Hill said. "It wasn't easy to stay positive. I was reading inspiring stories about Lance Armstrong and *Seabiscuit*. I watched *Rocky* a bunch of times."

One of the people Hill reached out to for help was his former coach Krzyzewski, who had made a comeback of his own in 1996 after missing most of the 1995 season due to exhaustion. "Coach K told me that he had had the same doubts, concerned that he would not be the same," Hill said. "He said that he had watched film of himself at his best, visualizing himself doing that again, because that is not only who he was, but it was who he will be again. I did the same thing."

For both Hill and Krzyzewski, it wasn't just physical; it was a mental challenge as well. And both of them worked on their mental approach in addition to rehabilitating themselves physically. "I had worked to get physically healthy, but mentally, I still had a lot to overcome," Hill said. "I needed to get back to who I am, to get that 'Eye of the Tiger' back."

Hill relishes the fact that he can still compete successfully at his age, and that he still has a lot to give. "At forty years old, I can still compete. I still enjoy it, and I still learn a lot," he said. "I am more disciplined, though. I eat right, and I take care of my body." In fact, Hill said he was in the midst of a "juice cleanse" right after the 2012 season to "detox" from some of the medications he had been taking during his eighteenth season in the NBA.

"I'm hungry." Hill laughed. "But I guess I need to be tough and push through it."

Hill has had to overcome injuries and the mental and physical hurdles that come with them, but has also had to adapt to change. The most challenging change has been delivered by Father Time. "It isn't easy being older and competing against people half your age," Hill said. "I have a different mind-set, and think a little differently in this area."

Hill refuses to concede that just because he is older, he has to slow down. Instead, he feels he just needs to be disciplined in his approach, and to be mentally tough enough to do what is necessary to be fully prepared. "I prepare differently than I used to: I eat right; I take the necessary steps to keep my body in the best possible condition. I have adapted to the changes in my body and my game, but I haven't slowed down."

Hill has also emphasized his strengths, and adapted to take better advantage of them, instead of just overcoming weaknesses. "I have a wealth of knowledge that you can't buy," Hill said. "It isn't fun having to do things differently, or not being able to do things the same way. But I am willing to prepare, to do what it takes. I am willing to work hard. I am willing to rest my body, listen to my body, work hard at it, and eat right.

"The truth is, many others aren't willing to do that. I am."

Grant Hill's willingness to do the difficult things to overcome his injuries, to overcome his doubts, and to adapt to his new reality are not just great examples of his toughness; they are his toughness. Hill has been honest with himself and he addressed his injuries, both mentally and physically, head-on. He was smart enough and tough enough to realize the difference between playing through pain and addressing injury, the difference between being tough and foolish.

In my own struggle with injury, I learned that difference, and that I needed to be tough enough to address my injury in a straightforward manner, and make certain that I was taking every reasonable step to make certain I was getting the proper care and doing things right to ensure that I was "right" physically. It isn't tough to play through an injury and pretend to be the strong, silent type. It is foolish. Tough people aren't foolish about such things. They are resilient.

CHAPTER 10

SELF-EVALUATION

Kevin Eastman, assistant coach of the Boston Celtics, is one of the finest teachers of basketball I have ever been around. Eastman believes in personal responsibility, and he believes in self-evaluation. In order to be truly tough, you have to accept the challenge of looking in the mirror and, with a clear head and clear eyes, evaluating the most important person in your life: yourself.

Eastman is constantly evaluating himself and those around him, striving to make himself and his team better. That is a measure of true toughness. Are you willing and tough enough to evaluate yourself and others honestly, and to do so to the highest of standards?

Michigan State coach Tom Izzo believes that self-evaluation is perhaps the toughest thing for any competitor to do. Izzo addresses the issue of self-evaluation with his team, and does so with regularity. "If you can't self-evaluate, to believe you need to get better—even when you are already really good—how can you truly make a difference?" Izzo said. "That is what toughness is: doing what it takes to make a difference. Toughness is not thinking or accepting that you have a ceiling, but that you have another step to take, another level to reach, another gear."

Krzyzewski wholeheartedly agrees with Izzo, and credited his belief in the importance of self-evaluation to his parents and his years at West Point playing for Bob Knight. For Krzyzewski, performance was the key, to strive to be at his best every day. But with that, Krzyzewski believes you have to honestly evaluate where you are, how you got there, and how you can get better. Even when you are at the top. "I know it sounds clichéd," Krzyzewski said, "but if you do that, it becomes a habit."

To Krzyzewski and Izzo, self-evaluation is about honesty. "You have to be honest with yourself," Krzyzewski said. "Where are we right now, and where are we going?"

After Duke was upset by Lehigh in the opening game of the 2012 NCAA Tournament, only the sixth time that a fifteen-seed had beaten a two-seed in NCAA Tournament play, Krzyzewski immediately evaluated his team, himself, and what he could do to improve and to make his team better.

"Of course, there is devastation there at first," he said. "But I refuse to stay there. I am not accepting that it is too hard, or that we're done. I accept that we didn't do a good enough job, or that we didn't play as well as we were supposed to," Krzyzewski said. "But I do not accept where we are, and I will not stay there."

Izzo echoes Krzyzewski. Izzo is among the greatest coaches in American sports and extraordinarily gifted, yet he still maintains a normal, blue-collar attitude and approach. He does not give in to complacency or self-satisfaction, and constantly self-evaluates with total candor and truthfulness to determine exactly where he is at this moment. "It isn't about blame as much as it's about accountability," Izzo said. "You evaluate where you are and who you are, but you still have higher aspirations of where you want to go. You have dreams, but you don't have illusions."

To assess oneself is not easy, and requires a certain toughness. "You need to be tough enough to challenge each other on what it takes to get there, and tough enough to actually do what it takes to get there," Izzo said. Whether a coach or a player, challenging yourself and those around you with honest appraisals requires trust and communication, issues we have discussed in detail. But the focus has to be on the most important people: you and those on your team.

Every day, North Carolina coach Roy Williams essentially gives his team and his players, as well as himself and his staff, a grade on their performance, on exactly where they are. "You evaluate your strengths and weaknesses truthfully," Williams said. "You work on shoring up your weaknesses, but you don't forget about your strengths."

Williams evaluates his team's strengths and weaknesses with regard to each individual game, not just for the season, and he isn't afraid to adjust the way his team approaches an opponent if it gives his team a better chance to win. "When we play Duke, we have to evaluate the three-point line," Williams said. "We cannot let the three-point line determine the outcome of that particular game, because that is what they do; that is Duke's strength. Our strength is to attack the basket; that's what we do." For Williams, the key in a particular game is to deny the opponent the opportunity to let its strength decide the game.

Instead, Williams's North Carolina team deals with and limits what the opponent does best, but does it without limiting what the Tar Heels do best. "We do everything we can to emphasize what we do best, and put ourselves in a position where our strength is the determining factor in the game," Williams said.

Jon Gruden always wanted the best coach coaching him, and that was Jon Gruden. "The best coach is you, coaching yourself," Gruden said. "You have to look yourself straight in the mirror and ask yourself if you are doing the best you can do, if you are as self-disciplined and self-motivated as you possibly can be. You always have to evaluate yourself first."

Kansas coach Bill Self believes self-evaluation is most important in the areas of effort and concentration. "I don't screw around with the players' minds regarding their ability or skills," Self said. "I want them confident in their abilities and believing that I believe in them. But I do challenge them on effort and concentration. What is more important than effort and concentration? Nothing."

For Izzo and Krzyzewski, self-evaluation goes far beyond the result of any game. It is about an honest approach to preparing to achieve excellence, and doing it consistently. "The first question you ask yourself is, 'What are you preparing for?'" Izzo said. "Are you preparing to win the game? Or are you preparing to be the best you can be, to be excellent? What is the ultimate goal?"

For Bob Knight, having a coach spearheading the effort to self-evaluate is essential. "I think self-evaluation can be hard for a player, because players usually have a more inflated sense of themselves than the coach," Knight said. "I want players that are willing to listen, honestly evaluate it, then act upon what they are told." But, Knight adds, a crucial element in self-evaluation and communicating the message to others is "why." "In teaching and evaluating, I always tell them why," Knight said. "Always."

Williams agrees, and strives to teach everything, including the reasons behind every action, every drill and every evaluation. "I want to tell them why, and explain why we do everything we do," Williams said. "I don't want my players asking why, but I guess what I'm really saying is this: I don't want them to have to ask. I want to take care of that in my teaching, to make the why a part of the process so they don't have to ask." Williams believes that his team's trust and confidence levels are related to how well he teaches. To Williams, the better he teaches, the more trust and confidence he builds. "And the more confidence and trust you build," Williams said, "the tougher your players can be."

Knight appreciates the importance of well-instructed players, but also welcomes their questions on the importance of a particular play or drill. "Why is not a question asked by a pain in the ass," Knight said. "Why is asked by a smart person, a smart player, a tough player. They need to know why."

Herm Edwards believes that players should do more than that. "Coaches can teach you what to do, but the great players, the tough players, *demand* to know why," Edwards said. When a player is willing to demand of himself to know and fully understand the "why" behind what he is being asked to do, that player and his team can hit another level. To Edwards, too many talented players feel like they don't have to learn the game. Too many players believe their talent will carry them through. Edwards sees that as a ticket to failure. Every player, no matter how talented, has to adjust in any game. When a team has talented players who understand the game and their place in it, and can adjust, you have special players, and a special team.

"We talk so much about talent, about the splash play, the Sports-Center play," Edwards said. "We are so enamored with that. Players grow up without knowing the game, without studying the game, truly understanding the game. That takes toughness too."

When Edwards was in college, asking "why" of a coach was even tougher than it is today. "I was a black player at Cal in 1972," Edwards said. "When I asked why, the coach would look back at me and say, 'Are you uncoachable? You're asking why?! Just do it. You do it because I said so, that's why.' By [my] asking why, they thought I was questioning their authority."

Edwards believes that teaching players why they are doing something, rather than just ordering them to do it, allows them to take ownership of what they are trying to accomplish individually and together as a team. "Knowing why gives them the tools to go out and execute it without hesitation," Edwards said. Knowing why allows the players to trust it, and when they trust it, they won't question it under stress.

To two-time U.S. Open golf champion Curtis Strange, self-evaluation is "paramount." Strange links self-evaluation to caring about what you are doing, and believing that it has great importance to you. "I hate it when people say athletes don't care," Strange said. "I cared about every shot. And I cared enough to prepare." Whether Strange performed well or poorly in a golf tournament or a practice session, he immediately wanted to analyze it and to learn from the "feeling" of a shot, or of how he reacted to a particular moment. "How did I feel over that shot?" Strange asked. "How will it feel when I am over it again? What do I need to do to handle that better the next time—because there will be a next time. I craved for there to be a next time."

Self-evaluation is a necessary part of a tough person's preparation. "It takes mental toughness to prepare every day, not just to win this game, but to do what it takes to be excellent, the best," Izzo said. "If you prepare to be the best every day, the games will take care of themselves. Preparation to be excellent can be grueling, because you aren't rewarded right then, at the time. It is a tough, hard thing to prepare yourself to be excellent. That takes self-evaluation."

Krzyzewski doesn't allow the final result to mask the important lessons, positive and negative, of the game or practice. "I don't care if you hit the last shot to win; it doesn't erase the plays before it," Krzyzewski said. "You still need to evaluate exactly how things are and not be fooled by the final result. You can't let wins and losses totally define the quality of performance and your progress, or whether you have met your standards."

Successful players and teams don't just appraise themselves by records or statistics, but by a standard of excellence that goes beyond a final score. Self-evaluation takes honesty, and the toughest teams and players do not con themselves. When I was playing for Coach K, he was often harder on us after a win than after a loss. He would identify areas of concern for our team and for individuals as "slippage" from our standards, and he was quick to point out that a lesser performance might have beaten our latest opponent, but it would not beat the best teams coming up in the future.

We weren't just playing against an opponent; we were playing to a standard. And it was a standard of excellence. Coach K expected us to give championship effort in every minute of every game, and in every drill in every practice. Even if we were ahead by thirty points and just mopping up, there was no such thing as "garbage time" for Coach K. Every minute of playing time was earned, and it was to be valued. And if we were down, Coach K expected his players to fight to the last possession and play through the buzzer to the highest standard.

Even though we would never play the perfect game, we strove to play perfectly, and give perfect effort.

I have never heard Coach K say, "A win is a win." He simply doesn't look at it that way. If we played poorly in a win, he was upset by the standard of play, and it could feel like we had lost the game. The environment around practice after such a performance was just like a loss. And in a very real way, it was: It was a lost opportunity. As a team and individuals, we moved on to the next thing, but we examined exactly where we were, where our deficiencies were, and took measures to correct our mistakes and improve as individuals and as a team.

Early on in our playing careers under Coach K, we would think, *What is he so worked up over? We won.* As a coach and a leader, he was thinking, *If we play this way against the best teams, we will not win. This effort won this game, but won't win against the very best competition.* Coach K often told us that our style of play or "system" was designed to beat the best teams. It depended upon how we performed in it. And we could not be fooled into thinking that everything was okay just because we won. We needed to be tough enough to evaluate ourselves honestly, especially after a win.

Coach K always told us he would never lie to us. But he also wanted each of his players to be real with himself. "Whatever success we have had, that is the biggest part of it," Krzyzewski said. "We address what just happened honestly and directly, we make corrections, and we move on together."

It is difficult not to be blinded by the bright lights of victory. But tough teams and tough people aren't fooled by winning, rather are still able to clearly evaluate areas of improvement, and never lose sight of their standards. It is much easier to take a hard, objective look at yourself after a loss than after a win. Winning masks a lot of problems and allows a lot of people to cheat themselves. In order to effectively address potential problems or issues, you need to confront them early. You need to do so while winning, and not wait for a crisis. Winning or having success can make you feel satisfied and complacent.

Harvard coach Tommy Amaker believes it takes a tougher person to move on after accomplishing something great, rather than after suffering through disappointment. It is easier to dedicate yourself to getting better after a failure, but harder to strive to get better after a triumph, when complacency and self-satisfaction can take over. Under Amaker, Harvard has experienced unprecedented basketball success. After tying for the 2011 Ivy League title for the first time in Harvard's history, an extraordinary and historic achievement, Harvard faced expectations for its greatest season ever, and Amaker knew that those expectations could get in the way of his team, if they allowed it.

Harvard not only met the expectation; it exceeded them. The Crimson finished the 2012 season with a stunning record of 26–5 and reached the NCAA Tournament for the first time since 1946. During the season, Harvard was ranked in the top twenty-five for the first time ever, and had attained such a lofty basketball reputation that, when the Crimson were twice beaten on the road, the opposing crowds stormed the floor to celebrate. Beating Harvard had become that meaningful.

For Amaker, the success achieved in 2012 was a measure of his team's collective toughness, and its willingness to learn while winning, to self-evaluate and to hold itself to its own standards. "It took some real toughness for our group to stay focused and meet our internal standards when external expectations were so high," Amaker said. "We accomplished a lot of 'firsts' in our history."

Amaker's team bought in, trusted each other and believed. But how do you get people to buy in and believe? In my experience, it is important that each member of the team invest in and take ownership of their personal development, the development and acceptance of their roles, and the development of the team. That kind of investment and ownership is not something that is demonstrated once and you are done with it; it has to be nurtured and emphasized every day. It has to be evaluated constantly.

Having recognized standards is important in self-evaluation. When Mike Montgomery was coaching at Stanford, I went to Palo Alto to watch his team practice and play. When Montgomery took me into the Stanford locker room, one of the first things I saw was a framed list of team standards and goals, and each member of the Stanford basketball team, including the managers and coaches, had signed it. The team had come up with the standards they expected to meet and the milestones they expected to reach that season.

At certain times when the team may have been falling short of those standards, Montgomery or any player could point to them and emphasize that they were not some directive from above; those were the standards they had all agreed to meet. They did not agree to meet them when they felt like it, or once in a while, but every day.

"Toughness is the ability to go from 'bought in' to 'locked in,'" Indiana coach Tom Crean said. "What it takes for you and your team, on a daily basis, to lock into what will make you better and make us better. How willing are you to absorb the mentality of change, contact and challenge?"

To Crean, too many people waste their time talking about buying in, instead of focusing on what it takes. "There are a lot of fakes in basketball—in any business, really," Crean said. "People talk about buying in, but most people really don't. It's just too hard. But if they do, if they lock in, the rewards are incredible, almost indescribable."

To "lock in" to toughness, to the principles and values discussed in this book, I believe that you have to commit to honestly and objectively assessing just how tough you are right now, where you have met your standard and where you have fallen short of it, and you have to address what you need to do, and are willing to do, to consistently meet that standard of toughness. In my own personal journey, I have fallen short many times of the standard of toughness I value and expect of myself, and that those around me value and expect of me. But through learned self-awareness, I strive to pick myself up and do better.

I know that I am capable of true toughness. I believe we are all capable of exhibiting the kind of toughness valued and emphasized in this book. I also accept that I am not as tough as I want to be, and that I have to continue to strive, every day, to be tougher—for myself, my team, and my family. Toughness isn't about bravado. It is about meeting challenges head-on and not shrinking from them. And when I get knocked down, I strive to be tough enough to get up and keep fighting. Based upon the principles in this book, those that I have learned from so many great people in my life, I know that I am tougher than I used to be, and I can and will be tougher tomorrow than I am today.

We can all be tougher, and we can be tougher together.

HOPE

Like any young kid, I started playing sports because it was fun. I looked forward to playing ball not because I was trying to set a record or achieve a goal, but because I truly enjoyed it. Playing ball was joyful. It was just plain *fun*.

Somewhere along the way, outside influences became attached to the playing of games. What was once just about innocent fun and enjoyment of the game suddenly became about other things. My identity as a person became wrapped up in the sport I played, and my performances seemed to be constant measures of my character and toughness. Expectations and influences of others began to creep into my play.

Those measurements and expectations brought pressure. Pressure brought tension. And tension is the enemy of performance.

I once had a baseball coach who said, "Having fun is doing hard things well." Even though we were working hard, striving to reach a level of excellence and desperately trying to win, we were supposed to be having fun. He told us the harder we worked, the more fun we would have.

When I was playing for Mike Krzyzewski at Duke, there was intense pressure, both internally and externally. His standards were high, and it was not easy to meet those standards on a daily basis. But Coach K worked hard to eliminate any outside distractions that could detract from our ability to perform. The standards that mattered were ours, not anyone else's.

Once, at the end of a hellacious, close, hard-fought game against archrival North Carolina, Coach K knelt down in our tense, pressure-packed huddle. I think we all expected a fiery statement from him, loud and with veins popping out of his neck, on the raw intensity and toughness we needed to finish this game and win it.

Instead, Coach K surprised us. He looked right at us, smiled and said, "Isn't this fun?!"

His message was clear, and it had a relaxing effect in such a frenzied, tense and pressure-filled environment: *This is important and we have a job to do, so play your ass off, and play to win.* He was reminding us to embrace and enjoy the richness of the experience and to savor the journey, in both peaks and valleys. This is a game that is supposed to be fun. So let's make it fun.

Having fun is doing hard things well.

When I look back, none of my fondest memories are of easy games. They are of the tough games, the games and practices when we had to lay it on the line, and things were the toughest. In my broadcasting career and my career as a lawyer, none of my favorite memories are of when everything went smoothly. They are of when something unexpected happened, especially in the biggest games and cases, and we were able to rise up and meet the challenge. Those were the most fun and the most rewarding challenges, and that was why we prepared so hard. I always try to remind myself to embrace those moments as fun.

What I am really talking about is proper perspective. Perspective is part of toughness too.

My friend Steve Kerr has great perspective in life and, as demonstrated by his insights in this book, tremendous toughness as well.

Steve is a five-time NBA champion with the Chicago Bulls and San Antonio Spurs, and a fifteen-year NBA veteran. Kerr is one of only two men in NBA history to play on four consecutive NBA title teams.

Steve Kerr is the son of Malcolm Kerr, the noted political scientist, professor and expert on Middle East politics at UCLA who later became the president of American University of Beirut in Beirut, Lebanon. Steve was born in Beirut, and lived for a time in Cairo, Egypt, before finishing high school at Palisades High School in Los Angeles, California. Kerr was lightly recruited out of Palisades, and accepted his only major scholarship offer to play basketball at Arizona for Lute Olson.

On January 18, 1984, during his freshman season at Arizona, Malcolm Kerr was assassinated outside of his American University office in Beirut. He was fifty-two years old.

Kerr credits his father for instilling toughness in him, and for teaching him about what is truly important in life. "In my life, the toughest person I ever knew was my father," Kerr said. "My dad wasn't an athlete, other than being a recreational athlete. But he was a tough guy."

Kerr's father taught at UCLA during Kerr's formative years. "He wrote books and was very outspoken on Middle East politics," Kerr said. When Kerr was a thirteen-year-old seventh grader, he was awakened when the family car was lit on fire in the driveway of the Kerr home. Those responsible had been angered by something Malcolm Kerr had written that was taken as sympathetic to the Arab cause.

"I was really freaked out by it," Kerr recalled, "and I remember my dad was so calm and matter-of-fact about it. He was so light-hearted, and tried to use humor in that situation. I learned to deal with adversity because of the example my father set for me." Throughout his life, because of his father's example, Kerr says he always tries to keep things "light" and in the right perspective, and Kerr believes that is one of the unheralded hallmarks of toughness.

"Keeping things in proper perspective is really important to me, and I think it is a form of toughness, really," Kerr said. That was especially true in his basketball career. "I was playing a game, and I was paid to play."

Throughout his career, Kerr would constantly remind himself to keep things in perspective, to lean on things he could count on to help him limit or put aside distractions. "I wanted to push aside the things that could get in my way or trip me up, if I allowed it," he said. "I had to get those things out of my way, and get out of my own way, by not allowing myself to think about those things.

"Maybe that's positive thinking," Kerr said. "For me, it was keeping things in proper perspective."

In my life, proper perspective was taught to me by my mother. When I was little, I was walking with her from the grocery store to the car at the Peninsula Center, a shopping area near our home. Heading into the grocery store was a lady about my mom's age pushing a wheelchair with a young girl about my age.

As we passed each other, my mother noticed that I was uncomfortable, and that I had looked away. After we had passed, she gently told me something I have never forgotten.

"It's okay for you to look. That little girl is no different from you," my mother said. "That's real life. You're really lucky. You haven't had to deal with real life yet."

I have never forgotten that.

It takes incredible toughness to deal with real life on a daily basis, and to do it with compassion and commitment. Nobody I know deals with real life more often and displays more true toughness in doing it than Dr. Henry Friedman.

When I came up with the idea for this book on toughness, one of the first people I thought of was Henry Friedman. I have known him a long time, and I knew that he could illuminate the concept of toughness unlike any other person I knew. I believed that Friedman had a unique perspective on life and toughness. The truth is, I had no earthly idea.

Friedman is a neuro-oncologist and the Deputy Director of the Preston Robert Tisch Brain Tumor Center, and professor of neuro-oncology at Duke University Medical Center. Routinely he has to provide life-altering news: that the patient sitting across from him has a brain tumor with a frightening prognosis.

"We lose the majority of our patients," Friedman said. "They die. And burnout rates of our providers are really high, somewhere in the range of twenty-five percent within twenty years. It isn't easy for anyone involved." For Friedman, the roller coaster of emotions really takes off upon diagnosis of a brain tumor. And it does not just involve the patient.

"The dynamics are different," Friedman said. "It is life-altering for the patient and for the family. It is, in every respect, a family diagnosis." The deep impact of the diagnosis of a brain tumor affects every member of the family in a different way, and raises profound questions. The first question, after the blow of shock and numbness, is "What's going to happen?"

The patients ask whether they will be there for their families, whether they will live to see the milestones of life, like a graduation or a wedding. Spouses ask whether they will lose their husband or wife, whether they will be alone, and how they can support a family by themselves. For the children of brain tumor patients, the experiences can be nightmarish. Those children have to process that their invulnerable protectors could be gone, sick or compromised.

The permutations are endless, and it is a scary, emotional ride, Freidman said. In his practice, professional people, psychologists and therapists, are involved early to support each patient's treatment. The issues to process are hard to fathom.

"It is a total and abrupt change in life," Freidman said. "All priorities change in an instant. Yesterday it was what to have for dinner or who won the ball game, or your dress for the prom. Now it's, 'What can I do to survive?' and, 'What is my condition?'"

For doctors, nurses and clinicians, the daily tragedy of catastrophic illness is extraordinarily difficult, and dealing with it requires a special kind of toughness. "You see such pathos, such horrible things," Freidman said. "You cannot help but grieve. But you can't grieve. You just can't.

"You have to have compassion, sympathy and empathy, but there is a line you cannot cross," Freidman said. "To be effective for your patients, especially over time, we have to find ways to protect ourselves and not get burned out by grieving." Friedman says he and his colleagues have to build up a "protective armor" over years of practice so they can overcome what they see, and so they can continue to be effective through such hardship.

But, Friedman says, no matter how hard you try, there are still chinks in that armor. When a patient looks like someone the provider knows or loves, that can hit very close to home. "It's incredible," Friedman said. "You feel pain and suffering in a very profound way."

Doctors and nurses have to take refuge in anything they can because the majority of their patients die. "We have to build up a core resiliency to not die a little ourselves each time," Friedman said. "You need tremendous toughness and will to fight these battles, and they are arduous battles.

"We have to focus on individual cases, but also a large number of patients," Friedman said. "It is tough to get our weekly memo that says, 'We regret to inform you that the following patients have died,' or whatever the phrasing is. It is really tough. We take care of someone, and we lost them. But we have to continue the battle. The fight doesn't stop, and we can't stop. It is an incredible challenge."

Friedman's philosophy on the foundation of true toughness is simple, and it is surprising: hope. Friedman believes that you cannot be truly tough without first having and embracing hope.

"I believe the most important thing in any endeavor is hope," Friedman said. "You cannot believe it is hopeless, because if you do, it is."

When a patient gets bad news, Friedman's immediate focus is

on hope, a positive outcome for that patient. "It is curable until proven otherwise. That is not the norm in our field. The majority believe that there is no hope, that you are a corpse upon diagnosis. That just perpetuates mediocre care, and makes them look smart when the gloomy prognosis comes true. But we want to win. We want survivors."

Hope is what Friedman believes makes him tougher, and makes his patients tougher. Friedman believes too many patients and medical professionals give up before they even start the fight. "If you have a team and you truly believe you can't win, you shouldn't even play," Friedman said. "But if you believe you can win, and you will win, you have a chance."

According to Freidman, hope is what gives providers and patients the toughness necessary to fight the fight. "You can't be tough without hope, a hope based upon the belief of a positive outcome." Friedman said that any athlete and any coach first starts with a foundation of hope. He asks how one can believe something can be accomplished without first having hope that it can be done. To Friedman, everything ultimately rests upon hope.

"We work from a foundation of hope," he said. "And it is more than just a cure today. If we can't cure you today, you must stay alive longer to take advantage of newer interventions that will come along to meet the needs we cannot meet today. The longer you live, the better chance you have to take advantage of our advances. Things will develop in your area of need. You need to fight to stick around to take advantage of them."

When I first spoke to Friedman about the concept of toughness, he stopped me in midsentence and told me that I needed to talk to a patient of his named Sabrina Lewandowski. He said that I would never know it by simply looking at her, but Lewandowski was tougher than any football player or basketball player I could ever find. In fact, Friedman said, if I took the toughest football players in the NFL and locked them in a room with Lewandowski, and only one of them could fight their way out, his money would be on Lewandowski.

In early 2002, Friedman first encountered Sabrina Lewandowski, and she came in a very small, blond, and dainty little package. Sabrina was a thirty-year-old fourth-grade teacher at Weatherstone Elementary School in Cary, North Carolina. She had woken up one morning with an intense headache that would not go away. In February of 2002, Sabrina was diagnosed with a grade-four glioblastoma multiforme, the deadliest form of brain cancer.

"At first, I was just in shock," Lewandowski said. "Here I was, being referred to as a corpse. I felt like I was down in a deep hole, and all I could think about was digging out. I'm going to get out."

Lewandowski believed she was strong, and that her attitude was everything. "I wasn't going to be a pushover. I don't look the part—I don't look tough," she admitted. "I'm thin, blond and nice. I'm actually one of the nicest people I know. But I am tough."

The hardest part for Lewandowski, at least initially, was telling her parents. "That was the toughest thing by far," she said. "I had to hold it together so they wouldn't crumble. I had to be strong and fight, because I was driving them through hell with me. I knew I could handle it. I just knew it."

Lewandowski had massive brain surgery at Duke in 2002, with a resection of her right frontal lobe. She immediately started a regimen of chemotherapy and radiation under Freidman's supervision. Four days after her discharge from the hospital following her surgery, Lewandowski had to go back to the hospital for a follow-up appointment with Dr. Friedman. She felt physically weak, to the point of being numb. When she arrived at the hospital with her family, she had no idea where to go. "We went through some automatic doors and I saw wheelchairs," she said. "It was a long walk, so I figured, why not? We took a wheelchair."

When Lewandowski saw Friedman, he had a very pointed question. "He said, 'What's the matter with your legs? You had brain surgery, not leg surgery.' Right away, I knew he wasn't going to cut me any slack. I had to be tough because he expected me to fight every step of the way."

Once they sat down, Friedman asked Lewandowski what she knew about brain tumors.

"Nothing, really," she said.

"Good. Don't go online and research it, because it will just say you'll be dead within six months," Friedman said. "It has been the same story for thirty years. We are focused on curing you. We have a plan A. If that doesn't work, we'll go to plan B. If that isn't effective, we'll go to plan C." With that, Dr. Friedman gave her hope, and Lewandowski said it served as fuel for her toughness.

Lewandowski suffered with neutropenia—a condition of the immune system—and lost her hair, but her hope remained steadfast. "Henry gave me the gift of hope," Lewandowski said about Friedman. "He told me he believed in me and he would stand by me. Henry comes across as brusque at first. But he has an amazing heart while at the same time being tough and driven. He inspired me."

Although glioblastoma has a survival rate of only 9 percent, Friedman told Sabrina there was reason for hope. "I told her that the diagnosis was not a death sentence. There was still an opportunity for a positive outcome."

Lewandowski embraced that hope, to the point that she looked up the word "hope" in the dictionary. But when she read the definition, she was disappointed. "The dictionary definition of 'hope' was so lame," she said. She decided to look up the word that was the opposite of hope, which was "despair," to help put hope into better perspective.

When Lewandowski read the definition of despair, the meaning of hope became that much more powerful. Despair was defined as "gloom; disheartenment; discouragement; hopelessness; total loss which may cause one to be passive or drive one to furious efforts; desperation; the abandonment of hope." The definition of despair helped Sabrina grasp the meaning of hope.

It was hope that kept Lewandowski tough and kept her going.

"Knowing the facts helped me step it up, to get tougher," Lewandowski said. "The percentages were not encouraging, but I thought, 'If it's possible, why not me?'"

There were incredibly difficult challenges along the way. Lewandowski endured a year of aggressive chemotherapy and thirty-three days of radiation therapy. "Radiation was tough stuff," Lewandowski said. "They put a mesh mask over my face, like a papier-mâché mask of me, and they would bolt it to the table. I couldn't move at all. I would just take myself to a different place. Sometimes I'd count, because I knew exactly how long it would usually take. I did anything I could to get myself through it."

Apart from telling her mom and dad, the hardest part was losing her hair, Lewandowski said. "I'm not a vain person, but when I lost my hair, that threw me. I looked in the mirror, and for the first time I saw an ill person looking back at me. That was really hard to overcome."

She met other brain tumor patients in different stages of recovery, and she witnessed many losing battles. Most of the patients undergoing treatment with her did not survive. As much as it crushed her, she knew she could not focus on those who might be fighting losing battles. To Sabrina, that simply was not going to be her. She was one of the 9 percent. "I had to keep myself separate from that," she said. "That was really difficult to do.

"But when you're in it and committed, you get used to the idea," Lewandowski said. "It was what I had to do, and I was determined to succeed. I was totally committed to doing what I needed to do just to have a chance."

Friedman emphasized to me that, even though my experience and touchstone was athletics, he could fathom no athlete who could understand or match the toughness of Sabrina Lewandowski. "No disrespect, but few if any of them have any clue of how tough that young lady is."

Lewandowski acknowledges her toughness. "It's not a competition, but I do know that I'm as tough as anyone, any football player, anyone," Lewandowski said. "I know it. I can prove it."

Yet, after all that she has been through, Lewandowski believes the brain tumor has been a real positive in her life. "It has helped me live a whole and meaningful life. I have met great people, an amazing network of great people, and I learned a lot about myself. I learned how tough I really was.

"I fought and I'm still here."

On February 9, 2012, just ten years after being diagnosed with a brain tumor, Sabrina Lewandowski and her husband welcomed a baby girl, Layla Grace, into the world. And she did so in remission, as a cancer survivor.

Lewandowski is proud of creating a new life after fighting so hard for her own, she said. And her toughness has inspired her health care providers. "Sabrina came back to Duke to give a presentation, and at the end of the presentation, she and her husband brought out the new baby," Friedman said. "All of us tough doctors, myself included, fell apart crying, and all looked in wonder at the next generation from a woman that wasn't supposed to be here—a woman who was 'incurable.'

"She is here because of hope, and the toughness that came from that hope," Friedman said. "I really believe that."

I have been so lucky to have learned about toughness from so many amazing people. With all of the tremendous coaches and athletes I have had the honor to be around, who would have ever thought that the most profound lessons in true toughness—and hope—would come from a fourth-grade teacher and her doctor.

Sabrina Lewandowski and Henry Friedman inspire me to be tougher, and to keep everything in its proper perspective. What difficulty could I possibly encounter that would approach what they have had to overcome? If I ever do have to fight such difficulties, I have great role models of true toughness to further inspire me. For that, I am truly grateful.

DEFINING TOUGHNESS IN COLLEGE HOOPS

By Jay Bilas
January 29, 2009
ESPN.com

I have heard the word "toughness" thrown around a lot lately.
Reporters on television, radio and in print have opined about a
team or player's "toughness" or quoted a coach talking about
his team having to be "tougher" to win.

Then, in almost coordinated fashion, I would watch games and see
player upon player thumping his chest after a routine play, angrily
taunting an opponent after a blocked shot, getting into a shouting
match with an opposing player, or squaring up nose-to-nose as if a
fight might ensue. I see players jawing at each other, trying to
"intimidate" other players. What a waste of time. That is nothing
more than fake toughness, and it has no real value.

I often wonder: Do people really understand what coaches and
experienced players mean when they emphasize "toughness" in
basketball? Or is it just some buzzword that is thrown around
haphazardly without clear definition or understanding? I thought it
was the latter, and I wrote a short blog item about it a couple of
weeks ago.

The response I received was overwhelming. Dozens of college
basketball coaches called to tell me that they had put the article up
in the locker room, put it in each player's locker, or had gone over it
in detail with their teams.

Memphis coach John Calipari called to say that he had his players post the definition of toughness over their beds because he believed that true "toughness" was the one thing that his team needed to develop to reach its potential. I received messages from high school coaches who wanted to relate the definition of toughness to their players and wanted to talk about it further.

Well, I got the message that I should expound upon what I consider toughness to be. It may not be what you think.

Toughness is something I had to learn the hard way, and something I had no real idea of until I played college basketball. When I played my first game in college, I thought that toughness was physical and based on how much punishment I could dish out and how much I could take. I thought I was tough.

I found out pretty quickly that I wasn't, but I toughened up over time, and I got a pretty good understanding of toughness through playing in the ACC, for USA Basketball, in NBA training camps, and as a professional basketball player in Europe. I left my playing career a heck of a lot tougher than I started it, and my only regret is that I didn't truly "get it" much earlier.

When I faced a tough opponent, I wasn't worried that I would get hit—I was concerned that I would get sealed on ball reversal by a tough post man, or that I would get boxed out on every play, or that my assignment would sprint the floor on every possession and get something easy on me. The toughest guys I had to guard were the ones who made it tough on me.

Toughness has nothing to do with size, physical strength or athleticism. Some players may be born tough, but I believe that toughness is a skill, and it is a skill that can be developed and improved. Michigan State coach Tom Izzo always says, "Players play, but tough players win." He is right. Here are some of the ways true toughness is exhibited in basketball:

Set a good screen: The toughest players to guard are the players who set good screens. When you set a good screen, you are improving the chances for a teammate to get open, and you are greatly improving your chances of getting open. A good screen can force the defense to make a mistake. A lazy or bad screen is a waste of everyone's time and energy. To be a tough player, you need to be a "screener/scorer," a player who screens hard and immediately looks for an opportunity on offense. On the 1984 U.S. Olympic team, Bob Knight made Michael Jordan set a screen before he could get a shot. If it is good enough for Jordan, arguably the toughest player ever, it is good enough for you.

Set up your cut: The toughest players make hard cuts, and set up their cuts. Basketball is about deception. Take your defender one way, and then plant the foot opposite the direction you want to go and cut hard. A hard cut may get you a basket, but it may also get a teammate a basket. If you do not make a hard cut, you will not get anyone open. Setting up your cut, properly reading the defense, and making a hard cut requires alertness, good conditioning and good concentration. Davidson's Stephen Curry is hardly a physical muscleman, but he is a tough player, because he is in constant motion, he changes speeds, he sets up his cuts and he cuts hard. Curry is hard to guard, and he is a tough player.

Talk on defense: The toughest players talk on defense, and communicate with their teammates. It is almost impossible to talk on defense and not be in a stance, down and ready, with a vision of man and ball. If you talk, you let your teammates know you are there, and make them and yourself better defenders. It also lets your opponent know that you are fully engaged.

Jump to the ball: When on defense, the tough defenders move as the ball moves. The toughest players move on the flight of the ball, not when it gets to its destination. And the toughest players jump to the ball and take away the ball side of the cut. Tough players don't let cutters cut across their face—they make the cutter change his path.

Don't get screened: No coach can give a player the proper footwork to get through every screen. Tough players have a sense of urgency not to get screened and to get through screens so that the cutter cannot catch the ball where he wants to. A tough player makes the catch difficult.

Get your hands up: A pass discouraged is just as good as a pass denied. Tough players play with their hands up to take away vision, to get deflections and to discourage a pass in order to allow a teammate to cover up. Cutters and post players will get open, if only for a count. If your hands are up, you can keep the passer from seeing a momentary opening.

Play the ball. See your man: Most defenders see the ball and hug their man, because they are afraid to get beaten. A tough defender plays the ball and sees his man. There is a difference.

Get on the floor: In my first road game as a freshman, there was a loose ball that I thought I could pick up and take the other way for an easy one. While I was bending over at the waist, one of my opponents dived on the floor and got possession of the ball. My coach was livid. We lost possession of the ball because I wasn't tough enough to get on the floor for it. I tried like hell never to get out-toughed like that again.

Close out under control: It is too easy to fly at a shooter and think you are a tough defender. A tough defender closes out under control, takes away a straight line drive and takes away the shot. A tough player has a sense of urgency but has the discipline to do it the right way.

Post your man, not a spot: Most post players just blindly run to the low block and get into a shoving match for a spot on the floor. The toughest post players are posting their defensive man. A tough post player is always open, and working to get the ball to the proper angle to get a post feed. Tough post players seal on ball reversal and call for the ball, and they continue to post strong even if their teammates miss them.

Run the floor: Tough players sprint the floor, which drags the defense and opens up things for others. Tough players run hard and get "easy" baskets, even though there is nothing easy about them. Easy baskets are hard to get. Tough players don't take tough shots— they work hard to make them easy.

Play so hard, your coach has to take you out: I was a really hard worker in high school and college. But I worked and trained exceptionally hard to make playing easier. I was wrong. I once read that Bob Knight had criticized a player of his by saying, "You just want to be comfortable out there!" Well, that was me, and when I read that, it clicked with me. I needed to work to increase my capacity for work, not to make it easier to play. I needed to work in order to be more productive in my time on the floor. Tough players play so hard that their coaches have to take them out to get rest so they can put them back in. The toughest players don't pace themselves.

Get to your teammate first: When your teammate lays his body on the line to dive on the floor or take a charge, the tough players get to him first to help him back up. If your teammate misses a free throw, tough players get to him right away. Tough players are also great teammates.

Take responsibility for your teammates: Tough players expect a lot from their teammates, but they also put them first. When the bus leaves at nine a.m., tough players not only get themselves there, but they also make sure their teammates are up and get there too. Tough players take responsibility for others in addition to themselves. They make sure their teammates eat first, and they give credit to their teammates before taking it themselves.

Take a charge: Tough players are in a stance, playing the ball, and alert in coming over from the weak side and taking a charge. Tough players understand the difference between being in the right spot and being in the right spot with the intention of stopping somebody. Some players will look puzzled and say, "But I was in the right spot." Tough players know that they have to get to the right spot with the sense of urgency to stop someone.

Get in a stance: Tough players don't play straight up and down and put themselves in the position of having to get ready to get ready. Tough players are down in a stance on both ends of the floor, with feet staggered and ready to move. Tough players are the aggressors, and the aggressor is in a stance.

Finish plays: Tough players don't just get fouled; they get fouled and complete the play. They don't give up on a play or assume that a teammate will do it. A tough player plays through to the end of the play and works to finish every play.

Work on your pass: A tough player doesn't have his passes deflected. A tough player gets down, pivots, pass-fakes, and works to get the proper angle to pass away from the defense and deliver the ball.

Throw yourself into your team's defense: A tough player fills his tank on the defensive end, not on offense. A tough player is not deterred by a missed shot. A tough player values his performance first by how well he defended.

Take and give criticism the right way: Tough players can take criticism without feeling the need to answer back or give excuses. They are open to getting better and expect to be challenged and hear tough things. You will never again in your life have the opportunity you have now at the college level: a coaching staff that is totally and completely dedicated to making you and your team better. Tough players listen and are not afraid to say what other teammates may not want to hear, but need to hear.

Show strength in your body language: Tough players project confidence and security with their body language. They do not hang their heads, do not react negatively to a mistake of a teammate, and do not whine and complain to officials. Tough players project strength, and do not cause their teammates to worry about them. Tough players do their jobs, and their body language communicates that to their teammates—and to their opponents.

Catch and face: Teams that press and trap are banking on the receiver's falling apart and making a mistake. When pressed, tough players set up their cuts, cut hard to an open area and present themselves as a receiver to the passer. Tough players catch, face the defense and make the right read and play, and they do it with poise. Tough players do not just catch and dribble; they catch and face.

Don't get split: If you trap, a tough player gets shoulder-to-shoulder with his teammate and does not allow the handler to split the trap and gain an advantage on the back side of the trap.

Be alert: Tough players are not "cool." Tough players are alert and active, and tough players communicate with teammates so that they are alert too. Tough players echo commands until everyone is on the same page. They understand the best teams play five as one. Tough players are alert in transition and get back to protect the basket and the three-point line. Tough players don't just run back to find their man; they run back to stop the ball and protect the basket.

Concentrate, and encourage your teammates to concentrate: Concentration is a skill, and tough players work hard to concentrate on every play. Tough players go as hard as they can for as long as they can.

It's not your shot; it's our shot: Tough players don't take bad shots, and they certainly don't worry about getting "my" shots. Tough players work for good shots and understand that it is not "my" shot; it is "our" shot. Tough players celebrate when "we" score.

Box out and go to the glass every time: Tough players are disciplined enough to lay a body on someone. They make first contact and go after the ball. And tough players do it on every possession, not just when they feel like it. They understand that defense is not complete until they secure the ball.

Take responsibility for your actions: Tough players make no excuses. They take responsibility for their actions. Take James Johnson, for example. With seventeen seconds to go in Wake's game against Duke, Jon Scheyer missed a three-pointer that bounced right to Johnson. But instead of aggressively pursuing the ball with a sense of urgency, Johnson stood there and waited for the ball to come to him. It never did. Scheyer grabbed it, called a time-out and the Blue Devils hit a game-tying shot on a possession they never should've had. Going after the loose ball is toughness—and Johnson didn't show it on that play. But what happened next? He refocused, slipped a screen for the winning basket and, after the game—when he could've been basking only in the glow of victory—manned up to the mistake that could've cost his team the win. "That was my responsibility—I should have had that," Johnson said of the goof. No excuses. Shouldering the responsibility. That's toughness.

Look your coaches and teammates in the eye: Tough players never drop their heads. You always look coaches and teammates in the eye, because if they are talking, it is important to them and to you.

Move on to the next play: Tough players don't waste time celebrating a good play or lamenting a bad one. They understand that basketball is too fast a game to waste time and opportunities with celebratory gestures or angry reactions. Tough players move on to the next play. They know that the most important play in any game is the next one.

Be hard to play against, and easy to play with: Tough players make their teammates' jobs easier, and their opponents' jobs tougher.

Make every game important: Tough players don't categorize opponents and games. They know that if they are playing, it is important. Tough players understand that if they want to play in championship games, they must treat every game as a championship game.

Make getting better every day your goal: Tough players come to work every day to get better, and keep their horizons short. They meet victory and defeat the same way: They get up the next day and go to work to be better than they were the day before. Tough players hate losing but are not shaken or deterred by a loss. Tough players enjoy winning but are never satisfied. For tough players, a championship or a trophy is not a goal; it is a destination. The goal is to get better every day.

When I was playing, the players I respected most were not the best or most talented players. The players I respected most were the toughest players. I don't remember anything about the players who talked a good game or blocked a shot and acted like a fool. I remember the players who were tough to play against.

Anybody can talk. Not anybody can be tough.

—Jay Bilas
ESPN